CHARLES
LLOYD

CHARLES LLOYD

A WILD, BLATANT TRUTH

JOSEF WOODARD

SILMAN-JAMES PRESS   **LOS ANGELES**

First Edition
10 9 8 7 6 5 4 3 2 1

Library of Congress Cataloging-in-Publication Data

Woodard, Josef, author.
Charles Lloyd : a wild, blatant truth / by Josef Woodard.
pages cm
ISBN 978-1-935247-13-5 (alk. paper)
1. Lloyd, Charles, 1938- 2. Saxophonists--Biography. 3. Jazz musicians--
Biography. I. Title.

ML419.L58W66 2015
788.7'165092--dc23
[B]

2015015907

Cover design by Wade Lageose
Cover photo by Paul Wellman

Printed and bound in the United States of America

Silman-James Press
www.silmanjamespress.com

to Charles

CONTENTS

INTRODUCTION...IN A FEW WORDS   IX

1. PRELUDE   1

2. MEMPHIS SOIL   11

3. OUT WEST, AND THEN EAST   31

4. MARQUEE TRAJECTORY   47

5. THE WILDERNESS YEARS   85

6. THE MUNICH CONNECTION   135

7. DIALOGUING WITH MASTER HIGGINS   171

8. NEW MILLENNIAL DANCE STEPS   193

9. POSTLUDE: HORIZONS ON THE RUN   219

ACKNOWLEDGMENTS   229

INTRODUCTION...
IN A FEW WORDS

ALTHOUGH THIS IS NOT an "authorized" biography, without the open and generous participation of Charles Lloyd in twenty-five–plus years of conversations with me—and Dorothy Darr's wonderful help in the process—this book would not have been possible. My role in the mix undoubtedly had a certain degree of right place/right time/right area code serendipity attached to it, given that I was a jazz-obsessed Santa Barbaran journalist with an open ear for Charles just at a time (starting in 1987) when he was eager to make his way out of his hermitage and back into the wide and notable musical world he had once inhabited.

As Lloyd returned to music's front lines, a nagging question repeatedly surfaced in our many (often epic and sometimes nonlinear) interviews: What about the general obscurity of his post-Sixties work and, more generally, of jazz itself in America? (Of course, jazz musicians' lack of acceptance in the United States is no secret, and many can seem like strangers in their own homeland.) But such questions are now largely behind him. By 2015, the time of this book's publication, Lloyd's music had reached broad new heights of acceptance: His life's work was very publicly celebrated and honored when the National Endowment for the Arts bestowed on him its NEA Jazz Masters Fellowship (described by the NEA as "the highest honor that our nation bestows on jazz artists"), and a few months before that he signed with the famed Blue Note record label.

As Charles told me, the day before his NEA honor was made manifest, "I have been acknowledged and honored in other countries, but somehow it is a sweeter confection to be honored in your homeland." In the same interview, the music man, at 77, surveyed his artistic future and reported thusly: "The possibilities are infinite."

1

PRELUDE

IN THE LONG, STRANGE, and twining arcs of the Charles Lloyd story, events have followed unpredictable and atypical rules of order. Chapters have sometimes been wild and fragmented. The rhythmic continuum of his career has been syncopated, and his path toward spiritual fulfillment has seen its fair share of twists and turns.

In the Sixties, Lloyd's moments in the broad public limelight were intense. Then, during a protracted self-exile/hiatus/hermitage from the jazz world in the Seventies, the saxophonist embraced the California coast, often a guest of rock 'n' rollers, as he devoted himself to personal enlightenment. The Eighties, however, saw his slow-motion segue back into the jazz scene and set the stage for what is possibly his longest, strongest period—the 1990s and the 2000s through to today, when, well into his seventh decade, his ever-questing music is intense, personal, and strong.

CALL OF THE FOREST: MONTEREY, 2006

Personal pathways and historic timeliness converged as Charles Lloyd stepped onto the fabled Monterey Jazz Festival stage in 2006. From one perspective, it was just another in a continuum of gigs coursing over almost five decades for the Memphis-born saxophonist, whose professional musical life began in the late 1950s. But from another perspective, the set was a key performance at the festival—marking the fortieth anniversary of the Charles Lloyd Quartet's auspicious debut at the annual event.

It was at this rustically outfitted festival on California's Monterey Fairgrounds in 1966 that Lloyd, in psychedelic regalia, crossed over from just another strong act on the jazz scene to something else altogether. Lloyd's performance in Monterey in 1966 was his cultural shot heard around the world. The next few years would find him rapidly soaring to great heights of popularity for a jazz artist, becoming an adjunct member of the counterculture's Summer of Love scene . . . and then burning out—leaping off the stardom train and more or less disappearing from the jazz world for nearly twenty years.

The popular recording of the quartet's 1966 Monterey appearance, *Forest Flower*, opens with a seventeen-minute performance of the title piece, a pleasantly rambling, liltingly modal two-part Lloyd composition that became the anthem of his Sixties work. The set also included easy-to-love and soon-to-be oft-played Lloyd originals such as his Caribbean-soul-jazz tune "Sombrero Sam" and his lovely ballad "Voice in the Night." Throughout the album, Lloyd's playing is clean and controlled and beautifully understated. The quartet format—here with pianist Keith Jarrett, drummer Jack DeJohnette, and bassist Cecil McBee—would remain Lloyd's primary, go-to instrumentation for decades to come.

A few months before his fortieth anniversary celebration at Monterey, Lloyd could be found nestled in his comfortable hilltop compound in Montecito, California, an affluent enclave south of Santa Barbara where he has lived for more than twenty-five years. On a crisp spring afternoon, as we enjoyed a stunning view of the Pacific Ocean far below his living room window, he wandered around his house and around a wide range of topics, periodically consulting on facts and details with Dorothy Darr, his wife and manager, who is also an architect, album cover artist, photographer, and sporter of many other hats.

During our conversation, Lloyd spun out ideas and unique refractions of those ideas, fragmented memories, and philosophical and spiritual asides in his inimitable Southern-gentleman-meets-post-hippie style. For this occasion, one of my numerous interviews with the man over a twenty-plus-year period, I wore my *Down Beat* journalist hat, and the result was Lloyd's first cover story in that magazine in decades.

He cast a fleeting glance at the red light on my tape recorder and said with a slight grin, "Oh, I didn't know you already started taping. I've got to be careful now."

I asked him, "Do you ever say anything incriminating?"

"Well, you know, I'm not wired for mediocrity or something, so I may say something that doesn't fit into the sound bite."

At the time, Lloyd was grappling with whether or not he wanted to put "Forest Flower" in his upcoming Monterey set, despite the efforts of the festival to seal the commemorative deal. "See," he said, "they wanted it to be with Jack [DeJohnette] and Cecil [McBee]. I said, 'Well, if you can get Junior aboard [Lloyd often refers to Jarrett as "Junior"], if all those guys want to do it, I would consider it.' I'm not like that. I don't bother people. If the spirit moves me, I might do it, but coercion is not on my menu.

"I never want taint to be on my thing. I don't like to be tainted. I rarely play it ["Forest Flower"] these days. Sometimes I play it. We shall see. . . . How am I going to re-create that? You can't re-create magic." (Fast-forward several months, and Lloyd is at Monterey, playing "Forest Flower" once again, and all is right with the world.)

Each musician in the jazz pantheon has a unique story to tell, and Lloyd's ambling saga takes him from a handsomely situated but also personally alienated childhood in Memphis to the California scene of the late Fifties, where he studied classical music at USC and played with the Gerald Wilson Big Band, an Ornette Coleman–linked crew, and others. After career-establishing stints with Chico Hamilton and Cannonball Adderley, his own brilliant solo career took off meteorically, tuning into the zeitgeist of an era when boundaries were being crossed in music and in audience tastes. Then came his long hiatus and various detours from the jazz scene.

He spoke to me at one point about the deeply ingrained seriousness with which he has taken his musical life, and his frustrations with the marginalization of jazz culture.

"I'm alienated by the treatment of music and culture. I have come to the acceptance that, to my work, I have a right. The fruits may or may not come. But I've been blessed anyway in this lifetime. I have a nice life. I'm able to live it in my lifetime and somehow almost endow my creativity. I have to jump out there sometimes and deal with the bankers and the marketplace, but I can do it spaciously. That is really good for creativity, if you can think about your work.

"For me, it's painfully slow. . . . I have to fess up: By the time you see me at intermission, I'm cool, because I've had the hit—you know what I'm saying? But before I go up there, I'm a nervous wreck.

"That's because you take it all very seriously," I interject.

"It's as serious as a heart attack."

Lloyd and Me

My own intersection with the world of Charles Lloyd came around the time of his re-emergence after his Big Sur–Santa Barbara "wilderness years" and was very much connected to our shared status as Santa Barbarans in love with their community and wanting to make jazz a richer part of the program in that city. I had a jazz radio show called Green Monday Street, *at KCSB, the noncommercial University of California at Santa Barbara station, and Lloyd would call up the station and launch into compacted versions of the verbal flights I would later come to know well.*

At the time, my awareness of Lloyd's life and times was limited, with my having been about twelve years old when he fled the scene. But I had jammed (badly) on "Forest Flower" in friends' garages in high school. And I knew of Lloyd as an ally of Mike Love, the business-shrewd Beach Boy who had established the cliff-hugging property/entity in Santa Barbara called Love Songs, and whose interest in Transcendental Meditation connected with Lloyd's interests in Eastern philosophy. During the years of Lloyd's jazz-world disappearance or hermitage, he could be found in the musical company of the post–Brian Wilson Beach Boys, sometimes joining them on tour and on record.

My first actual professional encounter with Lloyd was in 1987, before one of his regular concerts at Santa Barbara's powerfully evocative, historic Lobero Theatre (where he, with drummers Eric

Harland and Zakir Hussain, would later record his live Sangam *album at a 2004 memorial concert for his longtime friend and musical associate Billy Higgins).*

Lloyd is known for many things, including what some critics consider a reliance on softer-edged Coltraneisms. But his champions appreciate his playing's ethereal lyricism and impressionistically painterly qualities, mixed in with the sturdier stuff of his windblown timbres and craggy, expressive bleats and swipes—the residue of free jazz.

He also has shown an uncanny deftness for hiring well. His bands over the years have featured some top players, sometimes just before they ascended to great public renown. After ending his hiatus from public life, Lloyd followed up Keith Jarrett's position in his group's piano chair with the French pianist Michel Petrucciani (who is credited with helping lure Lloyd out of his hermitage), then the great Swede Bobo Stenson in the Nineties, then Geri Allen, followed by a brief encounter with Brad Mehldau, and in the late 2000s the mighty Jason Moran, shortly before Moran won a MacArthur "genius grant."

Over the years, the drum chair, where Jack DeJohnette sat in Lloyd's early quartet, has been artfully filled by Billy Hart, Billy Higgins (for an especially fruitful period, right up to Higgins's death in 2001), and, for the past decade, the uncommonly gifted and versatile Eric Harland.

AROUND THE HOUSE

One afternoon in 2008, Lloyd gave me a tour of his home, pointing out meaningful objects and memorabilia along the way, and also touching selectively on the breadth of his life. First stop: a pair of custom chairs in the large, open-feeling living room.

"You know who designed these chairs? Mies van der Rohe. They're from the Spanish Pavilion [the Barcelona Pavilion at the 1926 World's Fair]. I acquired a lot of these chairs. I remember when I first saw them. I was in San Francisco and I passed this Herman Miller show-room just off of Broadway. I was with Chico [Hamilton] then and making all of a hundred fifty dollars a week. This chair was sitting in the window and I walked in and I said, 'That chair is so beauti-ful. What does it cost?' 'Five hundred dollars. That's all right, young man—come back when you're ready.'" [laughs]

"So you came back when you were ready?"

"Yeah, she [Dorothy Darr] prepared me.

"You know who Joe Harley is? Audioquest. He also produces and makes a lot of records. So he hooks me up with these audio-phile people and they make this equipment available to me. These speakers are called B&W, they're British speakers. They're monitor speakers in studios in England. I just love them. . . .

"Then there are these people in Minnesota called Audio Research. They make high-end electronics. I also have some old tube tuners by McIntosh and I have a tube pre-amp. . . .

"That's a Theremin over there. That's a real Theremin."

"Do you ever use it?"

"I've used it in the past, yeah. . . . The guy who did the music for *Spellbound*, the Hitchcock film, Miklós Rósza, they used this Theremin for that score. . . . It's on *Moon Man* [Lloyd's infamous 1970 album]."

"I notice your piano there," I comment.

"It's a Steinway B. It's seven-foot and it's . . . the accelerated action [a Steinway feature that allows for faster repeated notes and very responsive action], the good ones that had the warm sound but that are modern instruments. . . . This instrument belonged to a guy named Keith Hardesty, who was the master piano technician on the West Coast. . . ."

Lloyd starts into a story about an instrument that is clearly dear to his heart: "During my years when I lived on the mesa with Mike Love, over at his compound . . . the Beach Boys had a piano techni-cian, and I asked this guy where I could find a great piano. He said the greatest piano technician was Mr. Hardesty. . . . He said, 'He has two pianos, and I think Brian [Wilson] wants one, but Brian is kind of out of it right now.' I said, 'I want a B.' He said, 'Well, call Hardesty.'

"He wanted me to have the instrument. We were living in Big Sur. We hired a technician from Monterey who flew down to Burbank and spent the day with this guy and said, 'It's one of the two best Steinways I've ever seen in my life.'

"It's . . . just so wonderfully built, and the sound is incredible. Michel has played it, Bobo has played it. Everybody has played it. Look how pristine it's built and all. It's pre-CBS." [Steinway & Sons was sold to CBS Musical Instruments in 1972.]

Our conversation takes a sudden detour when Lloyd interjects, "Oh good, it's raining. I want you to hear this."

We proceed to a bedroom with a window that offers a stunning view, overlooking an expanse of woods, with the Pacific Ocean and Channel Islands beyond. The gentle patter of rain completes a tranquil atmospheric picture. "That's beautiful," I say.

He slowly shakes his head. "I don't know how I got to be so blessed. I came around in the old days, and it was a simpler time. When I lived in New York, my first apartment at One Sheridan Square was $98.75 a month. . . . I was a composer and I had my publishing. They said it was 'semi-professional. You have to qualify for this apartment.' So I brought my royalty statements down. . . .

"But we could live in New York for a couple hundred dollars a month. We were all in the neighborhood. Ornette [Coleman] was around the corner. [Bob] Dylan was over here. [Don] Cherry was somewhere. Eric Dolphy would come over to my house. We were all in there."

We head downstairs into Lloyd's basement/studio, full of keyboards, audiophile gear, a Baldwin studio piano ("but it has a big sound," says Lloyd, an avowed Steinway man).

"Dorothy was going to have a studio down here, with the booth in there. But Higgins and I loved it upstairs, plus there was the fact that he was not so well." Lloyd is referring to the recordings made in his home for what became *Which Way Is East*, the acclaimed double

CD of duets recorded with Billy Higgins a few months before the drummer's death.

Darr enters the room and tells Lloyd, "Wait, you didn't show him the tape room."

Lloyd sniffs, and says with a laugh, "He don't want to see that. He might come back in the middle of the night." We move into a special climate-controlled archival storage room with shelves full of master tapes going back in time and tape formats. He whispers, conspiratorially, "This is where we keep our masters, man."

I ask him if he has digitized them. "No, that's the thing," says Darr. "They might fall off the face of the tape. Can you believe this? We've got a reel-to-reel from the Blue Note concert at Town Hall [in 1985]. How did we get that?"

Darr makes another discovery while gazing over the collection, "Oh, isn't that *Pathless Path*?" referring to the 1979 album Lloyd made during his jazz-avoidance period.

Lloyd: "You've got it, honey."

"But this is not the master," says Darr. "Somebody just wrote that they wanted to license the recording . . ."

Lloyd at home, 2015. (*Photo by Paul Wellman*)

Lloyd gestures to the archives and adds, "She's got video for days."

We head upstairs to a large art studio and archive of photos and other materials.

"Isn't this a lovely studio she has?" asks Lloyd, looking at the high ceilings and generous layout of the room. He leads me to various photos from his past. "Here's my grandfather here. He was very special."

Another large, hand-colored photo shows a teenaged Lloyd with a handsome upward sweep of hair. "See," he says, "that's when I was a singer. I wanted to be a singer, but I didn't have the voice. That's why I had to get a horn. That's what I'm trying to do on the horn—trying to sing."

2

MEMPHIS SOIL

MONTECITO

IT IS ANOTHER LOVELY day in Montecito, 2008, and Charles Lloyd, nestled in his hilltop abode, is verbally rambling down the byways of his early life back home in Memphis in the Thirties and Forties. Most conversations with Lloyd find their way to the powerful imprint left on him by his Memphis years. These memories are tinged with a sense of longing and, perhaps most importantly, a quest to understand the first chapter of his life as a musician, a son, and a spirit soon to be wandering the world.

As we chat, we are officially dealing with matters of house and hearth for *Jazz Times* magazine's "@HOME" series of photo essays on the digs and lifestyles of notable jazz musicians. An artist with a romantic attraction to the idea of a hermitage, Lloyd initially seemed reluctant about throwing open his house, history, and collected accoutrements of a well-lived life.

But his initial coolness and timidity yielded to a warm visit. We started out in the kitchen of the house that his wife, Dorothy Darr, designed in 1998 for a property tucked into the foothills. (From 1982 to 1998, they lived in a Mediterranean-style house down the winding road from here.) This spread has been a happy and idyllic home base for Lloyd's "second career."

Chopsticks

Lloyd digs into his freshly made salad with an eager appetite, wooden utensils in hand. "I like to eat with wood. I don't like to eat with metal utensils. I'll do it if I'm out there and traveling. But when I left New York and came back to California, after I disbanded the group in '69, I lived in Malibu, and I started eating with chopsticks. I also went into a serious detoxification thing.

"You know that saying 'Whatever you're looking for is looking for you'? Where I lived, in Malibu Colony—I went there in '69—I saw myself as an outpatient from New York. In New York, [Billy] Higgins wouldn't let me hang with him. One time in Brazil, when we were in a car, he said, 'I had to keep you away because I didn't want you to ruin your health.' I dipped and dived anyway.

"Back to Booker Little . . ." he says suddenly, referring to a friend from his youth in Memphis who went on to become a masterful and uncommonly lyrical trumpeter, living in New York City until his 1961 death from kidney disease at age twenty-three. Little, who moved east to New York as Lloyd moved west to Los Angeles, is something of a touchstone for Lloyd, who says, "I'm in his garden now. He told me really good, 'Don't do the fast lane. It's a waste of time, no question.' But when you're young and you're drunk with this music, and you love all these Hyperions that are there, we'd go exploring every night. We don't come back the same way. You live in a harsh environment, the way the society is set up, the way the game is set up. Like they say, 'Don't call it ebb and flow, call it rape and pillage.'

"You have dreams that all of God's children can run free and rise to their full potential. I never lost those ideals. I grew up in a society that fostered that. My grandfather built a school and a church and all that stuff, out in the country where they lived. I had these beautiful grandparents. And then there were my great-grandmother's Choctaw songs. There was all this richness around me. My grandfather's property was in Mississippi: I grew up there, on his place. He had sixteen hundred acres, really beautiful land, orchards for days. You could get lost there.

"I could only go there during the summers. Then I'd come to town to go to school in Memphis. But what was so beautiful was that I ran into these sages, like Phineas Newborn and these guys. . . . So now I bring all of that with me, because I stood on all those shoulders."

Returning to the subject of his Montecito home, he says, "Now, after we lived in New York, in lofts . . . I still want to live in a loft, you know. She [Darr] lived in Florence. From Florence, she says, 'Okay, he needs a loft, and I need the gentility of an Italian-Moorish house.' We had this land and she built this space. The beautiful thing is that you don't hear any sounds and you don't have people bothering you. I think it helps me to aerate, to go for hikes in the mountains and go swimming in the water. All of that stuff is still important to me.

"I'm still like a kid who is drunk from the music. By holding that dear to me, I never went for the okeydoke. . . . I like the exploration of something opening up and that freshness—of being refreshed in the ages of the infinite—and modernity, with the wisdom of the ancients just helping you. *If you're looking for it, they're looking for you.* 'Oh, another fish jumped out of the net. He got away.' Metaphors like that are what keeps me going."

He waves in the general direction of the open property around and above his house: "I also like that I can walk all around this land, 'cause I'm used to that, from walking on my grandfather's land. I'm used to walking, I hike a lot. I think that that keeps me in good trim. When I get out there on the trail, I can have all these permutations and songs and mathematical kinds of things that I like to look at, like intervals and stuff like that. I like something about, say, the Fibonacci numbers and things like that. They actually get that stuff from Africa. That stuff is old, it's from Egypt and like that. Even [Béla] Bartók, he would take those folk songs and smash them all around and put different kinds of equations on it. But I like the notion that . . . you have to leave that all behind you and just go into the music."

Of his home's elaborate yet warmly livable and inviting quarters, Lloyd muses, "She [Darr] made this full of light. . . . When I was in New York . . . there was always talk about artists being downtrodden and living beneath the sewer. I didn't think that was right. I thought that if a tree can't get water in its roots, how's it going to have wonderful blossoms and such?

"All of this is to say that the spaciousness of what happens when I can live in Dorothy's world here is that I'm able to move all around and be, on the outside and the edge of it. I can go exploring on tippytoes and then come back over here and get a bit of B-flat. It's like a lot of different options. But the options will close down on your ass if there's too much humidity and racism and too much b.s."

MEMPHIS

"Memphis was a strange place to be born. I look back in terms of process and it's very beautiful. It's a power spot. This is a magic place, as is New York and Memphis and Big Sur. It's how you use it and tune into it. The world's a gymnasium and this is a wonderful place to do study or exercise. I perceive that it's one life, and it's reflected through us; we're just vehicles or instruments and the Lord plays us. The closer we get to God, the Creator, the absolute being, the more purification is required in our nervous system, the more patience and perseverance for the vicissitudes of life.

"I think the ultimate notion is liberation through the chaos. I was born in this lifetime a musician. It's been my religion. I didn't have a formal religion, and music always had that spiritual calling for me. I've always been a seeker. Everyone is; we just do it at different intervals. I have a home here, but I'm not here all the time, because sometimes my work requires me to be away in solitude. Sometimes I can be in the middle of a New York jungle and there can be stillness in that. If you have to be only in the woods, then you haven't attained that balance. I'm trying to speak the balance."

Despite Lloyd's concerns about the racism and humidity he associates with Memphis, scarcely an interview goes by when he doesn't turn the discussion to fond reminiscences about his upbringing there. He is keen to reflect on the city's mythos as a great fount of American music, and a crossroads locality where rivers meet, literally and otherwise.

One of the documentaries that his wife made on him is entitled *Memphis Is in Egypt*, a reference he once explained, in his allusive way: "The notion is, there is a sphinx in Egypt, with pictures of birds. Bird [Charlie Parker] was conceived in Memphis—are you hip to that? Now, that alone is worth the price of admission. I'm interested in universality and sources, like that. The whole thing of Bird and the freedom flight of what he was saying, and the beauty, quality, and elegance of his song."

Lloyd was born in Memphis on March 15, 1938, a synthesis of African, Native American, Mongolian, and Irish heritages. He speaks of his earliest experiences in a semi-mystical way. "I was born anemic; I was called a blue baby. I used to go outside of my incubator and watch the trip all the time. I hung out on the ceiling. I could see myself and the doctors, people coming and going, I remember that. Later, when my mother told me that I was a blue baby, it came to me that I remembered this thing of witnessing from overhead.

"Also, it was revealed to me that my mother didn't want to have me. . . .

"Being serious, I saw what was wrong with the world. I was in a place to bitch or complain about it. At four years old in Memphis, I peeped that that wasn't where I was to be. People said, 'Well, why don't you leave?' I said, 'Hey man, I'm four. Give me a minute to get something together.' Not only was the humidity too much for me, there was also an appalling lack of opportunity, as I saw it.

"I was with my mother then. I didn't spend much time with my father. See, my father was Jack Atkins. He's one of the baddest cats on the planet. He was the football coach at Fisk University, in Nashville, for many years. They had some of their greatest teams under him. My mother married Charles Lloyd, who was a pharmacist. She didn't marry Jack Atkins.

"My father . . . used to come and visit me every so often. Charles Lloyd was distant. . . . He was in his own world most of the time. Whether he was a scientist or a scholar, he was deep into research, whatever it was . . . .

"My father had this quiet, dignified thing. He was very silent a lot. But I watched him when he coached, and he was very dynamic. I couldn't understand how he went from that modality to this other modality, where he lived in this lounge posture. But when it was time for him to go to work, it was all business. I realized later that he was gathering his forces.

"I realize now he was my hero at a certain time. Once I asked him why he didn't marry my mother, and he wouldn't tell me. After my mother died, he said to me once, 'You asked me once why I didn't marry your mother. . . . It wasn't that I didn't want to marry your mother—she didn't want to marry me. She didn't think my prospects were good enough.'

"My mother was very beautiful and elegant. She had ambitions, she came from a Brahman-type family. So it was hard on my father. I never knew that. He loved her very deeply, he later told me that. I remember during difficult moments he would call me. I remember after my mother died, we had been estranged, but he called me and he wanted to do anything he could. He was living in Arizona at the time. He actually taught there at a college in Tempe. . . . He taught humanities. I remember I visited his classes sometimes, and he would hold people spellbound. He was a beautiful weaver of tales and stuff.

"I realized, in some ways, I got something from him. He has a quiet side. My mother had this hyper charged-up energy. I was saddened by the lack of opportunities for my mother in the South. And yet, she made great contributions in the community. She helped in the community and did lots of things. She was a college graduate and developed herself. She was a nurse and married to Charles Lloyd. Then she divorced him and got a job with a company called Stanley Home Products. Within six months, she sold more than anyone had of those mops and brooms.

"I remember once we went to New York. She bought a brand-new Hudson Hornet in the late Forties. We drove to New York at, like, ninety miles per hour—the turnpike was so hip.

"My father had this thing of acceptance. He had a real positive thing. . . . In the final analysis, we have to really love ourselves and then we can love others. A lot of our problem is with fear. My father wasn't with my mother. We're all orphans. . . . We're orphans from something, and we're all fish out of water.

"For me, it has always been about jumping out of the net. You get trapped in a mold. But the music isn't about that. It's about being in the present, about having big ears and being able to hear around the corner and taking in the contribution of other music makers.

"That's the beauty of this music. It has this ability of touching in such deep places, and there is the camaraderie thing of making a world community. . . . Deep love and reverence and harmony with each other and that whole flow makes you want to see the world as a better place.

"You can blow an eight-hundred-amp fuse, if you want to look at it on a deeper level, by being stressed out by all that. I spent a lot of years just saddened by the condition of the planet and lack of harmony. But it's very complicated, because we all have different systems and different ways of being. It really gets down to 'Be good and do good.'"

GRANDFATHER INGRAM

Among the strong figures in Lloyd's family, his grandfather Ben Ingram ranks high in terms of being an influence, a source of inner strength, and a legend.

"I've been on the road every day of my life, since I was a little kid. I grew up in a dysfunctional kind of situation with my mother, but my grandparents were stable, so I had some stability sutra from my grandfather. He was a self-made man who owned a thousand acres outside of Memphis and sent twenty-one kids to college. He was very clear about education. I got something from him, a sense of quality. He didn't tap-dance. The only thing he bought was salt and coffee; everything else he grew.

"Everybody is equal in a certain way, but in another way, the power of emanation comes stronger through certain beings than others. My grandfather was one who was outrageous on fire. There was such a strong emanation of power coming from him that it would blind people. . . . My grandfather Ben was a wise man; his father was landed. His father was an Irishman, but the mother was part Cherokee. He was very fiery. He called us his 'little bulldogs.'

He flew up and down the road between Byhalia [Mississippi] and Memphis doing his cotton business. He was landed: We're talking about thousands of acres of land, as far as you could see. That's strange in the South, because you have the notion of the racist white man, the plantation and owning.

"I don't have so many words for my grandfather as I do power-ful feelings of being around him. He had long black hair combed straight back. He had very beautiful features, a very striking person. One example: One day we were driving with him. Whatever year it was, he had the newest shiny black car. . . . He was driving this car, dust was flying. He would drive flat out; pedal-to-the-metal was my grandfather. I remember one day a highway patrolman pulled us over and my grandfather was just outraged. He was so in a state that he told the guy, 'Stop some of those other folks who are passing me. I don't have time for this. I'm on my way somewhere.' I saw that guy with his mouth open, and he kept going. . . . That rubbed off on me: Certain things get planted. . . .

"I witnessed, from time to time, that people would try to con-trol him, to tell him to cool it. You don't stop a cop, especially a brother, you know? I worked with a guy named Tuff Green [bassist-bandleader Richard "Tuff" Green], and his trip was to get out of the car and tap-dance, saying, 'Yes, suh.' He'd do the tap dance and he'd 'Tom' his way out. But my grandfather did it with power and sheer vibes. His vibe was so strong. I watched him all the time. He never was inferior; he never tap-danced. Cats would always come around from the big fruit companies to buy from his orchards. . . .

Another tale Lloyd tells of his grandfather shows the man's strong influence in his community: "This guy was encroaching on my grandfather's land. He was a man of bad intent and kept encroach-ing on his land. My grandfather went in town to his attorney and said, 'What's with this?' Everybody loved my grandfather. He was a special man to all people of goodwill. The attorney said, 'No prob-lem, we'll just run the line and send the surveyors down and move his stakes to run the line properly.'

"This guy got arrogant and mad that my grandfather had the audacity to run the line and he got drunk in town and said he was going to go kill my grandfather. The postman ran ahead to warn him, racing in a horse and buggy. This guy came shooting at my grandfather and my grandfather took him out.

"They took him to jail, and the furniture company sent over mattresses, sent over fresh flowers—all this stuff was brought in and he was out in a moment's time. They didn't mess with him because he was Bud Ingram's son and because there were lots of skeletons in the closet. . . .

"So they had a trial, but that night, five hundred people gathered at my grandfather's farm, of all colors and hues and patinas, to keep the Klan away. That was in the days. This was 1919. They had a trial and the judge said, 'I want you to treat this man as a man, and don't play the game.' He was exonerated. . . . Hey, man, there were a lot of people who lived on the land and worked, sharecropper style, got their piece of the crops. But everybody dug my grandfather. He could communicate with whoever."

George Coleman

Lloyd's fairly comfortable situation in life in Memphis was sometimes set into relief by comparison with those of his friends and peers at the time. "I visited [Memphis-born saxophonist] George Coleman in his home, and his people were real humble people of very meager means. There was George, who, the first day he got a saxophone, played everything he heard on it. He has a kind of humility that doesn't have that endowment of strength and pride. . . . I could be wrong on this premise. I'm not trying to come off as that I'm better because of that station. I'm saying that station did give me an endowment of pride, for example. You can only talk about your own experience."

YOUNG MUSICIAN IN MEMPHIS

In his Montecito home in 2008, in the large room that held various archives, Lloyd pointed to a photograph of himself as a teenager, cradling an alto saxophone and, even then, conveying something of the airy charismatic gleam that he would carry throughout his long professional life in music.

"All my life," he says, "I've broken out into music. That was my burning desire—to get to the saxophone as soon as I could. It took me until I was nine years old to convince my parents to get me one.

"See, being in Memphis, I was in the right place at the right time. There were great masters there, some of whom I've told you about. One night, I was playing with Johnny Ace [stage name of R&B singer-musician John Marshall Alexander Jr.]. He was playing the blues so slow. I said, 'I'm going to figure out what this guy is doing, because it's impossible to play the blues this slow and maintain the consistency of beat and blues soulfulness. He could play the blues slower than anyone could ever play it. He didn't rush it or anything and he didn't miss a beat. He was just right there. One night I decided to figure out how he was doing it.

"I had become a mathematical genius. When I went to Catholic school, grades one through three, I was considered stupid and illiterate and not teachable; I couldn't learn. The nuns kept me after school every day and used to beat me on my hand with the ruler all the time. I was just in a state of shockeration. It was *out*.

"I couldn't learn anything. I was slow. They'd keep me way late after school. My folks had moved way to the other side of town by now. I had to catch two streetcars, transfer and all this stuff. By the time I get home, it's raining and it's dark. As a little kid, I was thinking, 'Wow, what is this?' I wasn't digging on it. . . .

"I liked something about the Catholic church. We had to go there for Mass. . . . We'd go to school early in the morning because we had to go to a seven o'clock Mass. After Mass was over, they didn't open the school; we'd have to crowd around outside the door and huddle, literally throw our bodies on each other to stay warm until the nuns would come downstairs to open the door. That's a little cold, but those are experiences everybody goes through in some form or another.

"In the fourth grade, I transferred to Melrose High School. [In the Forties, Melrose School incorporated grades one through twelve.] Mrs. Handy, this beautiful black woman, was up at the front of the class. She had these big bosoms. I'll never forget it. She had these white silk blouses on and black skirts. She looked like Mahalia Jackson, big dignity. She was so warm. She was just loving us so. I was sitting in the back and, one day all of a sudden a thing happened to me. It was a thing they talk about as religious experiences, a thing of enlightenment. I was sitting there and all of a sudden I rose up and started answering every question she asked. I knew every mathematical equation and I could multiply. . . . Everybody looked at me because everybody thought I was 'lights on but nothing is happening.' And she smiled when I started coming forth with the stuff. I became a genius. I was the class computer.

"So because I could figure out fractions and everything, I'm playing with Johnny Ace and playing blues. You hold these whole notes, and while I'm holding these whole notes, I'm checking him out and what he's doing on piano. As I was checking, lo and behold, I got zapped again with the lightning. I was no longer playing the music, I *was* the music. I was right in there. It was like [makes a wind sound]—it just *opened up*. It was no longer in time. It was just *whoo, whoo*. That experience was so powerful, it just set me on my way."

In filmmaker Eric Sherman's 1969 Lloyd documentary, *Charles Lloyd: The Journey Within*, Lloyd's mother talked about her son's formative musical life. "At the age of seven, he wanted to blow a sax. At night, he always kept his radio on. If he heard something, he would get something in his head. He said he didn't know how it got there, but he would get up in the middle of the night and start blowing or writing. He started working at nine in these nightclubs. Boy, it was rough around there at that time."

Later in the film she states, "He never really studied formally. He took music in school, and he would teach music on the side for twenty-five cents. As soon as he got a dollar, he would go to Professor Whitaker over at LeMoyne [College]. He charged him a dollar for a lesson. I had one of his teachers, Mr. McDaniel, buy his first saxophone for him at a pawn shop. . . . Then he started working with a group, 'Tuff' Green's little orchestra. From there he went to [trumpeter/bandleader] Willie Mitchell's band.

"He told to me one day, 'Mother, anything you want me to be, I'll try to be, but music is my life.' Every chance he got, he was trying to better himself in music. He said music was the only way he knew how to express himself. I have a peculiar feeling when I hear his music, because his soul is in it. His music is religion to him."

Perhaps music becoming a religious experience for Lloyd had something to do with his early musical achievements—but so did a strong sense of discipline and competitiveness. "As kids, we knew that we were the baddest," says Lloyd. "We 'shedded ["woodshed-ded," or practiced] every day, man. We'd get to school at nine o'clock. At nine-thirty, the band director would say, 'Professor Garrett needs Charles Lloyd in the band.' I would say 'Oh, no,' and run over there. This was when we had heard Bird records. He'd play 'Relaxin' at Camarillo.' We played through changes and listened to records all day, man. [Pianist/composer] Harold Mabern and [saxophonist] Frank Strozier were immediate contemporaries.

"I was in a beautiful place, because my best friend was Booker Little. We were little cats together, just practicing nonstop. That whole thing was just really full of music. He was my closest friend all through high school. We went to the Manassas High School. That was a wonderful school—just pregnant with the elixir of this beauti-ful music that gives us wisdom of integration of life. . . . He'd been practicing for three hours before I picked him up at nine o'clock, and we got to school for second period because we got to stay home and practice. We had a permit to do that, because we also worked together late at night in clubs.

"Check this out: We played from nine at night until four in the morning. That was over in a place in West Memphis. Memphis closed down at one o'clock, except on the weekends, when they were open until two. All our life, we were playing in these places. But the good thing about it, I must say, is that we did get to play a lot. That experience was really something. It doesn't seem to exist now, that youngsters come up playing as much as we did every night. As a youngster, from age ten on, I was pretty much playing every night of my life, and shedding every day. It was just our life."

In *Charles Lloyd: The Journey Within*, Lloyd recalled some of his early musical dues-paying. "I remember I was playing a place in Memphis called Mitchell's Hotel [on Beale Street], run by a proprietor who we called Sunbeam [Andrew "Sunbeam" Mitchell]. He would always stand back at the back of the room and watch us, to make sure that we didn't express too much of our feelings in the music. It was supposed to be totally an entertainment song. If our souls were to be sung, he would be there to watch us and make sure we didn't slip in any jazz or do too much like that. Actually, there was no such thing as a jazz club or anything like that, but there was a great desire to create and to improvise. There were many fantastic people in the Memphis area.

"I remember distinctly him standing in the back saying, 'Yeah, well. . .' Whenever he got in that kind of a mood, it meant we better play some blues soon. So we'd play from nine until two a.m. We'd play from nine to eleven-thirty, then take an intermission of about twenty minutes, and then we'd come back and play from ten minutes to twelve to two a.m. Steady like that."

As Lloyd says, despite its lack of a jazz club scene, Memphis in the time of his youth was fertile soil for jazz musicians of note—many of whom would make their stamp on the larger jazz scene and some of whom would remain local legends. "George Coleman had just graduated from high school before us. Booker and I would go to his house and he would show us stuff. He was a little older than us. Phineas Newborn was around, he helped us. There was a beautiful pianist, Charles Thomas, who you never heard of, who played in a manner not unlike Bud Powell. But he was his own person. The thing about us all is that we're all the same, we're all made of the same God-given stuff. But the thing is that, however, each of us is unique. We have our unique being. So although I say Charles Thomas played in a manner like Bud Powell, it was just simultaneously happening.

"In Memphis, of course, we heard those records of Bird and Diz [Parker and Gillespie]. To this day, when I see Diz I have to prostrate myself. They were putting out all this beautiful wisdom that let us know that this kind of apartheid down there was not to be an all-time feature in our life, and we weren't going for the okeydoke. We just had too much juice and too much stuff to go for that. So that's why I said when I was four I knew I had to split. But I had to do my time.

"I've always been a music maker. I was born into the world not knowing what to do, and yet I break out into song. In my lifetime, there were peers like Booker Little and many others that I have named, who helped me and encouraged me. Booker and I played and practiced together all the time. He was one grade ahead of me.

"He went to the Chicago Conservatory and I came out here to the University of Southern California. We met up again in New York in 1960. I was there with Chico [Hamilton]. I went to Birdland. It was a Monday night. Booker was playing with Eric [Dolphy], and they were burning. It was so beautiful to hear him. I was staying across the street at the Alvin Hotel. That's where Lester [Young] died. Towards the end, I remember a woman was trying to cut Lester's hair and the master said, 'No, no,' because it was just before he passed and his antenna was so sensitive it would have been painful for her to clip his locks."

Jazz passions and studies aside, some of Lloyd's earliest professional musical activities were in Memphis's thriving blues and rhythm-and-blues scene, playing with Johnny Ace, B. B. King, Bobby "Blue" Bland, Rosco Gordon, and the legendary Howlin'

Wolf. "I have never had an experience where a musician could shake the building to its foundation like Wolf used to do. He would start that 'shake that rattle and roll . . . ' with such power. He was a great man—big, too. At night we'd come back from those gigs and then, somewhere over in Arkansas, across the bridge—Memphis is right there on the border of the Mississippi and you go across the river to West Memphis, Arkansas—we'd go way over there somewhere to play.

"But with the Wolf, you could make ten or fifteen dollars. Wolf would always say, 'You play with the Wolf, you eat pork chops. You play with them other people, you eat neck bones.' I knew what he was saying. In other words, you had a choice. He'd come to town and say, 'You want to play with the Wolf?' 'Yes, Wolf, we want to be with you.'

"But when I played with Rosco Gordon and Bobby 'Blue' Bland, we would stop in Arkansas, and gunshots would be going off. They'd be shooting craps. I'm a little kid, scared because I'm hearing these gunshots going off. I never experienced nothing like that. . . .

"Anyway, those guys, man, would go and gamble all night, and it would be daylight when they came out. Then they'd take me home and they'd be mad at me, because I had four dollars and they were all broke and scuffling. They spent it gambling, trying to get some more bread, which is another metaphor for the whole thing.

"Beale Street does have a ragged song, but it's a cosmopolitan thing, because the brothers come up from Mississippi. Memphis is on the border of Mississippi and Arkansas. It's the cotton thing; Memphis is where they ship all the cotton out from. Downtown on Front Street is where they have all these cotton warehouses for the world.

"Robert Johnson is down there on the Delta. B. B. King is coming out of Hattiesburg [Mississippi] . . . and he had a show every Saturday on the radio, this black station, WDIA [in Memphis], sponsored by a drink called Pepticon. It was a patent medicine that you would drink that would cure whatever was wrong with you. Well, these boys from the New York tribe had come down there, they bottled some cough syrup or something and people were buying it because they were miserable. Who knows, maybe there was some codeine in it too."

As dapper young Lloyd traversed the blues' mean streets, gigging, dues-paying, he was also learning the more sophisticated musical ways of jazz. He had the advantage of living in a musically rich city, in jazz as well as other American idioms. Crossing over from one musical context to another, he soaked up the many varieties of Memphis's musical culture.

He remembers, "There was a guy named Bill Harvey in my hometown who had the best band around, and another guy named Willie Mitchell. These guys were elders who were pointing the way to me. They were also very modern. There was a guy named Onzie Horne, who was like our local Gil Evans. I remember he did arrangements on 'Joy Spring' and things like that—this really beautiful stuff.

"Memphis was a cosmopolitan place in a certain kind of way. Then there were the blues gigs or playing in white dance halls. There was the deep church experience—the sanctified thing, too. . . .

"There were all these incredible musicians. There was a guy named Edward Lewis Smith [a trumpeter], he was Booker Little's elder cousin. Booker Little's sister was an opera singer, she went to Europe and had a career there. Phineas Newborn [Jr.] was our little Art Tatum and our Beethoven, so to speak. He was quite inspirational.

"I thought my real mentor was George Coleman, but it was actually Phineas Newborn. . . . He was always a catalyst. I used to walk past his house and I would just stand outside and shake while they were inside playing.

"To hear that vibrancy and freshness at such a tender age was to know that that elixir that was coming through him was the real stuff. Also, I played with him for a couple of years in his father's band—it was Phineas and his brother Calvin [a guitarist]. It was a very powerful experience. He was always helpful, always playing Bird and Bud Powell records. . . .

"I met Phineas when I was ten. I listened to his record recently. I was so shocked at how great he was. Well, everyone knew he was a genius, but also, I was bowled over that he could do everything. Sometimes that's not good. He did it all. If he could just focus on one area of his depth. . . . But he came up in a milieu or environment, like he played commercial gigs with his father.

"He was too fragile to endure his lifespan, to live in his lifetime. We got to New York and the critics were ape over him, then they started tearing him apart. They called him superficial. It hurt him a lot. He didn't have the family stability, because his father was always a tyrant. He was afraid and thought, 'Something must be wrong with me.' He didn't grab onto that thing that I grabbed onto about *becoming*. It makes you become a better person, a better father. It's not easy to get up and tie your shoes and wipe the crud off your shoes every morning at nine o'clock. It's always a cleansing mechanism."

Lloyd continues reminiscing about his Memphis years: "I grew up around all of this. I think I was a loner. There's something of that in me only because I'm interested in trying to delve deeper and resolve something. It's troubling to me, the state of the world. . . .

"I played my first amateur show when I was ten years old . . . and got this huge adulation and first prize. I came off stage and Phineas said, 'You need lessons, bad.' So a master was there before I detoured too fast and got rich, before I learned how to play. Witness rock 'n' roll. Fortunately, Jimi Hendrix came and put them all in their place. When I was living in the Village I lived at One Sheridan Square for a long time, and then I moved over to West Third Street, at a brownstone. Jimi was over down the street at a cafe. I have a vague recollection of seeing him there, playing to four or five people. That was before he went to England.

"I always had a quest going. I was always around elders. I was junior this and junior that. Of course, my mother was married to a doctor, Charles Lloyd, so I *was* a junior. Anyway, there's something about revering your elders. I played these gigs with those standard charts, with all these great bands.

Young Lloyd with his alto saxophone. (*Photo provided by Eric Sherman*)

"Willie Mitchell had this big band that played like Dizzy's band. He produced Al Green and became a noted producer in Memphis. He was a wonderful musician and arranger. I played in his group. Across the bridge from Memphis was West Memphis, Arkansas, where they had dancing and gambling all night. There were several clubs over there where bands played, apartheid-style.

"I also played at the Plantation Inn [in West Memphis, Arkansas] with Phineas on piano and his brother Calvin on guitar. I grew up in this incredible milieu, I got to play every night from age twelve or so. I started taking these lessons, and Phineas would check in on me and see how I was doing. Then they put me in his father's band when I was about fourteen. I was matriculating around the changes pretty well. . . .

SAINTS AND SAGES

"The faith and surrender. I'm an ecstatic. Saints and sages. Reading the life of Buddha and *The Light of Asia* [Edwin Arnold's 1879 book about the life of Buddha], mother Africa—we're all descended from that. It was the first thing on the planet, if you look at the whole setup of that. You hit bottom, get up off the floor. The blues, Memphis, Phineas, 'Blue' Mitchell, Booker Little, Harold Mabern, Frank Strozier, this guy [alto saxophonist] Irvin Reason taught me those saxophone lessons. We could feel Bird and Sonny Stitt coming through real strong.

"Jimmie Lunceford taught at my high school. Harold Mabern has traced this: Bird was conceived in Memphis. *Memphis and the pyramids.* The river runs through there, that's something you should put in your memory banks. Conception is something, too.

"When I was a little kid, I went to see Duke's band with Johnny Hodges and all. I went backstage and they told me, right up front, 'Son, go be a doctor or a lawyer. Don't do this stuff.' But I knew that was what I had to do. It's only something that you let somebody do if they have to do it. Don't get into music if you want to be a trillionaire—whatever that's all about.

"Music is all I have. I love it. It's my all and all. My journey's been a different journey. The New York school . . . it teaches you that you have to be indestructible, so you have to get with that. Plus, the fact was that all the masters were there when I got there. They were all saints and sages to me. I bowed down to that.

"I heard Clifford [Brown] in Lionel Hampton's band when I was a little kid. Quincy [Jones] was in that band, Jimmy Cleveland, Jerome Richardson, a lot of guys. I'd go backstage and they'd tell my mother, 'Don't let that boy be a musician. Let him be a doctor or lawyer or an Indian chief or something like that.' But I couldn't deny the music thing.

"I remember one time, Lionel Hampton was staying at our house when I was ten or twelve or so. My mother would put up some of the musicians in our house. I'd bug them all to death. He said something beautiful to my mother. He said, 'Try to get him a Selmer. He needs the best horn he can get, because if a professional can't play a bad horn, how do you think he's going to play it?' You always give kids some secondhand old horn that can't inspire them. They need their tools.

"My mother said after I went to high school, I could go to the college I wanted to. That's a nice thing for a mom to do—although maybe she can't afford it—to set a standard, something to shoot for. My mom always laid the trip on me. She said, 'I don't care what you do, just be the best at it.' That was after she gave up on me being a doctor or lawyer; I went to USC and was going to major in pre-med."

But fate and Lloyd's musical passions had other destinations in store.

3
Out West, and Then East

LA

Prospects for studying jazz in any concentrated, academic way in the 1950s were a world away from the dense landscape of jazz education options for today's aspiring musicians. In 1956, when the young Lloyd headed west out of Memphis instead of northeast to the jazz mecca of New York, he was pursuing a path of marginal resistance but also of deep passion. He had, among other things, a passion for classical music, which he would study at USC, where his teachers would include composer and acclaimed Bartók scholar Halsey Stevens.

But a richer seedbed for Lloyd's Los Angeles education lay in lessons discovered and pursued outside of the classroom. The gestalt of the time and place set a ready stage for him. As the glory days of LA's famed and fabled Central Avenue scene of the 1940s and early 1950s waned, some of jazz's adventurous young voices began carrying out experiments elsewhere in the city.

In the late Forties and early Fifties, LA-bred bassist/composer/bandleader Charles Mingus was making his way into the greater cultural world, as was ever-inquisitive master alto saxist/bass clarinetist Eric Dolphy—and Dolphy's 1959 departure from Chico Hamilton's LA-based band would pave the way for Lloyd's first major gig.

The boldest jazz muse out West during the late Fifties was Ornette Coleman, who came to LA from Fort Worth, Texas, and built a visionary jazz-based music of his own devising—"The Shape

of Jazz to Come," as the cover of one of his early LPs proclaimed—
abetted by an eager and empathetic quartet featuring Charlie Haden
(who had recently come to town from Iowa to study at LA's Westlake
College of Music) on bass, trumpeter Don Cherry (an Angeleno
since age four), and LA-native drummer Billy Higgins, who would
decades later figure strongly in Lloyd's musical life.

Young Lloyd, besides attending to his classical music studies by
day, interacted with a variety of players on the scene—including
some who would join Ornette Coleman's group, as well as future Bill
Evans ally bassist Scott LaFaro. Lloyd also worked in a late-Fifties
incarnation of the Gerald Wilson big band, an anchoring presence
in LA jazz for more than fifty years.

About his early years in Los Angeles, he recalled, "I went there
in '56 to go to college, for summer school, because I was run out
of Memphis. I was playing with a bunch of outlaws, with Willie
Mitchell, Al Green's trumpet player [Lloyd sings Green's classic
"Let's Stay Together"]. Girls would start chasing us at night. So I
came out here and met this whole community. There was a man
named Mr. Brown [Samuel Brown], who taught at Jefferson [a Los
Angeles high school where Brown's students included bandleader
Horace Tapscott; saxophonists Dexter Gordon, Eric Dolphy, Sonny
Criss, Big Jay McNeely, Frank Morgan, and Vi Redd; vocalists Ernie
Andrews and O. C. Smith; trumpeters Art Farmer, Don Cherry,
and Clora Bryant; trombonist Melba Liston; and drummers Chico
Hamilton, Larance Marable, and Bill Douglas]. When I was going
to USC, I had to get a music education and was going to teach. My
mom, from the South, said, 'You have to have something to fall back
on.' So I was going for a teaching degree. I was majoring in music
composition, and playing the clarinet. . . .

"Look, I came to California at eighteen. My peers went to Chicago
and other places, but I came here, and it was fortuitous. I met
Ornette Coleman and Eric Dolphy. We'd woodshed. The Gerald
Wilson big band was very important; it was like an institution. We
rehearsed every week, like going to prayer meeting every Monday
night. Walter Benton was playing tenor, Harold Land played, Don

Cherry, Billy Higgins, Frank Butler, all kinds of cats were playing in Gerald's band. There was a thriving community when I came out here.

"We were playing all the time. There were so many places to play, too. We were what you call 'outsiders' or something. We weren't relating to the scene of Shorty Rogers and Shelly Manne—the whole thing of what was called 'West Coast cool' music. But Scott LaFaro was out here. Charlie [Haden], Frank Butler, Elmo Hope, and Don Friedman were out here. Walter Norris, Sonny Clark. Clifford Jordan came out for a while.

"When I first got there, there was a place called Stadium Club, off of [the USC] campus. There were a lot of clubs everywhere, and sessions were going on around Western Avenue. There were all these places—the It Club, the Hillcrest, Alhambra, the California Club. There were Monday-night jam sessions with Frank Morgan and Larance Marable.

"When I first got out there, it was this cauldron. We were always getting together and playing at people's houses. Chauncey Locke, a trumpet player, Lester Robinson, a trombone player in Gerald's band. Gerald's band was like this messianic thing he had. He had beautiful arrangements. It was a Holy Grail.

"Ellis Marsalis was out there. Did you know that? He was a good friend of mine. He heard me at a session. He was older than me. He always had the teacher kind of thing he has now, that professorial thing. I was going to USC and was maybe a freshman or sophomore. He was in the army, at El Toro, the Marine base down there. He would come up on the weekends—I had a little house off campus—and get me. . . .

"We would make all the sessions. He had that thing like his boys [Wynton and Branford] have, kind of brash. We'd just walk in on the scene and start playing, move the piano player over and just started playing. He was very helpful to me. . . . I remember Horace Silver had a record out, the song called 'Room 608' [starts singing a beboppish line]. He wrote that stuff out for me. We'd go and just tear these places up playing that stuff."

Speaking of the musical talent roaming Los Angeles at that time, Lloyd remembers, "I had a group with Bobby Hutcherson, Scott LaFaro, and Billy Higgins back in '56, playing at a place in Pasadena called the Dragon Wheel. We were on it. Don Cherry played with us sometimes. Then they started playing with Ornette later.

"There were very few gigs, but we got to play all the time. It wasn't about bread. There was no bread. It cost a dollar or two to go somewhere. It was based on the hunger—the starvation for the elixir—because the life didn't work. It's just like now, the life doesn't work for folks, even if they've got plenty. What happens is that you need peace first, and then prosperity. Prosperity without peace ain't no kind of prosperity at all. That's part of the dilemma of so-called modern society.

"It's the peaceful sutra. Well, where do you get that from? The arts, from beauty. Beauty inspires and lifts one's spirits up on the human journey."

Lloyd continues: "I was in a beautiful 'college' in Memphis. Phineas [Newborn Jr.] played with us. . . . Booker [Little Jr.] and I played with Phineas and all those guys. Then, in LA, there were Eric [Dolphy] and Charlie Haden and all those peers. Paul Bley was out there.

"There was a trumpet player, Martin Banks, who was wonderful, too. There was an alto player you never heard of, called George Newman, who was out of the Bird tradition, but he had his own unique individuality. He sang so beautiful on his horn. Oftentimes, they were putting him in mental institutions. Don Cherry was a friend of his. Don Cherry would bring him around and we'd all be happy because George Newman was there. . . . He could wipe us all out. He had that original impetus, like Bird playing. Great cat. Cherry used to bring him to the sessions and sit in the back and watch him go—he'd sic him on everybody. People just stop in their tracks, couldn't play after that. . . .

"There was another friend, who was also a journalist who worked for *The New York Times*, named George Goodman. His folks own a paper down in Los Angeles called the *Sentinel*. [Founded in 1933, the *Los Angeles Sentinel* is the oldest and largest African American–owned newspaper on the West Coast.].... Anyway, George Goodman was a wonderful tenor player and he put his horn away and picked up the pen more. But I remember he oftentimes would play. I heard him play one night at the 911 Club on Jefferson [Blvd.] there in Los Angeles and he sounded beautiful.

"But there were a lot of people around there. Sonny Criss was down there. Dexter [Gordon] was around there. Older guys. Harold Land was there, and Buddy Collette was the one who recommended me to Chico [Hamilton].... That was a rich period."

Ornette

Lloyd's early LA period was especially supercharged by his proximity to the emerging iconoclastic firebrand Ornette Coleman, and the musicians Coleman both inspired and irritated with his new ideas.

"I've always loved Ornette," Lloyd states excitedly. "His Studebaker had smashed up his horn, so he had that funky old plastic horn out. [He] said, 'Okay, you can play the saxophone, but dig this.' I was going to USC. He was out there on the streets mining gold. I remember I used to watch him go to sessions. I remember once he was sitting in in a place called the Stadium Club, over by the Coliseum. It was a bar, and it said 'Jam session on Sunday'....

"Ornette tried to sit in with Dexter and those cats. They were playing one of those songs, like 'There'll Never Be Another You.' They turned the microphone off. That was in '56. We were all pushing, trying to get up there. They took an intermission.... I don't know whether I got in on that date, because I didn't understand the rules.... But I did get to witness how cruel it can be, and I witnessed how we die to play this music. We *have* to play this music.

"Ornette was on shaky ground, because he couldn't play changes to the tune, but he had this natural thing and nobody was accepting him on his own level then. He was talking about harmolodics then: 'If you take a B-flat, the natural note is always E and then an F-sharp will always come from that and any kind of C will *sound* on that. It will always have a sound, because any kind of note matches with another note and if you hit it at the same time, you will get a B-natural sound, because a piano is not built right. . .' He was always talking like that. We all had his script down.

"Then you'd go to his house and he had all this manuscript paper lying around with no bar lines, all this little crazy stuff on it. But it was hip [hums an Ornette tune]. He kept mining the stuff, though. He had these little tone poems that were just pure gems."

BUDDY

Reflecting on the crucial turns in his musical life, Lloyd looks back with particular admiration on the influential saxophonist/flutist/ clarinetist Buddy Collette: "Buddy Collette is Mingus's spiritual father. That should be known. Buddy is a beautiful man, a beautiful soul. See, he had kids and he had to raise them up. Something happened with the wife situation, I don't exactly know what happened. He is also Dolphy's spiritual father, a bunch of cats: James Newton. Myself, for sure, because when Eric Dolphy left Chico to go with Mingus, Buddy calls me on the phone. At that time, I was teaching school to save enough money to get my master's, to go to New York, because Ornette and Eric and everybody had gone. I was still left out here; coconuts were hitting me on the head, and I was just trying to get to New York.

"Buddy called me and said, 'I know you want to play. It's your time.' Read *Central Avenue Sounds* [the 1999 book coedited by Collette chronicling Los Angeles's famed jazz-filled haven from the Twenties through the Fifties]. They caused the merging of the unions. They had the thing segregated in Southern California. They also had these Southern cracker cops. Buddy has some stuff. Mingus was such an activist, but there was a time when Mingus wouldn't stand up to Buddy. Buddy was a beautiful man, and a sensitive soul. He told Eric who to study with, but he said, 'But just stay with this cat for a little while, because you don't want to lose your thing. The cat will teach you to read around the corner, but you want to keep your warmth.' Eric was always a very studious cat.

"The other thing with Buddy was that he sacrificed himself for his family, which is a noble thing. He's had a stroke and stuff, but to this day he is still vibrant. [Lloyd was speaking about Collette in 2000, two years after Collette had a stroke. That same year, Collette published an autobiography, *Jazz Generations: A Life in American Music and Society*.] He's so beatific now. Something happens. We come through life and then you matriculate and all these cats have something. I would sit down there at the Vanguard with Mr. [Coleman] Hawkins. He'd be drinking that scotch and looking at me, tuning me up. I was a kid. He's the father of the modern tenor saxophone, with that big, beautiful sound. . . .

"Then, Gerald Wilson was like a Duke Ellington cat for us. He comes out of Memphis, too. We went to the same high school, Manassas. He was there years before me. . . . Jimmie Lunceford taught at Manassas too, there was great musical tradition there. . . .

"All these cats inspired me so much. I'm still drunk, man, and armed and dangerous with what they gave me.

"Buddy Collette came to New York to do the music for Mingus, help him organize his stuff for the Town Hall concert back in the Sixties. . . . Buddy was the brains behind that. He was a rocket scientist, he put all that music together. Buddy came to New York for a month to put that together, and stayed at my place in the Village, at One Sheridan Square. More people came to my apartment in that month when Buddy Collette was there than came in the whole ten years that I rented that apartment. I owe him a huge debt of gratitude, so does Eric. . . . People around the world still tell me, 'Boy, we were at your apartment when Buddy was there.' So, although he didn't get to live in New York, he was set up there. . . .

"Buddy was a teacher of all those cats, like Mingus. . . . He's been there with Ella and Sinatra and all different people. He's a very special man.

"Here's the kind of man he is: One man walks up to a wall and looks over, and he jumps, because he figures, Why stay in this vale of tears? He sees what's on the other side. Another man walks up to the wall, climbs up and looks over on the other side and he's gone. The third man looks over the wall, looks over and sees what it is, and he carefully climbs down and wants to serve suffering humanity. That's who Buddy is. He stayed to take care of his kids. He worked with all of that studio stuff, as one of the first cats who integrated into the studios, with Groucho Marx's [TV] show band and all that stuff."

SCOTTY

Lloyd had a special connection with bassist Scott LaFaro, whom he calls "my dearest friend when I was a kid down in Los Angeles."

"Do you know Scotty used to be a clarinet player? And Scotty copied Bird's solo on 'Just Friends' for me, when I was a kid in college. We used to hang out all the time. He looked like Steve McQueen and he could drive a car like McQueen. He could drive a car through a little spot, said 'Watch this,' *phew* . . . pedal to the metal. You'd just close your eyes. He would rub his hair. He'd play those metal strings. I remember when we were kids, we played a lot together.

"Scott could drive a car through a needle. It was strange that he died in a car accident. He was a very beautiful being, also. He also was on one of Booker Little's records. He left us one time in LA to go play in a band with [pop singer/actor] Dick Haymes. Guess who the drummer was—Elvin Jones! [Laughs.] You don't think about guys like that with guys like Tony Bennett. But Tony Bennett did some stuff with Bill Evans. Remember that Lady Day record, *Lady in Satin*, with arrangements by that guy [Ray Ellis]? Lady's voice was gone, but she was still able to bring forth the mysticism of sound. You have to lay down and weep with that.

"Well, man, that's all I know. I'm still drunk from that kind of experience. And I was around these guys who created this music. Duke Ellington, Strayhorn, and all that stuff. I'm still like a kid who has all of these synchronicities of all of that stuff, and how it opened up and affected me."

A World of Music

Tracing the musical evolution and stylistic components of Lloyd's music through the decades of his professional life can be a slippery exercise. Deep in the tangled roots of his music, elements of classical and pre-jazz Western musical thought mix freely with the ideas of the great composers and performers of jazz and elements from various non-Western musics. "In music, I live for removing time. I love when the music is happening. Don't misunderstand me: I come from a tradition. I play out of Duke and Bird and such, as well as Bach and even the medieval cats. I like those cats. I love music, man.

"I liked Ravi Shankar and music of Asia and Africa. I've always liked 'world music,' before they gave it a label. When I was going to USC I would always talk about Duke Ellington, and they didn't know anything about that. They'd always talk about Beethoven and stuff. Cool, Beethoven's a brother. Did you know that Beethoven was a Moor? He's a descendant of the Moors. They traced him back.

"Anyway, I love Beethoven, those late quartets—that's some bad shit. So I loved all that stuff, but they could be so shortsighted not to dig Duke. He's America's composer.

"One thing bothered me at USC. They said it was three hundred years of European classical tradition. I said, 'What are you talking about? What about African and Indian music, and Duke and Jimmie Lunceford?. . . What are you all talking about?'. . . They were telling me it was just about Wagner. Well hey-hey, I love Wagner, man—that *Ring* stuff and *Tristan und Isolde*. . . . I was listening to Wagner in Switzerland recently, the whole *Ring* cycle. I listened to it all night long. I couldn't believe it. I think I wet my bed, that stuff was so powerful.

"I love music. There was a man named Cool Jones, who used to work for my grandfather in Byhalia, Mississippi. I remember he used to sing the blues, and he sounded like Howlin' Wolf or something. That affected me. I remember hearing music in the church. My grandfather built a church, and on Sunday, they would just go *out*, singing and stuff. Sisters would just be jumping up, testifying. I loved *that* music.

"Then in high school, I used to play this Edvard Grieg stuff, and I liked that music. But then I heard Bartók and Stravinsky and those cats, that really perked my interest up. That's why I went to USC. I applied to Juilliard and all those places, because my mother said that after high school I could go to any school I want.

"The thing I didn't understand was that she struggled to make it possible for me. Parents make sacrifices and such. My mother, although she came from a wealthy family, died without much money. She was very sensitive, way ahead of her time. The environment wasn't so receptive or conducive for her. Had she been able to live a little longer, I think she would have gotten more accepting. . . .

"My father had extreme patience. He lived into his eighties. We were real tight. . . . Once, I asked him, 'Dad, what do you do when you and your wife have an argument, when you have a fight?' And he said, 'I have my say, and then I clam up.' [Laughs.] That was some deep wisdom. He answered my question. I remember the students in Phoenix loved him.

"I digress."

CHICO AND CANNONBALL, AND ON TO NEW YORK

Lloyd recalls that by the dawn of the Sixties his coterie of Los Angeles jazz allies was shrinking. "Scotty had left. Ornette and Eric had left. Guys were starting to leave around '59. In '60 I graduated and stayed on to work on my master's. Then I got this teaching gig, but I got a call from Buddy Collette saying, 'Eric just left Chico to join Mingus. I know you're teaching, but I also know you want to play.'

"*Bam!* That was my ticket out. I immediately moved east, because all my partners had gone before. I said, 'Send me a ticket.' He said, 'The plane ticket's on the way.' He gave me my start. He got me out of there. . . . He was the one who was the Underground Railroad for us. . . . If we had stayed in LA, nothing would have happened. That's just the nature of it."

Later, Lloyd gazes fondly at a shot of himself with Collette: "You tell people that's my hero. I owe everything to him. To this day, I might have been over there, teaching school. Nothing wrong with teaching school, except sometimes you have to do too much babysitting or something. But the other thing was, I noticed that, after the first payday . . . all the teachers were broke again after a week. That's not right. I thought, 'If it's this way, I might as well help myself do bad. I can do bad on my own.' So I wasn't worried. The students liked me and the principal said, 'Well, Charlie, anytime you get tired of those smoke-filled rooms, you can come back.'"

For Lloyd, the transition from school life to "real" life happened quickly, and on a fast upward trajectory. He had already been honing his chops and skills, and exploring new stylistic avenues as a young player full of vigor and curiosity on the Los Angeles scene. Suddenly, the Chico Hamilton gig not only gave him a public jazz platform upon which to showcase his talents, but in that band he assumed a directorial role, "finding himself" on the job.

"Chico said, 'Well, I'll reorganize around what you want to do.' I said, 'Cool.' I brought in [guitarist] Gábor Szabó and trombone player Garnett Brown. Later I brought in trombonist George Bohannon, because Garnett was a little too stiff. Albert Stinson was on bass. We got into it. Chico was a gentleman, like Cary Grant. He had his dignity. The cat lived in his fantasy. All these jazz musicians have their fantasies. I have my fantasies. I want to eat out of my own garden—those are fruit trees down there" [pointing to his yard].

With Hamilton's group, Lloyd landed in the right spot to launch a career somewhat separate from predictable palettes of sound and style. The LA-born Hamilton had established himself, starting in the mid-Fifties, as a bandleader and drummer with a great deal of flexibility in his attitudes about style and instrumentation. And he had assorted encounters with the film world, both in soundtracks and in onscreen performances. In 1941, he showed up in Fred Astaire's backing band in *You'll Never Get Rich*. In 1952 he was on the soundtrack for *Road to Bali*, a Bing Crosby–Bob Hope lark.

And in 1957, he and his band, with flutist Paul Horn and guitar-ist John Pisano, showed up in the gritty film classic *Sweet Smell of Success*. Hamilton's bands during the Fifties included such noted players as bassist George Duvivier, guitarists Howard Roberts and Jim Hall, Buddy Collette on flute and sax, and the mighty Eric Dolphy, who featured prominently in the Hamilton group seen in *Jazz on a Summer's Day*, a documentary shot at the 1958 Newport Jazz Festival.

Lloyd's imprint on the Hamilton band was indelible, and the experience itself seems to have provided Lloyd with a blueprint for much to come in his life. Hamilton's 1961 album *Passin' Thru* was a harbinger of a new jazz aesthetic in the making, including the cheery Caribbean sheen of the Lloyd-penned title track. But it was Hamilton's 1963 album *Man from Two Worlds* (a fitting phrase for Lloyd's musical identity) that solidified the emerging voice of Lloyd as a bandleader—even if he was not credited as such. Lloyd laid out the repertoire, writing the album's tunes, from the mix of modal waxings and tropical breezes of the title song to alternative blues tunes and tender resonances of softer material, such as "Child's Play" and "Love Song to a Baby," a Bill Evans like waltz number featuring Lloyd on flute.

That album also sports the first recording of Lloyd's most widely known piece, "Forest Flower," in a ten-minute version that moves around the contours of its chord changes in swing and beguine grooves. It's a mild-mannered prequel to the "Forest Flower" that would win legions of new fans several years later in Lloyd's freer and more volatile band with Jack DeJohnette and Keith Jarrett.

The *Man from Two Worlds* album has a sound all its own, espe-cially when compared with what else was happening in jazz at the time. Lloyd's mercurial and sometimes mumbling sax work—sweet, soulful, and brushing up against abstraction—blended empatheti-cally with Szabó's spindly, clean-toned, and vaguely Gypsy-flavored open-string-leaning sound, while Hamilton kept time and beauti-fully complemented the evolving sensibility of this Lloyd-led band.

Lloyd looks back on that innocent, simpler time with a certain qualified wistfulness: "The world's different now, because we're in the universal living room. With computers and airplanes, you can be anywhere like that [snaps his finger]. But in those days it was all about station wagons, driving across the country to play with Chico at Newport—the only gig he had. We made four hundred dollars. Then we'd go down to New York and sit in the Shaw [Artists Corporation] office and try to get on the phone and get some gigs out in places like Pittsburgh, where we'd make twelve hundred fifty dollars a week, gross, for the whole quintet and a road manager. . . .

"Cannonball [Adderley] called me and said he wanted to have a meeting with me. I'd been playing with Chico for three and a half years by then. They [Hamilton's group] were playing with that cello and guitar sound, kind of a chamber music sound. It was a niche. Billy Strayhorn was doing some arranging, nice stuff. But I wanted to emote and express myself, so I told him [Hamilton] after a while that I had to go. . . .

"I joined Cannon in '64, and that really broke Chico's heart. But I saw that I had to do it, because we were struggling. That was a fine group, but we were struggling, big-time."

Hamilton Reflects on Lloyd's Departure

In 2006, I talked briefly with Chico Hamilton. His memories of his experience with Lloyd seemed to reflect his disgruntlement with his young bandmate's sudden departure.

How did you first hook up with Charles Lloyd?

If I remember correctly, Charles graduated from USC, and the day he graduated I gave him a job. As a matter of fact, he lived in my house for quite a while. It was he and his wife, Joan, right? I haven't seen Charles in over twenty-five years. . . . As a matter of fact, I haven't seen Charles since he left my group. . . . I haven't heard from him, either.

How did you first hear about him?

First of all, I was reorganizing my group. I don't know who recommended him to me. As a matter of fact, he was playing alto at that time; he hadn't started playing tenor. Strangely enough, everybody wanted me to fire him [laughs]; they didn't like the way he sounded at that time. But I gave him an opportunity.

Did he actually replace Eric Dolphy?

No. That group with Eric was the last time I had a group with cello. I made a complete change from that. The group with Charles consisted of Gábor Szabó, Albert Stinson, and George Bohannon.

Charles made the switch from alto to tenor while he was in your group?

Yeah, that's right.

Was that his own idea or did you nudge him into it?

I think it was his idea.

That was a good group, with an unusual instrumentation.

I've never had common instrumentation in any of my groups.

How long did you play with Charles?

You mean how long did Charles play with me?

How long did Charles play with you?

Okay. I guess it was a couple of years anyway. When Charles left my group, I had no idea he was leaving. I heard on the radio that he was leaving my group to join Cannonball. He never did tell me. He was living in my house, playing in my group. I made him musical director of the group. And when he got ready to leave, I had no idea he was even leaving. I heard it on the radio.

About his coming into Adderley's band, Lloyd recalled, "Cannon loved my playing. He had a meeting with me and he said, 'I know you're great and are going to be greater. I want to hear you play every night, so I want you to join my group. I'll pay you *x* dollars.' In those days, we worked for about two hundred fifty a week, fifty-two weeks a year, all around the country. We'd go to Philly and Pittsburgh, Cleveland. He said, 'I'm going to put your name up there with me and my brother.'

"I was ambitious and young. I remember we were in some town and my name wasn't up there. So I went to [bassist] Sam Jones, who was the general in the band—'Mr. Home'—he was always giving advice. 'My name isn't up there, and Cannonball said he was going to put my name up.' He looked at me and said, 'You know how you get your name up there? Every time you go up on that motherfuck-ing bandstand, you play your ass off. That's how you get your name up there.' I was selfish, you know. Now these things come to me, these stupidity things of youth."

In the career scheme of things, Lloyd's 1964–65 stint with Adderley was short-lived, with Lloyd's work as a leader of his own band overlapping with his time in Adderley's, which at that time included keyboardist/composer Joe Zawinul (whose "Mercy, Mercy, Mercy," a tune he wrote during his Adderley stint, became a soul-jazz classic), trumpeter Nat Adderley, bassist Sam Jones, and drummer Louis Hayes.

Adderley's ensemble played its jazz fairly straight, with touches of harmonic sophistication mixing freely with strains of gospel/soul on such recordings as 1964's *Cannonball Adderley Live!*, which fea-tured Lloyd's tunes "Sweet Georgia Bright" (later revisited on some of Lloyd's own albums, including *Discovery!*, his 1964 debut album as a credited leader, and 2008's *Rabo de Nube*) and an extended version of his ballad "The Song My Lady Sings," which included an interesting *tête-à-tête* between Adderley's crisp alto phrasings and Lloyd's more broken-toned, modal-ish tenor lines.

In 1965, the Adderley band with Lloyd on tenor and flute issued an album of swinging, easy-does-it versions of tunes from the cur-rent Broadway hit show *Fiddler on the Roof.*

Lloyd felt that "Cannon's group was more traditional than I was interested in, but it was a way for me to blossom to another level of playing. I did it. He also played my pieces. It was a beneficial thing, and I stayed with him for about a year and a half. It's the apprentice process.

"Then, after that, I started with my group, four hundred dollars a week at Slug's [Slug's Saloon, a jazz club active on NYC's Lower East Side from the late 1960s through the early 1970s], for the whole quartet. But in those days I had great bands. I had Herbie [Hancock] and Pete La Roca, Ron Carter, Henry Grimes, Steve

Kuhn, Joe Chambers, you name it, all the cats. It was New York, and a beautiful time.

"I had heard Keith [Jarrett] while I was with Cannonball. He called me once when he was on the road with [Art] Blakey and was unhappy. I was out on the road with Gábor, Albert Stinson, and Pete La Roca. He wanted to play with me. I said, 'When I get back to New York, we'll talk about it.' So when I hit it with that band—with him and Jack [DeJohnette] and Cecil McBee—when we played our first gig in Baltimore, it was special. The band took off.

"There was a special chemistry, and everybody knew it."

4

Marquee Trajectory

Forest Flower's Flowering

Listening with hindsight to the eighteen minutes that make up the tune "Forest Flower" on the album *Forest Flower: Charles Lloyd in Monterey* can be a strangely crystallizing experience. This performance of this tune was a potent, fulcrum moment in Lloyd's musical life and the catalyst for what would become one of the first jazz records to sell a million copies, as well as the track most likely to be rattling around in the mental recesses of his ever-growing legion of fans—especially his young fans from outside the jazz world.

Lloyd penned the tune, with its gently restless harmonic structure and idyllic spirit, while in Chico Hamilton's group, with whom he performed and recorded it earlier (1963). But in comparison with those earlier performances of it, his 1966 Monterey Jazz Festival rendition, with his band of young virtuosos—Keith Jarrett, Cecil McBee, and Jack DeJohnette—turned out to be something altogether different. Although Jarrett steals the show in some ways, as later pianists in Lloyd's groups sometimes have, Lloyd also puts forth a commanding performance on both movements of the two-part tune—its core "Sunrise" section and its extended vamping coda, "Sunset"—with a voice that alternates beautifully muted, searching statements with bursts of boldness.

As Lloyd's manager, the noted record producer George Avakian, wrote in the album's liner notes, "The music speaks for itself—a comfortable cliché, but nevertheless true, for it is a unique and personal music which communicates universally. While it has a distinct individuality—Charles Lloyd has created an expression all his own—it draws on every kind of music imaginable." Well, that may be an overstatement, but in 1966, before the term and concept of "fusion" in jazz were commonplace, the Lloyd quartet's collective vocabulary must have seemed more inclusive than exclusive or locked into any particular -ism.

Avakian ends his notes by commenting that, during the Monterey set's finale, "some measure of the joyous atmosphere in the crowd might be inferred by an incident that took place during this final piece [the quartet's spirited version of the jazz standard "East of the Sun"]: someone let loose a blue balloon and the crowd happily kept it bouncing in the air throughout the performance. Buoyancy through group cooperation is, indeed, one of the results of the happiness generated by the Charles Lloyd Quartet!" Avakian's use of "buoyancy" and "universality" perhaps points toward the potential of this intellectual yet high-energy-espousing band to reach heights of popularity rarely attained by such bona fide jazz musicians.

In 1997, I asked Lloyd about the delicate dance between art and commerce he navigated in the Sixties, especially after his *Forest Flower* album blossomed into a great public forum that created a broad fan base for him and his band. Did he feel at the time that he was being sucked into some sort of commercial machinery that he wanted nothing to do with?

"Absolutely," he replied, "because the merchants saw something there, in that I had an audience and some appeal. . . . It wasn't because they promoted the records—they were shocked that it was selling."

ON BORROWED HORNS, WIND, AND YOUTH

"After [the Monterey Festival performance], we went to San Francisco. . . . I left the horn on the curb. We were at the El Matador in North Beach. Joe Henderson is in the audience, [as were] a bunch of saxophone players and musicians who were all at the festival. I didn't even have my horn, and I wasn't concerned. Jimi Hendrix and I had just been hanging out. I was *ripped-boom*.

"I remember there was all this noise around me and then something happened. When you're in the *now*, there's only now, and I don't know what the commotion was about, but finally Joe handed me his horn. It may have been hours later. I remember he had a really soft setup. When you're in the state that I was in, like, Sandoz-altered [referring to Sandoz Laboratory, which first produced LSD in the 1940s], I could adjust.

"Bird had to do that all the time, because he was always borrowing someone's horn. You heard the story about Miles and Art Farmer? When Miles was in bad shape, somewhere in the Fifties, he didn't have a horn. He would pay Art Farmer to use his horn. He would rent his horn, basically. One night, Art said, Miles came to him and said, 'I need your horn. I got a gig.' Art said, 'I've got a gig tonight, too, Miles. I need my horn.' So Miles said, 'Man, I didn't think you were that kind of cat.' Art said, 'Miles, I'm not in the horn-renting business.'

"You have to adjust, so I adjusted to this guy's setup. I like resistance in my setup; it's about wind going through the thing, you know. See, I'm working on the sound. It's all wind. I study the ocean, the sound and how the wind comes off it.

"Coleman Hawkins messed me up. . . . He didn't weigh a whole lot, but he could blow you off the stand with such hugeness. That's what I was doing every night. I couldn't get that sound. Well, I wasn't going to drink that much scotch.

"See, Coleman was out in California, and so was Bird. It was happening out here. Then there was Buddy Collette, playing that alto. Here was this big guy. I didn't understand. I thought he played like . . . [sings] *toot-toot-toot*. I didn't know anything when I was young. Then he'd go to the studio and make some bread and drive around in a Cadillac.

"Youth is kind of a messed-up stage sometimes. I also thought, when I was extremely young, that I wouldn't have a saxophone in my mouth when I'm fifty. I thought jazz was a young man's music, it was that 'Live fast, die young, leave a beautiful corpse' idea. The point was, I thought that you had to burn the candle and go ahead and go for it. I'm learning now, more than ever. And I'm closer to finding my sound.

"When I was a kid, the old guys in Memphis used to say, 'You know, it's going to take thirty years.' I would say, 'What are you talking about?' They said, 'You'll find out.' They would talk about Johnny Hodges and people like that. They didn't want me to have delusions of grandeur. What they were really saying was that it takes a long time to get a sound, and then it takes a long time just to understand this campus."

OF COURSE, OF COURSE—OF COURSE

For Lloyd, the road to the afternoon of the *Forest Flower* recording, and the success it paved the way for, was hardly a matter of happenstance. Before that concert's soon-to-be-classic quartet came into being (a band introduced on the 1966 album *Dream Weaver*, its only studio date), Lloyd was establishing his unique voice with his first two albums under his own name: *Discovery!* (1964) and *Of Course, Of Course* (1965), both produced by George Avakian.

Discovery! is a fairly tame outing by the standards of what was soon to come from Lloyd, and not really worthy of that exclamation point, at least in retrospect. Greater promise and fruits came from his transitional album *Of Course, Of Course* and then *Dream Weaver*.

A candidate for the Album Deserving Wider Recognition category, *Of Course, Of Course* shows Lloyd in strong, searching form amid a seductively airy but bold rhythm section featuring bassist Ron Carter and the young, flexible drummer Tony Williams. Gábor Szabó's notably spare and often conversational guitar parts show a cool kinship with the bandleader. The record opens with the free-ranging, swinging amble of the title track, which is followed by the boppish, Birdlike line "Apex"; two Lloyd classics in the making, "One for Joan" and "Voice in the Night"; the Monkish blues tune "Third Floor Richard"; and the standards "The Things We Did Last Summer" and "East of the Sun (and West of the Moon)," with Szabó's sense of restraint contributing to its distinctively less-is-more vibe.

Stanley Crouch penned the liner notes for the Mosaic label's 2006 CD reissue of *Of Course, Of Course*. Here, Crouch addressed a subject that has dogged Lloyd for most of his solo career—the Coltrane Comparison Factor. Crouch wrote, "What makes Charles Lloyd an important artist is not the ingredients that we can recognize as part of his identity but the fact that he has the kind of artistic temperament that pushed him in an individual direction. In a time when so, so many young tenor saxophonists were taken by John Coltrane, Charles Lloyd found his own way. He was not as overwhelmed by Coltrane's energy and the furious accumulation of notes that went from chordal structures that were characteristically difficult all the way over to the opposite direction of simpler, often minor modes that had little chordal motion but were approached through scales delivered with the same dense fury as his arpeggiated approach to harmonic materials. Charles Lloyd was surely influenced by Coltrane's two basic approaches but he was not pushed so far away from himself that he became a part of the indistinct darkness that merely shadows the motion of an innovator."

Coltrane Reflections

Throughout his life Lloyd has had a deep and abiding love for Coltrane's sound and vision: "I wasn't around Bird; he died before I got to hear him. But I feel real fortunate in my lifetime to have been around Trane. I heard Trane for the first time in about '55, when I was out in California at USC.

"It saddened me. I had a difficult experience. I remember one concert I was talking to Trane at intermission. He was so complimentary and encouraging. He always was with me. I said, 'You sound so beautiful tonight'; I always said that because he always did. I'd go to sit in the back room at the Five Spot or wherever he was. He'd played the shit for an hour and a half or two hours—one song—and the audience would be bathed in water. Everybody knew they'd had an experience. Elvin would be bathed in water. He was full-on. . . .

"And then I'd go in the back room and say, 'Trane, you sound so beautiful.' He said, 'Oh, Charles, I just can't get it tonight.' And he had found every high out of every deity that there ever was. He had articulated truth from Bombay to Berlin to Karachi. He was God incarnate; God was coming through him, electrified. When he played, it was like holding court . . . holding church. . . . It was that Pentecostal thing, just so strong.

"That's why I'm a little shy about what I do in terms of being a player. I notice a little backlash every now and then from some cats.

"I witnessed Trane playing at the Village Theater in the late Sixties—that was before it became the Fillmore East. He was up on the stage and he had a bunch of cats with him—a large group. Rashied Ali was playing. At this particular concert, Alice [Coltrane] was there too. This was before he took sick. The place was close to packed; you could hardly hear the sound system. This was before Bill Graham and technology stepped in. Say whatever you want about cats like Graham, but when I played there, I heard Archie Shepp talking to Ben Sidran on NPR, saying, 'You know, I went to the Village Theater one night and heard Charles Lloyd. What impressed and moved me was that you could hear what the bass player was doing. You could hear every note.' It was the Fillmore then.

"Ever hear Milford Graves? I liked him because he actually sat there at the drums and played like this [flails with arms in a loose and bouncy way]. Who's that guy who played with Cecil Taylor? Yeah, Sunny Murray. He played a certain way, but Milford Graves, man, really played organic mumba-jumba.

"Getting back to Trane, he'd heard Pharoah [Sanders]. Pharoah's name was 'Little Rock.' He came from Little Rock to San Francisco. I used to see him there; he played at all the jam sessions. He played in a manner kind of like Trane. Coherent. Bebop. He was getting it together. He was kind of mystical, quiet, not giving up a whole lot. Later he came to New York and then he turned his mouthpiece upside down and he told me he put his teeth on his reed—experimenting with sound.

"One day I was playing at Slug's Saloon—on the Lower East Side, on Third Street and Avenue C. Sawdust on the floor. It was kind of a beer bar. Pharoah came in and jammed. My group played the first set—that was before Keith joined. It would often-times be Herbie Hancock or Steve Kuhn on piano, Ron Carter or Henry Grimes on bass, Pete La Roca on drums, or Jack DeJohnette. Miles was sick a lot, so Herbie and those guys were off a lot. They would play with me. . . .

"They came in and tried to play 'There'll Never Be Another You,' and I was shocked, man. They couldn't play bebop no more. They had lost it, they couldn't play the eighth notes anymore. I'd heard Pharoah earlier in the Village play some hip stuff.

"I still maintain that if a cat doesn't swing, I don't know what that's about. When I played with Cannonball, they always talked about swing—he and his brother and Zawinul. Zawinul in those days was very influenced by Bud Powell and Barry Harris. . . . They'd always talk about who could and couldn't swing, and I said, 'Why do you cats always talk about that?' I was more inter-ested in the content of what was played. I took swing for granted. I thought that was a basic. A cat had to be able to swing.

"Duke said, 'It don't mean a thing if it don't got swing.' He also said, 'Nice guys are a dime a dozen. Give me a prick who can swing.' Coleman Hawkins said, 'A cat's stuff don't sound the same when he gets to New York for the first time.' I've experienced all that."

I spoke with Lloyd about *Of Course, Of Course* at the time of its CD reissue:

Gábor Szabó's role is really interesting on Of Course, Of Course, giving the ensemble palette a different feel than the piano-based rhythm section on Discovery!. John Abercrombie, who was in your band briefly in the Nineties, once spoke to me about how that influenced him.

Yeah, that was a big influence on him. That's a beautiful thing that Abercrombie and I hooked up, because I hadn't played with the guitar in so many years, and I missed that. . . . Gábor and I had such a special hookup.

When Of Course, Of Course *was made, was it a transition between your work with Chico Hamilton and your own quartet?*

No. When I left Chico, I went with Cannonball for a year and a half. I spent three years with Chico and then, in '64, I went with Cannonball for a year and a half, and it was during that period that I recorded that. Gábor and I were playing together with Chico, so I brought Gábor into those recording sessions. Then I had Ron [Carter] and Tony [Williams].

I liked to have confluences like that. Ron and Tony had this rapport and of course Gábor and I did, and of course I had a rapport with Ron and Tony, too. We were like young guys who were moved by modernity and how we could move through space and create waves through sounds. We had sat on the shoulders of all this tradition. We were modernists. We had a need.

I grew up around guys who were like taskmasters, guys like Phineas Newborn and George Coleman and Booker Little. Those guys had grown up with tradition. Ron is from Detroit, and Tony was from up in Boston, around Roy Haynes and all that kind of stuff. . . .

They were with Miles at the time. . . . He was having some health problems, so he didn't tour a lot. Whenever Cannonball was off, I would go off with them. Or sometimes I would play with Louis Hayes, [Joe] Zawinul, and Sam Jones. That was nice too. That was a beautiful rhythm section. They had a beautiful synchronicity, too. Nobody could walk like Sam, you know. Louis had that swing, and Zawinul, in those days, was coming out of loving Bud [Powell], Barry Harris, and all that.

This was your second album as the bandleader?

Yeah, the first album [1964's *Discovery!*] was with Roy Haynes and Richard Davis, and Don Friedman played piano. He was from California. We used to jam out here. He was one of the early ones to go to New York, and we used to play together a lot in New York. Also, Herbie [Hancock] played with me a lot, with Richard Davis or with Ron [Carter], or with Pete La Roca. Those guys I played with a lot, interchangeably. Reggie Workman played sometimes with me at the Vanguard and different places. Henry Grimes used to play with me.

One night, we'd been playing a waltz for a long time. After we came off the stand, Pete La Roca said, "You know, while we were playing, Henry Grimes leaned over to me and said, 'Are we in 3/4 or 4/4?'" And we had been playing for twenty minutes! We were just *gone*, man.

But, you know, I come from the time when we were drunk with the music. It was like a quest. I came from a time when that was so strong. That's what I don't understand about civilization and society today, how the beauty of this music and its forwardness—if you think of Prez and Bird and Lady Day and Trane, Hawk, and Miles and Mingus, all of this beautiful music—it just really validates the journey so much. For me, it set up a tone so strong that I can definitely do it into the coda, into the sunset, with the effulgence of all of that. It's so rich.

Being able to sit backstage with Coleman Hawkins, the father of the tenor saxophone and with all of this tradition and majesty, being able to be around Monk and Duke and Strayhorn and Johnny Hodges and Harry Carney . . . there's a feeling that I can't express in words.

In Memphis, there was a school, and in California, there was a school out here. Master [Billy] Higgins was close to me and [Don] Cherry, and Scott LaFaro, and there was Gerald Wilson's big band. . . . Then . . . we all migrated, because we had to get to Mecca, and so we left. We all just hooked up again. That time was so rich, there was so much music going on all the time.

Many of us lived downtown. Rents were inexpensive and we could find a place to live. We could go from the Vanguard over to the Half Note over to the Jazz Gallery, to the Five Spot, up to Birdland, and on and on. You keep going, and you end up, at four or five in the morning, and last call was at Birdland. New York was truly a twenty-four-hour city. You'd end up in Smalls' [a noted jazz club from the

1920s through the 1960s], up in Harlem. you'd just keep going. All we did was live and breathe music. My peers from Memphis were there. I was living with Booker [Little] when I first got there.

I got derailed just thinking about the beauty and the richness of it, and the deep spirituality of it, that affected me so much. I was so affected by being around the Holy Grail, when these giants were roaming the earth. It fills me so much. I got there just after Prez [Lester Young]. Of course, Bird left early. But Prez was there. I think we're so fortunate to have had all this.

Good Notice

In an August 1965 Down Beat, *critic Don Buday reviewed a show with Lloyd as leader, joined by his Adderley allies Joe Zawinul on piano, bassist Sam Jones, and drummer Louis Hayes. Buday was duly impressed: "Whether Lloyd is scaring any other tenor men I don't know, but judging from this hearing, he should be. No sudden luminary, he has apprenticed with several name groups (including his current tenure with the Cannonball Adderley Sextet) and now seems on the verge of really breaking out. His influences behind him, the voice is clearly his own.*

"More lyrical than most tenorists, Lloyd can drive with power and still coax out all the nuances. Equally deft on flute, he does not overuse the horn, as do so many others, but employs it merely to add scope. Tenor, he admits, is his horn. One of the new image-makers, his scholarly appearance and general stage presence command an attentive audience. . . . It seems only a matter of time before Lloyd sets out on his own. Enthusiastic responses such as those received at this concert may soon produce such a move. A strong writer and performer, he bears watching."

DOUBLE SCALE

Lloyd recalls the economics of the jazz world in the early Sixties: "Andrew Hill asked me to play on his fourth record [*Point of Departure*]. I had been playing at Birdland and around the world. He took me to a rehearsal with Richard Davis. Alfred Lion [the co-founder of Blue Note Records] and those guys were licking their chops, saying, 'We got a good one, we got a good one. He's the new discovery.' That was me, a new tenor guy on the scene.

"But then I was playing with Cannonball at the same time, and he told me, 'Now that you're playing with me, you really should get double scale when you record with anybody, because that's what I'm going to pay you.' Double scale means that instead of getting ninety dollars for a session, you should get one hundred eighty dollars. Well, so I said to Andrew: 'Cannon said I should get double scale on a recording.' He said, 'Sure.' But he made the mistake of telling Alfred Lion that 'this guy gets double scale,' and he [Lion] said, 'Oh well, we just undiscovered him.'

"So there's some weird stuff along the way in Babylon."

On the Road

"I played with Cannonball in '64 and '65, and then I went on the road with Gábor and Pete La Roca and Albert Stinson. Great band, man. Them two cats were junkies, Gábor and Stinson, and me and Pete were acid guys, smoking and coke. We'd drive across the country in a station wagon. There was no reason we should have made it.

"One time, out in the middle of the country, we had a kilo in the back of the station wagon. Pete was going back to New York. I think the other cats stayed out here. I remember it was just Pete and me in the car. Man, it was snowy and there was ice on the road in New Mexico or somewhere. Do you know, a truck jack-knifed in front of us and we both closed our eyes. I was driving. I don't know how it happened, but we ended up on the other side.

"I'm telling you straight-up: I've had experiences like that. I was driving a Ferrari, upstate New York, coming back down to the city. The car kept running off the road. I just said, 'Lord, you've got to keep this together for me. It's up to you.' Upstate New York is just these huge big mountainous, sheer drops. I had a doctor's appointment in the city. I could've stopped and spent the night in a motel, but I had an appointment with Dr. Needle, my dentist. What a name. So I pulled into this garage, and Richard Pryor

was in there. He looked at me, like the way I got out of the car,
I had been through hell and back. I thought, Boy, Richard with
his insights, he must have thought I was really out there, with a
cowboy hat on and a red Ferrari."

THE JARRETT CONNECTION

It was during Lloyd's Cannonball years that Keith Jarrett, and the
prospect of working with him, entered his life. "When I was with
Cannonball, I'd be downstairs at the Jazz Workshop and Keith was
upstairs playing with a girl singer. He was playing his buns off. He'd
be running down there to hear me and I'd run back upstairs to
hear him. He said he wanted to play with me. I said, 'Well, I'm with
Cannon, but when I get my thing together, we'll hook up.' About
a year and a half later, I got my group together. It was mid-'65 or
somewhere in there.

"On the road, Keith called me. He was with Art Blakey, but he
wanted to play with me. I said when we got back to New York, we'd
talk. So I put the band together with Jack [DeJohnette], who was
always calling me, and Cecil [McBee], also. . . . And that was a special formation, obviously. Birds of a feather, the synchronicity. . .

"But then my life, personally, turned because of all these excesses
and stuff. What's the guy say? Think of all the famous men who had
to fall to rise again—pick yourself up, dust yourself off, start all over
again. . . . Booker warned me: 'Don't do this fast-lane stuff.' I did it
anyway. I don't know what to tell young people about that."

In the documentary *Charles Lloyd: The Journey Within*, Jarrett
talks about connecting up with Lloyd: "The way I got together with
Charles was kind of strange, because I was playing commercially
and he was playing in the same building, but downstairs. I had gone
downstairs to hear him. I had never heard anything like that, at
least nothing that moved me so much. It was something that I felt
that I had known could happen, but that I had never experienced
hearing happen.

"I think art can show the people involved in it, through their art, if they're sincere, laws and truths about their art which are parallel to the laws and truth of the world and the universe, and . . . the knowledge of those can be applied to their lives. For instance, everything in nature flows. It's in the laws, and without that, probably art wouldn't be as important a thing.

"I enjoy hearing us more than I enjoy hearing anybody else. The thing about this group is that it's more complete more often than with anyone else I've ever heard. There's a feeling we seem to share with each other, a feeling for different kinds of prettinesses and different kinds of beauty. But it has a strength, though, that a lot of times is lost when something gets pretty."

Jack DeJohnette, who would leave the band shortly after *Charles Lloyd: The Journey Within* was made, underlines Jarrett's comments: "You can play with strength, but still yet not be violent. I like things to just flow. Whatever force or vibe, we just let it come through us. The music turns me on to life. I try to make my life reflect what the music does. You should be able to just close your eyes or open them and just relax and let the music take you on a little trip."

Lloyd once told me, "Keith is a true master and he plays with such inspiration and grace. That's the thing about this music: It's all-encompassing. It has this ability to dance on all shores. He comes from Allentown and I come from Memphis, and yet he's a dervish and maybe Memphis is in Egypt. Or maybe, as my grandmother said, our Cherokee ancestors came from Mongolia. She traced us back to there. Maybe some of my fieriness comes from my grandfather, who's a mixture of African and Irish. So it's all in there, but the song is a song of eternity and it shouldn't be about races and class systems.

"It's really time for us to get beyond all of that. It doesn't matter who you are and where you were born. It just matters that you get to that loving nature that's in you and share that with your other brothers and sisters. If someone's rude to me out there, I try to be mindful and say, 'Thank you very much.' I try to learn. It's all your

Charles Lloyd Quartet, Copenhagen, 1966 (left to right: Jack DeJohnette, Lloyd, Cecil McBee, Keith Jarrett). (*Photo provided by JazzSign/Lebrecht Music & Arts*)

attitude. As you are inside, so be it. It's not [that] you want circumstances to be great and then you will rise to the occasion. No, you have to carry that with you. You must carry your attitude of positiveness and open-mindedness.

"I tell you something: I got a feeling—this is intuition—that people, whether they know it or not, are very hungry for the beauty of the music again. The rock 'n' roll stuff has been promoted. I'm not trying to negate that. It actually comes from Robert Johnson and the Delta. Those boys around here putting a surfboard on Chuck Berry's stuff and the Little Richard thing and the Howlin' Wolf thing and the Johnny Ace thing. Bobby Blue Bland with the honeydripping stuff, and B. B. and all that. These little boys put a silk dress on it and bring it back and spin it around two or three times and somebody can merchandise it and stuff like that. I'm not nutting on a phenomenon like Elvis; I don't want to botherate with that. But the point is that there are sources of this stuff."

DREAM WEAVER

The album *Dream Weaver*, the Lloyd-Jarrett-McBee-DeJohnette quartet's first recorded outing, announced the arrival of an important new band that intended to stretch notions of what jazz might be. As if to telegraph both its departure from and roots in tradition, the album's first track, "Autumn Sequence," is a twelve-minute expansion of the standard "Autumn Leaves" into a three-part suite that features Lloyd's swirling and searching flute lines framing an expansive Jarrett solo that raises the piece's heat to a notable plane.

The title tune, which would become a staple of his concert song-book for decades to come, is in two sections, "Meditation" and "Dervish Dance," which ramble expressively for eleven minutes. A beautiful and reflective rubato tenor solo opens the piece. It leads into a bouncy one-chord vamp that gives way to a Jarrett solo that takes harmonic, abstract, and narrative turns all its own, hinting at the Jarrett solo piano persona that would blossom in the Seventies.

On Side Two of the LP, three other Lloyd tunes—"Bird Flight," "Love Ship," and the sweet-spirited two-chord crowd pleaser "Sombrero Sam"—fill out the program.

"When I see Keith now," says Lloyd, "I'm very touched with what he's done with his music and his life, and also Jack. I see them from time to time now. It's real beautiful, because Keith has this very wonderful balance. He's actually, probably in his soul, a dervish. He's got that thing deep in him. I remember on *Dream Weaver*, he would weave some very beautiful spells. I think we both had in common the love of the ecstatic. I think that's what music has always meant to me, that ecstasy.

"As I've matured more now, I still have a freshness and a feeling for that. Whatever my path and my tradition and the great masters that I've come through, we each are unique and we must bring our feelings and our creativity to it. What I think I bring to it is a culmination of all of those experiences and feelings, and yet my own unique individuality, which is something that is a blessing.

"I'm just thinking in the moment about the original quartet. We had such wonderful communication. That was such an orchestra. Jack was just so *right there*. Of course, Cecil was fine, except that Cecil was trying to keep us grounded. We were really space cadets. We were heading on out into the stratosphere. He was, like, 'I'm trying to keep this music together now, fellas.' We would be gone some nights. Cecil is wonderful. We called him the Sheik. I think Jack named him that. . . .

"How proud I am of Gábor and how his talent blossomed, and Stenson, and then working with Keith and those guys."

TV LAND

Lloyd, then as now, is a combination of gregarious self-knowing and retiring introversion, and he has a strong sense of the musical value of the Lloyd-Jarrett-McBee-DeJohnette quartet. At the time it was active, he was eager to have this band appreciated in a much broader forum than the then-current jazz world would typically accommodate.

Looking back at the time before this quartet found a broad audience, he says, "I remember I played on *The Pat Boone Show*, with Keith and Jack. I went to William Morris and I said, 'Hey, man, I got a great group. We can play our asses off. What's going on? We aren't being exposed. We're over here in these little clubs—Shelley's Manhole. . . . I think we ought to be exposed.' Groups were playing on TV shows. So they got my band on all those shows—*Joey Bishop*, whatnot.

"I remember, Michael J. Pollard had just made *Bonnie and Clyde* with Warren Beatty. He saw me in the dressing room and he just went crazy. Stephanie Powers was backstage and she was *fine*. She wouldn't give me the time of day. Michael Pollard was bowing and scraping, saying, 'Your music, man, is the first music to break out. It takes you places.' And then she said, 'Oh, I'm so sorry,' hitting on me, but then it was too late. I do remember when a joint fell out of my pocket and I saw it on the floor when I was playing flute and I had to shove it away."

Flying at Slug's

"I was playing at Slug's Saloon, with people lined up around the block. A painter friend said, 'What's happening?' I said, 'What do you mean what's happening? I got people digging my music. I'm having a good time.' During intermission, they'd take me outside and get me ripped. We would smoke! Then one night, people would come up during intermission and say, 'You were flying.'"

CROSSING BOUNDARIES

In the Sixties, Lloyd unabashedly crossed the lines of demarcation between the jazz and rock worlds, playing the Fillmore (a highly noted rock venue in San Francisco) before other jazz artists—including Miles Davis—and undoubtedly luring in some rock fans from that period who remain tuned in to his music now, whether or not they pursued other jazz interests.

Even so, he cherishes his link to the lineage and the "elixir of the masters" in jazz. In his overview of his own musical trajectory, he places himself squarely in the narrative and respected echelons of jazz (as well as certain strains of pop music).

"When I had the original quartet," he told me, "one day I was staying at the Hyde Park Suites in San Francisco and someone knocks on my door. Who was it? Diz. That was in the Sixties. That was a real honor. I've had Bob Dylan knocking on my door in the Village. That was an honor. I had Eric Dolphy, I had Trane. I've had great masters knocking at my door. But with Dizzy, at that particular point in time, I think I was at a searching, low point. Dizzy knocked at my door and it was kind of a real affirmation, a real kind of upper. You get what you need if you're ready for it and are ready to receive it."

I spoke with Lloyd in 2006 about that period, and the paradoxes attached to his cultural sidestepping.

Ravi Shankar often talked about his frustrations over the attention brought on by George Harrison's interest in his music, which led to a large audience but one with a shallow connection to the music, and

who mistook drug-induced euphoria for spiritual meaning. Thinking about the opening up of ears to jazz, world music, and other serious forms outside of pop and rock, did you have ambivalent feelings about circulating in rock circles?

First, when I was approached about playing a set at the Fillmore by these guys from the Committee Theater [the Committee was an improvisational theater group] in San Francisco . . . they said to me that they really didn't like jazz but they liked us and they came to hear us every night, since their theater was up the street. We were at the El Matador in North Beach, having gone there after Monterey [the year *Forest Flower* was recorded there].

This guy from the Committee told Bill Graham about us. Graham said, 'Well, bring them over on Sunday.' They told me there's this place called the Fillmore and they thought the young people would like us. I said, "Well, who plays there?" "Muddy Waters, the Grateful Dead, Chuck Berry . . ." And I said, "McKinley Morganfield [aka Muddy Waters]? I love him." There was the Delta staring me in the face. I had played with Howlin' Wolf. So I said *sure*.

We were supposed to play forty-five minutes, and the audience wouldn't let us off for an hour and a half. Bill Graham immediately started booking us. I didn't make a judgment about the audience, I just did what we do. . . . I remember the Grateful Dead, Jefferson Airplane, Janis, Steve Miller, and Jimi—they always wanted to be on the bill with us. And Carlos Santana has told me how he would stand at the front of the stage yelling, "Free the people, Charles, free the people."

It was a Holy Grail kind of thing. And I felt that I was on a mission to change the world. I later came to find out I needed to change myself first.

The Dead began to see how we would open up the music and improvise, and it influenced them. The Dead and the Airplane always had the best dope. Janis Joplin had Southern Comfort, which tasted like cough syrup.

Ornette and Miles criticized me for playing there, and the next thing I knew *they* were both playing there. I know that I am a music maker and I can't always control where I get to sing my song. I come from a time when we were always looking for it. So I go inside the music . . . and when I come out, they tell me an hour or two has gone by and it feels like a few minutes. It's a beautiful thing when the audience is ready to receive it, because then it helps us to go higher. You see, we're in service.

But you could be right: They might have had short attention spans. It's not for me to judge them. I was dipping and diving myself in those day—I had been up at Millbrook with Tim Leary and Richard Alpert in the early Sixties. [Both Leary and Alpert were psychology professors known for advocating the use of LSD; Alpert would go on to become the spiritual leader known as Ram Dass. Millbrook was an estate in the New York town of the same name where Leary and Alpert conducted some of their LSD experiments.]

Was the **Forest Flower** *phenomenon a double-edged experience— both blissful and also disorienting? Did the pressures connected to that album precipitate your getting off the music business bus and heading to Big Sur?*

I think, somewhere, Big Sur was always calling me, even when I was a kid in Memphis. I think it was Benny Carter who had a song called "Malibu." When I played it as a teenager, I had tears. But when I got to Malibu it had shifted, so I headed north to Big Sur, for the solitude and healing. In the process of going forward, there can be lapses and banana peels. I have fallen down many times. The important thing is to get up. That goes for all of us.

Success is a heady thing. I was young, and by the end of the Sixties I had lots of excess. Life on the road, life in the fast lane, had become unsavory. I was suffering inside and out. The music was suffering. The business people were talking about putting us in stadiums. It didn't seem to have anything to do with me or the art form or about uplifting humanity.

Yes, there were times when the Mack truck had me pretty flat—and, yes, the music business was a drag. That's the beautiful thing about life as school: We're all here to evolve and serve, whether we know it or not. "So here we are today," as Master [Billy]

The quartet in the late Sixties, with Jarrett doubling on soprano saxophone. (*Photo provided by Eric Sherman*)

Higgins liked to say. "We did all those wonderful things and all those not-so-wonderful things, but we're on a different airplane now." Eventually, you hope to get it right so that you don't have to come back and do it all over again. I want to be free of the wheel of birth and death.

An Era

Even though he was chased by inner demons and outward distractions during his Sixties heyday, Lloyd recognizes and appreciates the unique historical cultural convergences of the era. "I think the Sixties get a bum rap in a lot of ways," he says. "We've had a lot of casualties and few survivors, but there was a very deep culmination of what had gone before. For me, it was powerful and positive because lines of demarcation were breaking down. We were fed up with the narrowness of the stage set, of America's constipation and 'Pass the peas.' It was a worldwide thing and content was oozing. Even the radio format they made—'freeform radio'—you could hear Ravi Shankar and then Bill Evans and Bird and Maria Callas. That was something."

TALKING MILES, AND MILES TALKING

In the Nineties, Lloyd spoke of the hindsight on the Sixties that he received from his then-drummer Billy Hart. "Billy says wonderful things about me, which is surprising. He says I'm the one who changed the music in a lot of ways. Of course, everybody thinks Miles did. Of course, Miles did, through the decades. Hart was saying that you [should] look back and hear what Charles was doing.

"Miles was trying to get me to play with him early on, before I started my own group, when I was with Chico and Cannonball. But he and I couldn't get along. I had great love for his music, but sometimes he could be an interesting bunch of guys. Some of them I wouldn't want to march with. Miles was something, man. Whenever we would play, he would always be there. He was trying to get me to play with him all the time, but he and I couldn't get along like that. He had a way of messing over people. I didn't want to go along with that part of it. But he was very, very special."

The trajectories of Lloyd's and Miles's careers crossed in strange ways, including the sharing (or borrowing) of players, including Lloyd working with Carter and Williams in the *Of Course, Of Course* days and then Jarrett and DeJohnette going on to play with Miles after the Lloyd quartet self-destructed.

In *Miles: The Autobiography*, his famous 1989 "as told to" book with Quincy Troupe, Miles spoke of the period in the late Sixties and the Lloyd story as he saw it:

> A lot of things were changing in music around 1967 and 1968 and a lot of new shit was happening. One of them was the music of Charles Lloyd, who had become very popular. When his band was really happening he had Jack DeJohnette and a young piano player name Keith Jarrett. He was the leader, but it was those two guys who were making the music really happen. They were playing a cross between jazz and rock, very rhythmic music. Charles never was any kind of player, but he had a certain sound on the saxophone that was kind of light and floating and worked with what Keith and Jack were putting under and

around it. His music was very popular for a couple of years so people started paying attention.

Our two groups shared a bill at the Village Gate at the end of 1967 or early 1968. Man, the place was packed. I knew Jack from when he filled in for Tony, and when Charles's group was in town I would go over for a listen. He started accusing me of trying to steal his musicians from him. Charles didn't stay around for too long, but made a lot of money during the time he was hot. I hear he's rich and selling real estate today, so more power to him.

Psychedelia

Lloyd talks, a bit cryptically, about a natural by-product of life in the Sixties fast lane: recreational drug experimentation and tripping—"flying without a license," as he puts it—with Timothy Leary and others. "I spent time doing research, authorized and unauthorized. I was going up to Millbrook and places like that. I remember one time Herbie Hancock and I went up there. Mingus, too. Millbrook was the estate that the Mellon family [heirs to oil and banking fortunes] owned, and Tim Leary and Dick Alpert had a facility up there where Sandoz lab was sending over research materials. We were doing research with, uh, internal stuff. . . .

"We saw ourselves as anthropologists from the twenty-first century inhabiting a time module set somewhere in the dark ages of the 1960s. On this space colony we were attempting to create a new paganism and a new dedication to life as art."

THE BYRDS AND . . .

In a nostalgia-waxing moment, Lloyd remembers, "I was talking to David Crosby down at one of my favorite eating places, La Super-Rica. We were reminiscing. . . . My group had Gábor Szabó and Albert Stinson and Pete La Roca. Crosby was with the Byrds. . . . This was around '64, before things broke open. I was on Columbia at that time, and so was their group. I said to the people at Columbia, 'You really ought to record us together, because it would really be something.'

"Dave told me something far out. He said that Miles told Columbia, 'You should sign those white boys there.' Miles had heard them somewhere down there in the Village. It's strange how things go.

"I told David Crosby about that. . . . That's something that would have been interesting. They were doing 'Mr. Tambourine Man,' and 'Eight Miles High' in those days.

Dylan was a friend, because I was living in the Village in those days. We were all hanging out. Jimi Hendrix was playing down the street for nothing at some little place. Jimi was a very close friend, a very sweet guy. We also planned to do something together.

"When I wanted to do something with the Byrds, there was a guy at Columbia named Billy James who was for it, but the powers that be said, 'No, no, no, we're not going to mix this stuff.' They weren't ready for it. It was too early—we're talking '64. Everything was compartmentalized—jazz over here, rock over there. . . .

"We had these other friends—Robbie Robertson and the Band, with Dylan. We used to hang out and spend time together, up around Woodstock. Robbie and I were very close friends. They were very wonderful. They had that Arkansas-Canadian thing, because Levon [Helm] was from Arkansas and then there was Robbie, Rick Danko, Richard Manuel, and Garth [Hudson]. They had something really soulful." [Robertson, in fact, appears in a jangly cameo on the bonus track "Sun Dance," included on the 2006 CD reissue of Lloyd's *Of Course, Of Course*. As Lloyd put it about that track, "Robbie played some nasty breaks, man."]

Lloyd continues, "We don't need all these polarities and hatreds and stuff. It seems like things are getting back to the Fifties or something. I don't experience that when I play, but in a secular sense I feel that. When I play, it's very sacred. It's all I have, and I give it my life's breath. But just matriculating around the world, I sense that there's a kind of harshness—again, going back to the quality of the arts and the sacredness of a vision or something uplifting. If you don't have that in a culture. . ."

THE ACOUSTIC WORLD

Throughout his life as a bandleader, and as jazz musician in the company of rock 'n' rollers and a performer at rock palaces like the Fillmores East and West, Lloyd has maintained an allegiance to the purity of acoustic instruments, occasional brushes with clean-toned electric guitarists notwithstanding.

As he says, "I still like the warmth of breath in music. I don't know about the modern world. You can deal with the computer chip and all of that. I've got that stuff at my house, but I don't know."

Does it leave you cold?

Yeah, I think so. No, it's about the soul of the person. I remember this guy Walter Carlos who was doing the *Switched-On Bach* on the Moog synthesizer, and he changed his sex later on [becoming Wendy Carlos]. I stayed at his house. . . . He made dinner for me, because I was interested in the Moog synthesizer when the thing came out. He took me over to the factory where they made those things. I've always been curious.

Herbie Hancock was always curious, and he really went off into it. I had Keith playing those things, some electric keyboards, for a minute.

I guess Jarrett didn't take to it.

No, but he played it with me for a minute and he also played it with Miles. We were all kids, interested in looking into new ideas, but then you get deep into the breath and the *prana* [Sanskrit for "life force"]. Then again, there are different temperaments for different people. I still love the organ. I plan to do something with that someday.

IN THE USSR

In 1967, in a strong gesture of support from its readers, *Down Beat* magazine's Reader's Poll named Lloyd "Jazzman of the Year." The award was deserved, particularly given Lloyd's meteoric rise in acclaim and widespread public attention and the success of his quartet's tours of the US and Europe.

In a *New York Times* review on May 6, 1967, just before the band made a historic visit to perform in the Soviet Union, at a jazz festival in Tallinn, Estonia, reviewer Theodore Strongin sized up the band's performance at New York's Town Hall.

> The Charles Lloyd Quartet roughly qualifies as an avant-garde group. There are other groups who play wilder and more concentrated jazz, and still others who work up more impetus than Mr. Lloyd and his men. But few are as free in their associations. Few can pivot as easily and instantly from a straight swinging line to a funeral march or a bit of Latin rock or a belly dance—or to the kitchen sink, for that matter. The quartet uses any sound that comes to mind.
>
> Mr. Lloyd himself alternates on flute and tenor saxophone, mainly. But when necessary he will switch to maracas, making them hiss like rattlesnakes as he propels the other quartet members along.
>
> His pianist, Keith Jarrett, has a collection of bells and other noisemakers inside the piano, and he periodically brings these out, or strums directly on the piano strings, or even wails into the microphone, Arabian style. In one number there was a fine duet, with pianist and drummer (Jack DeJohnette) each wailing while playing, and Mr. Lloyd, on maracas again, and Ron McClure, the bassist, spurred them on.
>
> The point is, they made all this grotesquerie seem natural, even ingratiating. They are avant-garde in the sense they embrace whatever sounds and associations that come to mind, without regard to convention. But they are also old-fashioned enough showmen to relieve the concentrated moments with episodes of solid, loose-limbed, swinging jazz. They will probably go over big in the Soviet Union, after the first impact.

Reuters News Service gave a succinct account of Lloyd's May 15 concert at the Tallinn Jazz Festival (an intense and rollicking performance preserved on the 1967 LP *Charles Lloyd in the Soviet Union*):

> The Soviet Union's first international jazz festival ended tonight after the Charles Lloyd quartet from the United States received a standing ovation from thousands of fans in Tallinn, Estonia.
>
> The way-out American group had been refused permission to play before live audiences for the first three days of the four-day festival. Soviet officials offered to allow it to play before a limited audience of festival organizers or in an empty hall for television, but Mr. Lloyd refused.
>
> Today, however, the officials relented and he was given the opening spot in the evening program. His tenor saxophone and flute playing probably gave Soviet jazz fans their first direct experience of what's happening in American jazz.

Looking back on that historic trip, Lloyd sees it as a watershed moment, not only musically but in terms of transcending political blocs and cultural blockades.

"We were going to Russia to play over there. We had this invitation from the people. It wasn't from the government, it was from the people.

"It caused such huge dissension and weirdness with politicians. They jumped in, and it had nothing to do with them. It had to do with people who invited us as musicians to come and share this experience. The politicians got in there. They called and said, 'A group called the Citizen Exchange Corps [a nonprofit cultural-exchange organization founded in 1962 to sponsor visits to the USSR by private US citizens] is going to underwrite your trip.' I said, 'What are you talking about? Who are these people? What do they want?' I had a binocular. They said, 'Well, they just want to underwrite the trip.'

"Sure enough, they thought I was outspoken or something like that, and they decided that the Russians wanted me to come over there because the Americans had escalated the war in Vietnam. I just finally fired back and said, 'I'm just coming in the spirit of music, which transcends politics. You guys have got to cut the rhetoric, 'cause it don't hold no sway here. . . . These people have invited me. It's not about your kroner. I'm not asking for any of it. I have my own kroner. I'll underwrite it.'

"That blew everybody away. They backed off, because they thought I would be like a showbiz guy in a blue suit and go over there and play, and come home. That was what it was about for me.

"I'd gone around the world, played Russia and all that stuff. I would speak up about injustice and stuff like that. The whole thing in the Soviet Union is that they didn't want me to play. We were invited to Estonia to play. We get to Estonia and they wouldn't let us play because of politics. Then they would send different cats around, saying, 'Will you do a clinic for the musicians and a TV show?' They wanted to keep me anywhere but in front of the people—there were about five thousand people waiting for the stuff.

"We had been invited by the music committee. The other thing was, the Vietnam War was escalating and they said, 'We don't want you to come because of the war.' I said, 'Hey, I'm a musician, dealing with the spirit of peace. I'm not advocating war.' I wanted to go, as a citizen of the planet. It's like Cuba. . . . Those people are suffering, but at least they've got medicine. In France, man, you get sick or something, in that country, you go to the hospital and fix you up and give you a bill for forty dollars. What's going on?

The quartet in the late Sixties. (*Photo provided by Eric Sherman*)

"But we finally played and the people loved it. Then we went to Moscow and Leningrad. One place, in St. Petersburg, we went to a concert where the audience was locked in. They told us not to come in. But the underground people had an alternative venue, because they knew this was going to happen. So they took us out to the country somewhere, and people were waiting out there for us. They were going to get it, one way or the other."

The album *Charles Lloyd in the Soviet Union* was recorded on May 14, 1967, in the Kalevi Sports Hall in Tallinn. The LP's four tracks—"Days and Nights Waiting," "Sweet Georgia Bright," "Love Song to a Baby," and "Tribal Dance"—lean toward the epic in length (with "Sweet Georgia Bright" logging in at over eighteen minutes), and the quartet's playing is both exploratory and expansive.

ACTION-PACKED LATE SIXTIES

Within a short, densely packed period of time the Charles Lloyd Quartet took on the world, broke new records for the jazz business, and abruptly imploded. This was also a period well documented through a handful of live recordings rushed out by Atlantic Records.

The generically titled *In Europe*—possibly the strongest ever officially released by the group—was recorded in Aulean Hall in Oslo, Norway, in 1966. Albums with the Summer of Love–appropriate titles *Love-In* and *Journey Within* (both with bassist Ron McClure replacing Cecil McBee) were recorded at San Francisco's Fillmore West on the night of January 27, 1967.

Naturally, there was backlash in the midst of the heady rush of attention, global touring, and various rapid gains for the Lloyd group. In *The New York Times* on September 15, 1968, well-known critic Martin Williams floated some questioning notions in a column with the loaded headline "Will Charles Lloyd Save Jazz for the Masses?":

> Tenor saxophonist Charles Lloyd has won a "Jazzman of
> the Year" award from Down Beat magazine, has been written
> up in several slick magazines, and has represented American

culture abroad in a tour of the Soviet Union. He is also destined, according to one observer, to carry contemporary jazz to mass audiences, including rock audiences—even to save jazz from hopelessly esoteric forms and practices.

Lloyd certainly puts on a show of sorts. With wildly bushy hair, military jacket, and garishly striped bell bottoms, he looks like a kind of show-biz hippie. He usually sounds like a kind of show-biz John Coltrane.

Williams's piece about jazz populism included a dismissive review of the 1968 Lloyd album *Nirvana*, featuring tracks recorded a few years earlier (in 1962 with Chico Hamilton's band and 1965 with Lloyd's Szabó–Carter–La Roca group), which Columbia released to cash in on the late-Sixties Lloyd buzz. Soon thereafter, Lloyd's Jarrett-McClure-DeJohnette band cut its final album, *Soundtrack*, recorded at NYC's Town Hall on November 15, 1968. The album ends with a seventeen-minute version of "Forest Flower" (called "Forest Flower '69," as if anticipating the impending demise of the band and Lloyd's high-flying public profile in that final year of the decade, in all its tumult and ecstasy).

JACK DEJOHNETTE, LOOKING BACK FROM 2006

I spoke with DeJohnette in 2006, on the general theme of his formative period in Charles Lloyd's quartet, especially post–*Forest Flower*.

***Do you have strong specific memories of the performance or the period that produced* Forest Flower?**

The Charles Lloyd Quartet was the first band that got me and Keith and Cecil international recognition. It came about around the time when the climate for music in America was more experimental. The group was quite innovative in that it was one of the first jazz groups that crossed over, that played at the Fillmore West, Bill Graham's venue. We have some recordings from there.

But the first record, *Dream Weaver*, actually created quite a bit of attention. We have a tune on there called "Sombrero Sam" that got a lot of airplay, and things started opening up for the group. It was one of the first crossover groups to receive international attention. Subsequently, we followed that up with going to Russia. That was an incredible experience with the group, in communist Russia.

That was in Estonia?

Estonia, St. Petersburg, and then Moscow. I remember we got a chance to go to the Hermitage there.

It was a group that was pretty eclectic. The group had musical flexibility and it was kind of a visual group as well, between Keith and Charles. Visually, it was an exciting group to watch.

Yes, those guys don't just stand and deliver. It's interesting to listen back to that group. There's an intense quality between the musicians. I don't quite know if there was anything similar at the time. Was there?

There were some other groups around. There was a group that didn't get as much recognition as we did, called the Free Spirits. It consisted of the late Jim Pepper, the Native American saxophonist, Bob Moses, Larry Coryell, and Chris Swanson. I don't even know if their records are still in print. They were doing experimental genres and different types of music. There were a few groups around, experimenting doing different things.

There was another group called The Fourth Way, with Mike Nock and Jerry Hahn, the West Coast guitarist. It was interesting: The Charles Lloyd Quartet predated Miles's playing the Fillmore by a few years. The Charles Lloyd Quartet was there first. Subsequently, other jazz bands played there and then Miles was at the Fillmore— Fillmore West and Fillmore East.

We were out there in the hippie period and doing shows with people like Jefferson Airplane, the Grateful Dead, Janis Joplin, and Big Brother and the Holding Company. There was Elvin Bishop and the Paul Butterfield Blues Band, a band called the Electric Flag, with Buddy Miles in it, and also Cream. It was a very interesting period, a really exciting time.

The thing about the group was that we had a lot of freedom. . . . Charles gave us a lot of liberties to take with the music. Each time we played the pieces, they turned out differently.

You're mentioning some groups that were paving the way for fusion and bands with electric instruments, but your group was acoustic and coming out of the Coltrane mode, wouldn't you say? It had the same instrumentation.

You might say that, although I think the intent was trying to reach a wider audience with it, but still have the musical integrity be intact.

Were you surprised when **Forest Flower** *became a huge sensation?*

Not really. It's kind of a catchy tune. I'm not surprised by that. Simple melodies have a better chance of becoming popular. It's a very catchy melody.

This was the beginning of a long and fruitful connection with Jarrett?

Yep.

And then there was **Rutya and Daitya***, your 1971 duet album with Jarrett, after you played together with Miles, right?*

Well, we did that album while we were with Miles, during that period. Keith and I came together for a Kenny Wheeler album, *Gnu High* [1975], and then hooked up again through Miles's electric period. After that, Keith formed the trio. I think it's been twenty-three years. That's still going on.

I can hear the chemistry between you and Keith on **Forest Flower.**

Yep. I don't know. Maybe we played together in another life. We don't have to speak too much about what we do when we play. It's just an intuitive, natural chemistry that we share. It has just continued developing throughout the years.

JOURNEY WITHIN

Filmmaker Eric Sherman's documentary *Charles Lloyd: Journey Within*, though hard to find, is a fascinating and eccentric piece of filmmaking, lacking the glossier, more traditional documentary feel of later films made by Lloyd's wife. Hints of the saxophonist's forthcoming hermetic life intermingle with valuable archival footage and illuminating interview segments.

At one point in Sherman's film, Lloyd comments, "I find that, ideally, I have a great desire to go out and play for flowers and trees." That segues to shots of him in a free-form duet with Jack DeJohnette, playing in the woods with scarcely another soul around. In another scene, Lloyd plays solo flute in a natural setting, then stops and points to the ground: "See the snail there? He came out of his, uh . . . thing. He's grooving there." Then he continues with his serenade for the snail.

In one of his interview snippets in the film, Lloyd states, "My music is a love offering. . . . I still dream of the day when man can live in harmony. It's a struggle out here. That's nature. That's the order of things. The thing is to attain liberation and fulfillment amidst all of the struggle. I'll find ways to continue to make music and I hope to continue to evolve in all ways. . . . There's all this ugliness out there. I want to wipe it out with beauty.

"Although I believe in love and understanding and I hope for a kind of joyous communication amongst us all, I have often found, during my life, a kind of lonesomeness, I guess. I'm seeking an ideal world that doesn't exist, and that has brought me to be a lonesome child. Although I have a great deal of optimism, I also realize that there's a great deal of sadness sometimes."

Live concert footage in the film includes a scene with Jarrett, dressed in a snug, spangled Nehru jacket, playing soprano sax, interacting with the leader, who's dressed in a long coat. During the vamp section of a performance of "Forest Flower," the visuals shift to shots of a nude Lloyd, cavorting in the wilds and running on the beach at Big Sur—imagery that may be viewed as a harbinger of the post-public life shortly to come for him.

THE DECADE—AND THE MAN—WIND DOWN

As the Sixties drew to a close, things were wearing down within Lloyd—even as his career was, from all outside appearances, soaring. His famed quartet began feeling the pressure and creative inequities of working under a leader whose playing and musical focus were slipping, even as he held fans—some of whom weren't equipped to detect musical problems or lapses into laxity, but who found him an exotic Svengali figure—under his charismatic sway.

In Ian Carr's biography *Keith Jarrett. The Man and His Music*, the pianist recalls a fateful moment at a post-concert reception after a particularly bad university concert. As Jarrett recounts, Lloyd "was sitting in the lotus position in the midst of group of reverential students, in his usual role as guru, and Jack and I were there reluctantly, knowing we had this on our minds—that he had been playing badly ... Jack said to me, 'We have to tell him. We have to do something!' I said, 'Yeah, we have to do something and it can only be both of us doing it; it can't just be one of us because then he'd say, "No, sorry, I'm busy.'". ... So Jack and I both went in among this bunch of ogling people and he was there being the flower child and everything. We said, 'Charles, can we talk to you for a minute?' He came out of his trance for a minute and said, 'Oh, oh, not *now*!' Then we said, 'Yes, *now*! Now, we're talking to you, now ... come on! We want to talk to you *now*!' So Charles came out on the porch and we all sat on the porch for a minute, then Jack and I said, 'Listen, Charles ...' I think Jack was the one who spoke most on this. He said, 'I don't know what the word is to call it, but you have been playing flat, it's like there's nothing happening, it almost sounds debauched, like the music is plain debauched.' And Charles said, 'Well, maybe I want to play debauched.' And Jack and I looked at each other and said, 'OK, it's the beginning of the end of the band, I think.'"

As Lloyd says plainly, but without fully explaining the complex backstory of his fateful escape into self-imposed hermitage, "At the height of my thing in '69, I disbanded the quartet. What happened was, I never want to fire nobody. I know when something has run its course. There got to be vibes and signs ... and stuff like that. On the other hand, we weren't making any bread, no real bread.

"That was before bread was around for jazz musicians. It's still not around. After you got through paying for planes and hotel rooms, which you had to pay for in those days, a gig might pay a couple thou or something, and then you had to pay the agent and the manager. I think I probably never made more than five thou for a gig. The point was, you could do more with the money in those days, with the equivalent of what a dollar meant compared to now. A dollar then would be almost ten now.

"My rent was $98.75 a month in the Village, at One Sheridan Square, and I had a nice big apartment. Now, that apartment would cost me three to five thousand dollars. Guys can't live in Manhattan. They have to go to Jersey or someplace else. It was a real community in those days. We were all running around to the clubs all night. It was a different time. We would play all the time.

"In '69, I had a bee in my bonnet. My mom had died. Booker had died a few years earlier, and I just wanted to deal with this time-space thing. I wanted to find out how to stop it, and how to transcend it, so to speak."

Orange Juice, Monk, and Enlightenment

In a Lloyd remembrance that I've encountered more than once, he tells a seemingly meandering tale about a particular incident that he holds as among the more fateful of his life. The subject is orange juice—at least on the surface.

"So [Thelonious] Monk . . . and I . . . played together weekends at the Village Gate, alternating sets. The [Monk patroness and bebop guardian angel] Baroness Nica Rothschild was there. She was always bringing Monk there in the Bentley. . . . I had a bunch of stuff, and one of the things I had was . . . orange juice no more than six hours off the tree. Monk would drink my orange juice every night, which was cool. . . . One night, I came in and said to Nica . . . 'Tell Monk not to drink the orange juice tonight, because it's rancid.' She said, 'Oh, thank you, Charles, thank you.' So Monk came in later and Nica said, 'Oh, Thelonious, Charles says don't drink the orange juice. It's tainted.' So Monk was just dancing and walking around and carrying on. About ten minutes later, he danced on by the place where the orange juice was and he picked up the pitcher. He kind of danced by me and drank the whole pitcher down. He looked at me and said, 'Tainted, huh?'

"That flipped me. Later on, I realized what he was saying. That's the whole Milarepa thing and the Buddhist thing, the tantric thing of you ingest poison and turn it into soma, the elixir. When you're enlightened, it's like . . . 'Tainted, huh?'

"It's like when Max Roach was recording some of Monk's tunes and he and Abbey [Lincoln] wanted Monk to come to some of the sessions. Monk came to the session and Abbey was singing this stuff. They worried about what Monk thought. Abbey came over to Monk and said, 'What do you think?' And Monk said, 'Make a mistake.' [Lloyd laughs.]

"That's something that's beautiful about music. Dissonance is important with consonance, it can't just be all missionary position. Somehow, you've got to always have the sweet-and-sour sauce. Booker used to talk to me a lot about that—dissonance. He was really working with the minor second a lot. He really had a thing for it. Check out [Little's 1961 album] Out Front, *if you can find it. He was very creative and very beautiful.*

"One thing that I've often lamented about . . . one day, maybe I was with Cannonball by this time, Monk's manager called and said, 'I'm inviting you to go and play with Thelonious. He wants you to come up his house and play, so why don't you go to his house and play with him?' Well, I was so shy and so reverential and respectful of Monk and I didn't understand the function of intermediaries or buffers in those days. I thought, if Monk wanted me to play with him, he would call me. I didn't have a manager. I didn't know what that was about.

"That would have been a wonderful growing experience for me to play with Monk. Then, Charlie Rouse was playing with him. That's something that I missed. I used to listen to him a lot. Monk was such a beautiful master."

Lloyd has a keen and poetic sense of his unusual life trajectory so far, and tends to seek out points of resonance or perhaps divine mapping along the way. One day among many in our years-long series of interviews, he fell into one of his trancelike channeling moments, as if hovering, half-detached and half-engaged, over the Charles Lloyd saga so far.

"I left Manhattan, went to Malibu . . . all these M's: Memphis, Manhattan, Malibu, Montecito. . . .

"As a kid, they said, 'Listen, you've done pretty good. We're ready to put you in arenas. You've just got to act right, boy.' At which point I said [claps his hands], 'I'm out of here.' So, in the still of the night, I hit it. For me to be in arenas, I would have to really do something to my music, and I don't think I was prepared to do that. You have to be serious product, and man, I like it loose.

"See, here's where I'm at, man: I come down to space and time. In the music, you can move them around, you can obliterate them. In my music, there's a lot of spaciousness, because I always heard that. I don't think you can be too spacious in arenas. Don't get me wrong: I can live in a humble room. All I have here is a little room. I sleep here many nights. I just don't leave what I'm doing. . . .

"The thing about music is that you can move it around. What I'm trying to discuss, politely, is flying. I always dreamed about flying when I was a kid. Kids' imaginations are amazing. So I heard Bird [Charlie Parker] when I was nine, and I thought of flying. Well, his name is *bird*. I know what he does. So I got my cape on at night, with the sheets, and fly all over the place. I've had dreams about flying on my back. A lot of flight.

"Then I went from flight to manifestation. In Big Sur, I used to look up at the stars and you see stuff moving and taking up way too much territory to be normal. I'd drink some more of that *yerba buena* tea. We had the yerba buena plant which grows up there. Ever had that tea?"

ALL KINDS OF MUSIC

"I haven't found anything, to this day, that has impeded my love for this art form. I love music. It's like Monk told a guy, who asked, 'What kind of music you like?' 'I like all kinds of music.' 'You like country music, Mr. Monk?' 'The guy must can't hear good. Once you say you like all kinds of music, that's it.'"

Lloyd in the late Sixties. (*Photo provided by Eric Sherman*)

5

The Wilderness Years

Coastal Californian

"We break camp at various times. I guess we're Bedouins or something."

It's 1987, and Lloyd is sitting in his Montecito living room, reflecting on his life's often meandering path. It is a ripe moment in the long arc of his musical career, as he has just rededicated himself to working his way out of his long retreat from the traditional jazz scene. Soon he will embark on a second-wind career as an ECM Records artist. But for now, he is indeed a Bedouin in transition, reminiscing about the things that led him out of jazz's fast lane in 1969 and into a series of coastal retreats: Malibu, Big Sur, and finally, his nature-centric place in Santa Barbara.

"There's something here in Santa Barbara that keeps drawing me here. I feel a real warmness here. The people are real friendly and sweet and they give each other space to be and to grow. I think I first played here at Earl Warren [Showgrounds], with Buffalo Springfield. That was the nice thing about the Sixties—that eclectic things could happen."

Dorothy Darr, his wife and constant companion since his Big Sur era, is in the room, and she mentions another strange bill from the genre mash-up days of the Sixties: Lloyd playing alongside Frank Zappa's Mothers of Invention and Vanilla Fudge.

"I want you to hear my Santa Barbara tone poem." He plays a tape of bright, unperturbed tropical music. "This is Santa Barbara, way before commercial enterprise—Chumash [pre-conquest Native Americans living in the coastal areas of what is now Central and Southern California]. I tried to get into the spirit of what it is. It's guitars, coconuts, kotos—I got the islands in there, too. . . ."

"Fortunately, because I can live in simple elegance, I don't really envy people's lifestyles. How could I? We live in a wonderful garden here. Also, I like that I can live in this town. People don't bother me. I got to the place in New York where I was being bothered on the street. I had never expected that from New York. I thought it was way too sophisticated for that—for that to happen to me, someone who was making an esoteric statement, or an artistic statement. I didn't quite understand. It made me really thrive on privacy.

"You've got to understand something about me. It's called 'Universal Living Room.' What every artist does in his lifetime is the same thing: You keep working at what it is—union with the Supreme, that place where there's no little Junebug in the way. It's just radiant, effulgent self. When you're playing and it's right, it's *there*, it's effortless. That's what music's always held for me—that possibility of transforming the world. There's a war going on. It's a madhouse, the world. Pleasure and pain, the dualities. It goes like that.

"There's no way to get rid of the ego. All you can do is pray to Mother that she makes your ego ripe. You try to efface it, and it jumps back. All that I strive for being about is being a clear channel for that essence to come through. We're servants, we're musicians. There's no more beautiful way to serve than with music.

"I love it when unity is present, when there's no divisiveness or lines of demarcation or boundaries. Back in the Sixties, we used to play with the Dead [Grateful Dead] in various venues around. I don't know how that all came to be. That's the blessing that I've had. . . . The timing was right with that Sixties band.

"I love people. I love musicians. But there are seasons in your life. I've lived in the cauldron, back in New York, playing with Roy Haynes and Ron Carter and Herbie [Hancock]. When Miles wasn't playing, those guys played with me a lot. I played at the Five Spot. Jackie Byard played with me. There was all that intense experience.

"Then, later, I pulled back to reflect on it all. . . . That was a strange move, because in those days, they were trying to get me to take my music into arenas. I had made the so-called crossover, playing at the Fillmore and being very appreciated in Europe. I'd come back here and play colleges and such.

"I found a way to do my music where I could live in my lifetime. But at the same time, the tumultuousness of travel and the experience of the mechanics of the tollbooth and going through it two hundred times—[while] aiming for a higher ideal and wanting to share something of great beauty . . . it's not helpful to any of us.

"I was wounded and hurt in the sense that, as a young man, I wanted to change the world. As I've said before, I came to a realization when my mom died, when I was thirty, that what I best better be about is changing myself, because I saw mortality right before me. My mom was fifty-four when she died [Lloyd's age at the time of this interview]. She was very beautiful and she always gave me that loving encouragement. . . .

"After my heavy experience of living in New York in the Sixties and the early Seventies—I kept my place in New York until 1975—I bought a house on the beach in Malibu Colony because I wanted a laboratory, to face the mirror again. I needed the sea, because of my Pisces nature.

"I went to Malibu for a little time, and it was a little congested down there on the beach. [Actors] Larry Hagman and Peter Fonda were very sweet friends to me. Peter had just made *Easy Rider*, and we'd go sailing every day. . . . Those cats were very brotherly. . . . We had meals and spent the night at each other's houses. That camaraderie and the soulfulness of Larry and his wife, Maj, was very beautiful, but I had to get more deep into solitude. That's why I went to Big Sur. . . . I always listen to my own bells and the drummer within."

Darr was an important ally in Lloyd's post-Sixties life out West. Lloyd states. "She came and helped me to straighten up and helped me to carry the load.

"I remember when I came back to California, Herbie [Hancock], Wayne [Shorter], Miles [Davis], [Joe] Zawinul, Horace [Silver]—none of those cats were out here then. I remember everybody said

I was doing a dumb thing coming back to California. I was up at [Bob] Dylan's place in Woodstock. We were standing around and his manager, Albert Grossman, had a pool. . . . We're looking in Grossman's pool, with cracks in it, and Dylan said, 'Man, why are you going out there?' I said, 'I gotta go back to heal a little bit. I went to college out there and I'm gonna go be by the sea and not wear any clothes and become a fruitarian.'

"He said, 'Man, that place will fall into the ocean.' I said, 'Yeah, so be it.' Then one day, I'm sitting in my living room in Malibu and there was the Band, ironically, almost in front of my house taking a picture for an album cover. I said, 'What are you guys doing?' It was Robbie [Robertson] and Levon [Helms] and all of them. Robbie and me were close in the old days."

Ultimately, Malibu and Southern California weren't aiding Lloyd's restive soul-searching. His thoughts and compass tilted northward.

"I have to heal. I find these healing places. I needed seclusion and moved to Big Sur."

Tales of performing artists who, at a high point in their careers, make a conscious decision to jump off of the fast-moving bus of fame and acclaim are rare. Usually they involve those stressed and pushed into action by some need for reboot or rehab—often triggered by debilitating substance abuse or some spiritual/mental tailspin that makes the limelight suddenly unbearable. An artistically frustrated young Sonny Rollins famously retreated from the jazz world for a time and practiced under the Williamsburg Bridge to find his way back triumphantly with the 1962 album *The Bridge*. Miles Davis famously, and infamously, had his own self-imposed disappearing act for the last half of the Seventies, sidelined by drugs and health issues, in a transitional period between his edgier and experimental seventies music to his more populist—and final— Eighties era.

Lloyd, whose urge for flight from the jazz spotlight at the age of thirty-one involved a complicated cocktail of rationales and demons that even he can't exactly articulate, was in a position to follow his heart as far west and as far adrift from the jazz cosmos as he could go. Logistically, he had the advantage of coming from means, coming out of a lucrative period as a leader, and also having some shrewd business savvy on his side to subsidize his life/career flight plan.

THE ROAD WEST

Lloyd gave me a fairly tidy summation of the plots and subplots leading to his sabbatical from public life, as such, and his general east-to-west move.

"All through the Sixties I spent in New York, living in the Village. I came back in '69. I kept my place in New York and moved to Malibu. I remembered the beaches here. I was getting to be an out-patient and got off the bus. I was doing a tour on the West Coast. I had a Ferrari and would put it on the plane, cost like three hundred dollars. I'd fly on TWA, get off the plane and drive up and down the coast in my Ferrari.

"I didn't start that example—of course, Miles was into it before me. I loved him, too, but he was a weird guy. He was always trying to get me to play with him, but he was a strange guy to be around.

"The [early] Seventies I spent in Malibu, on the beach, working on myself. I was too close. I wanted to be in solitude, because Booker [Little] had died, my mother had died, Scotty [LaFaro] had died. I'd seen death. I moved up to Big Sur. I had this calling: I wanted to be in service of spiritual practice. I got into Transcendental Meditation, but I wanted to go deeper. When I was up there, Mike Love [of the Beach Boys] came around and got me to come down here [Santa Barbara] to start this 'Love Songs' operation. I came down here and loved it around here. I was finishing up with TM. I came here because the Vedanta Temple was here. That's how I moved up on this hill. There was a swami down there, Prabhavananda [founder of the Vedanta Society of Southern California], a beautiful man.

"I first got turned on as a kid when I read *The Light of Asia*, by Sir Edwin Arnold, about the life of Buddha. That whole thing as a seeker made sense to me. We seek in the music all our lives. That's the hookup, that's the connection with me. I've found that, around here, I can have a rural setting, but I can still find cosmopolites around. From my sense of it, this has always been a progressive place, open to things. Outsiders and seekers can find some kind of way to function without being put away. We're not normal people."

Moon Man Landing

Once he had effectively seceded from the jazz scene, Lloyd headed west into an increasingly reclusive way of being. But he still played, in studios and on stages, as a sideman to pop artists. The first recorded venture of his own into some new way of musical being turned out to be one of the more anomalous projects he ever made—*Moon Man*. If this album, released on the Kapp label in 1970, was Lloyd's attempt to ease into the then-new but fertile jazz-rock world, it was an odd attempt. (The oddly interesting and quirky venture is probably better appreciated now than at the time it was released.)

As he says, in retrospect, "In one of my most down periods, I made a record called *Moon Man*. People sabotaged it. I can't sing. You know how sometimes I sound like verbal diarrhea. I had to get these ideas across. I was just in a real weird place. But Ornette and Jimi Hendrix came and said they loved it.

"I couldn't sing anything, but I was just so ODed by the lack of humanity in our civilized world, on a level of caring and education and sharing and all of that, that I just broke out into this verbal diarrhea. Don't go up there and spy on everybody and make all those crystals and not feed people and not care. I'd been around Buckminster Fuller and guys like him who always thought there was really abundance on the planet, dancing around waterfalls and like that.

"The interesting thing is that the more I grow . . . It led me to a spiritual focus, because this music is a spiritual music."

As we talk, Darr brings out an old copy of *Moon Man*, Lloyd gets wide-eyed and excitedly grabs it. He starts singing the lyrics—or

Sprechstimme-style intoning—suddenly transfixed, as if he just wrote them yesterday. "Moon Man, don't you take my place now / Way in space like you done before . . . They know you killed Geronimo / They know you done took the gold . . ."

"It sounds like some of Hendrix's stuff," I volunteer.

"Oh, Hendrix said he loved it. Jackson Browne says he still loves this one [he starts to sing his tune "Sweet Juvenia"]. . . . That was *out*. What it was, was a reaction to these guys who just got on the moon. I knew what they were doing, they were spying on people's backyards. My mom just died and Atlantic [Records] was ripping me off. The Erteguns [brothers Ahmet and Nesuhi Ertegun, heads of Atlantic Records] blackballed me and said I couldn't record. They wouldn't let me record because they said I owed them records. They had me giving them three records a year for three years, and I wouldn't do it."

"I don't know what to say. It wasn't about free, but it was about something. An artist was doing something."

True enough. A legendary semi-orphan in the vast Lloyd discography, and in the annals of experimental asides by jazz artists, *Moon Man* may once have been one of those half-lost aberrations in a veteran artist's past, an item from the "hard to find" category. And that situation was possibly to Lloyd's liking. In the Amazon.com age, though, you can find it on used vinyl, or as an expensive European CD reissue/collector's item.

What may be surprising is listening to the project in the clarifying light of expectations and biases four decades later and finding an album that has its own sense of adventure and bohemian savvy, alongside its perhaps half-baked aesthetics. Rather than the kind of proto–New Age vapors encountered on some of Lloyd's dismissable records made in the Seventies and early Eighties, *Moon Man* is an intriguing, bizarre amalgam of hippie jazz-blues-jam ramblings, sociopolitical poetics, and detours and diversions of the sort that would be, in any genre, commercial and, mostly, critical suicide.

In an album framed by two versions of the title song, Lloyd presents his rambling lyrics in a loopy, soft-spoken *Singspiel* style reminiscent of his friend Jimi Hendrix and also, oddly, Captain Beefheart, as guitarist Ned Doheny leads the music's rhythmic charge in a style more akin to Robbie Robertson and Steve Cropper than to any jazz attitude. Atop this, Lloyd sings in his special way and occasionally pulls out his tenor saxophone, but leans more on flute, and even sprinkles in some swooning Theremin, for distinctly moon-manly color.

Of the album's eight tracks, the most peculiar charmer is "Sweet Juvenia," which morphs from a hazy, Rolling Stones *Exile on Main Street*-y gospel song into a free-play improv section, as Lloyd's vocals drift off into a hallucinatory ether of consciousness-streaming references. His lyrics venture into a jumbled admix of poetry, references to show biz folks (including musicians Neil Young, Herb Alpert, and drummer James Zitro), and opaque allusions to the "tollbooth," a Lloydism for commercialism.

On the wave-length
Neil up in the north country
Dancin' down the riverside
Over the side, over the beautiful sky
What a travesty. Yes, what a travesty
Told the broad, say, come aroun' the corner
Don't nobody know and don't nobody know whether it's a law.
An' I asked 'em and seventeen people stop and stare
Everybody looking and don't nobody know nowhere
Say it Zitro
Bang—You dig?
In Asylum Wapucha shesayla you know but the soul Juvenia knows
Ow . . . Mr. Alpert's studio
Ow . . . In your studio
Ow . . . in your studio
I've been in America before the dudes say . . .
Hi, hello . . .
Communications network
Chicago calling London, Connecticut . . . anybody there?
Computer man say

Hey man, is anyone home?
Fuck the tollbooth, man
I can dig that but Oh . . . say: I been lovin' you
Say: oh, but you know
Sweet Juvenia

Token simple sitar riffing joins Lloyd's Indian-flavored flute work on the jam-heavy psychedelic-kitsch track "Heavy Karma," and the Indian musical vibe continues on the album's single instrumental, the five-part "Hejira" (a transliteration of the Arabic word *hijra*, which means "journey"—years before Joni Mitchell popularized the term with her great album of that name, which was engineered by Henry Lewy, who was also behind the studio controls for *Moon Man*). "Hejira" is the track that hints at the New Ageish, watery jazz to come in Lloyd's recordings of the Seventies. The album trails off into an extended version of "Moon Man" in a floating group-improv atmosphere as antithetical to the pistons-firing intensity and intellectual probity of the Jarrett-DeJohnette–driven quartet as could be imagined.

WARM WATERS AND WAVES

A second album for Kapp Records, *Warm Waters*, from 1971, found Lloyd traveling in some ever ever-starrier pop music circles. The musician list includes guitarists Dave Mason and John Cipollina, whose vibrato-quivery blues touch was a signature of the Quicksilver Messenger Service sound, joining Tom Trujillo, Lloyd's regular guitarist at the time. The album featured vocals that signified his strengthening link to the Beach Boys, with Mike Love, Brian and Carl Wilson, and Al Jardine in the mix, as well as Billy Cowsill of the Cowsills band fame. *Warm Waters* also featured drummer Woody "Sonship" Theus III, with whom Lloyd would have a long if spotty working relationship during his reclusion period and up through his recordings with pianist Michel Petrucciani in the Eighties.

In 1972, Lloyd bumped up to the major label world again with *Waves*, one of two albums for Herb Alpert's A&M label (the other being 1973's *Geeta*). On an album that featured his old ally Gábor Szabó on a few tracks, Lloyd further pursued his strange brews of jazz lite, soft rock, and jammy excesses. The album opens with a lovably kitschy tribute to his newfound spiritual practice, Transcendental Meditation (with harmonizing Beach Boys kookily crooning "TM, in the AM, and PM . . ."). On the title instrumental track, Lloyd's friend Roger McGuinn lends his twelve-string guitar jangle to a rolling and cresting folk-rocky modal rumble that includes both Wolfgang Melz's electric bass and the acoustic bass of a young Roberto Miranda (who would go on to play regularly with LA musical legends Horace Tapscott, Bobby Bradford, John Carter, and others). Again, the lighter-minded Lloyd opted for flute over tenor sax as his main expressive ax.

NYC FOR A MOMENT: 1972

After Lloyd had disappeared from the jazz scene, and hadn't played in NYC—"The Town that Matters"—for a handful of years, he made a token reappearance there in 1972. *The New York Times* took note of the prodigal son's fleeting visitation, as critic John S. Wilson recounted, on August 12, 1972. To those aware of Lloyd's prominence only a few years earlier, just the article's headline—"Program Is Given by Charles Lloyd"—may have been startling.

> In the mid-60's, Charles Lloyd, the tenor saxophonist and flutist, was one of the top names in jazz. But about five years ago, he seemingly disappeared. There were no personal appearances in New York and no recordings except for an odd album two years ago on which he performed primarily as a singer of his impressionistic lyrics.
>
> This week, Mr. Lloyd is back in town at the Village Vanguard leading a quartet which, it turns out, he has been playing with on the West Coast for the past two years. He hasn't been heard in New York, he says, because he has not been invited to play in such places as Central Park and because he had thought of playing in clubs as "very degrading."

But, as a vegetarian and fruitarian, he feels he has cleaned himself out.

"There are no stresses now," he says. So, he was invited to play at the Lighthouse in Hermosa Beach, Calif., Monday nights in July. He tried it and found that he was no longer faced with the "beer tavern mentality."

"There were young people there who were interested in getting to the music," he said. As a result, he is trying a couple of club dates while he is in the East playing some concerts.

His music at the Village Vanguard comes out as a cross between what he was playing in the mid-60s and his more recent efforts as a songwriter. His pieces are long, extended, sprawling works that cover a variety of changing moods and tempos, sometimes including lyrics declaimed with dramatic intensity by his drummer, Woody Theus.

On saxophone, Mr. Lloyd ranges from the gently singing approach of his familiar "Forest Flower" to a richly guttural attack that is often paralleled by the spiky guitar lines of Tom Trujillo. In Mr. Lloyd's concept, their solos are not so much the individualistic, spotlighted affairs that one usually hears in jazz groups but are part of an over-all atmospheric coloration. It is an approach that allows for a lot of variety within a given piece, but, by the same token, it produces pieces that eventually seem somewhat similar.

Solitude

Whatever the critics and those in the jazz world were making of Lloyd's conspicuous absence and strange new musical potions, the man himself was busy on an inward journey. Getting approval from official sources was the last thing on his mind at the time.

"Those years of solitude were prayerful for me," he recalled years later. "Music is the highest form of worship. Since I wasn't doing music, I had to take those years to try to change my character. I knew that if I could do that, it would affect the music, without question. You are what you eat.

"Sitting here talking to you, I can see the canyon by the sea where we lived in Big Sur. For a time, we lived on the point by the ocean. The house is very dramatic and is perched out over the sea. When I first lived in Big Sur, I lived in a little goat shed with a lemon tree outside.

"My financial estate was tied up in my Malibu property. I had left that marriage with Joan [his first wife] and had moved to Big Sur, because she and I had grown in such different directions. I was called to solitude. She stayed there in the beach house, which had a pretty big value, but she wouldn't sell it, and she wouldn't move to Big Sur with me to try to work out our life. I lived simply.

"So when I first went there, my economic base was not strong. I ended up renting a property. . . . It was just a glorified goat shed, made of stone with a tin roof or something, with an outside shower. It was very dramatic. You had to hike a ways from the highway to get to it."

Certain recurring themes arise when Lloyd considers the mix of events and feelings leading him to escape the fast life, to retreat from the outside world and into himself at Big Sur.

"I was affected by Monk having sent me away with that notion of 'Tainted, huh?'—like you may think this is tainted, but it doesn't affect me. I had read about Milarepa, and how he changed his life from a life of wreaking havoc because of the way his mother had been treated. . . . I had read the *Bhagavad Gita* and the life of Buddha.

"There was always something telling me that you have to make something. Not everyone wants to take that step out and take that chance. In my case, it was a calling that I had no choice but to heed. It was like I had to dive deep to see if I could bring anything back. And in that diving, something got cultured. I got a glimpse of something.

"When I left New York at the end of the Sixties, I moved to Malibu and bought a house on the beach there and wanted to live simple. I began to fast and change my diet and meditate a lot. I was trying to deal with seeing mortality. I had seen my friend Booker die at twenty-two or twenty-three. I had this experience. Then my mom died. As a young person, seeing someone profoundly close die, it affected me.

"Many of the great musicians died at really young ages. Scott LaFaro was also one of my best friends when I came out here to go to school at USC. He and I played a lot around Los Angeles. . . .

"I had been on the road constantly for ten years—three and a half with Chico Hamilton, a year and a half with Cannonball, and about five years with my group. I had played with all these great musicians, all the best—Jack DeJohnette, Elvin Jones, Pete La Roca, Joe Chambers, Clifford Jarvis, Ron Carter, Scott LaFaro, Gary Peacock, Henry Grimes. . . . I always found great pianists. There was always this love attraction. Gábor Szabó and I were also very close.

"After ten years of that, this inner thing was calling me so strongly, I didn't know how it was going to manifest. But I knew there was something about solitude that I would have to acknowledge. I was going to have to grow in ways that I couldn't in the world. As I look back on it now, I think it was very rich and wonderful. It taught me to be comfortable with silence and being alone. I learned to walk in the dark. Maybe I had that anyway. I'd walk at night.

"Anyway . . . I left Malibu in disarray and didn't have an economic base. So I began to teach students in Big Sur. I taught flute, saxophone, harmony, theory. Some would do exchanges with various barter arrangements. I lived very simply. One day a student said, 'You should be living down there, at the Point House.' It's a very dramatic house that's been in *National Geographic*. It hangs over the cliff and is a two-story, cement and glass, a kind of Howard Roark, *Fountainhead* kind of notion.

"I was reading Rilke and Meister Eckhart, all kinds of poets, Thoreau and everybody. I was also very moved reading the *Bhagavad Gita*, and a lot of deep spiritual texts. I was just reading and studying. I said, 'Yeah, I'll sign up for that.' Sure enough, a few weeks later, they arranged for me to move into this house. The landlord rented it to me for a very reasonable rate and I moved in there.

Then my situation was getting better in Malibu so that funds were available to me. But I liked living the simple life with high thinking."

Lloyd's first marriage, to Joan, was coming apart. "We were in divorce court by then because we couldn't agree. That was a horrendous thing, which took four or five years and tons of money. All this time, I was still meditating and living simple. I became an artist-in-residence at Esalen Institute [a retreat community in Big Sur] and would give seminars, sometimes in flute, *shakuhachi*. I had my Chinese oboe and would play my saxophone out in the woods. I wasn't playing anywhere in an organized way.

"Some people knew who I was, but I lived real low-profile. After a while, I got into the simplicity of that life. I didn't come into contact with the so-called music world, except that I'd see a *San Francisco Chronicle* or a *New York Times* every now and then and it would jolt me, to where I'd think, 'Hey, I should be there.'

"But after a while, I began to make a little progress in spiritual life, so it was like something was happening. What I'd been looking for was very hard to find, but because of my sincerity and digging deep, something happened. Then, the divorce thing was settled and I was able to build.

"While I was up there, I was involved in the fringes of TM, and Mike Love—who was always coming around—talked me into going to one of those six-month courses with the Maharishi. I did that in the mid-Seventies somewhere. Then he wanted to start a company with all of us, so we started this company called Love Songs. I was going to do my jazz things and he was going to do his rock 'n' roll stuff. This other guy, Ron Altbach, was doing classical and rock 'n' roll stuff. He had this group King Harvest, which did [the hit pop song] 'Dancing in the Moonlight.'

"So I dabbled in Santa Barbara. I'd come down here sometimes for that. The divorce happened and then my economic base was stronger. I bought property in Big Sur and down here, also. Dorothy built this beautiful Japanese country house up there.

"Then this little guy comes through—Michel Petrucciani. I had been reading this spiritual text. There was some kind of dynamic there, some kind of providence that made that come together. Here's this little guy with this bent frame, and I'd been reading about this sage with a bent frame.

"So I took it as something talking directly to me. I decided to take him around the world, because the elders had helped me. I did that for a couple of years and got him going. I had this place here by then. Once I got him going, I tried to go back to Big Sur and do what I was doing, and resume my spiritual life, but I had been bitten by the cobra by then."

THE LOVE CONNECTION

Gazing at the strange arc of Lloyd's Seventies saga, the plot both thickens and thins when it comes to his association with Mike Love, who has a fairly dubious reputation in pop culture. Love is perceived by many as a business-savvy, power-mongering commander of the Beach Boys brand, with minimal musical talent but a willingness to profit from the band's success—as well as Brian Wilson's great musical ingenuity and mental instability over the years. He has sued Brian Wilson, and invoked widespread ire among music fans as recently as 2012, when he infamously cut short an acclaimed fiftieth-anniversary reunion tour featuring the long-absent Beach Boys songbook mastermind.

Love also infamously disparaged, at least initially, *Pet Sounds*— the Beach Boys' masterpiece and one of a handful of classic pop albums of all time—which was largely conceived and realized by Brian Wilson in the studio. (Lloyd himself has thus far recorded two *Pet Sounds* tunes, "God Only Knows" and "Caroline, No." Personally, I keep waiting for him to record the most harmonically jazz-informed song on the record, "Don't Talk, Put Your Head on My Shoulder." Maybe one day.)

Looking back, Lloyd has mixed feelings, leaning toward regret about the Love link. "Mike Love kept coming around in the Malibu days. As a matter of fact, in my New York days he tried to meet me. I held that suspect. Some guys want to talk about New Age music nowadays, and I want to take out a machete. Hearing that some Beach Boy wants to talk to you, it's machete time. Those guys put a surfboard on Chuck Berry and the Four Freshmen.

"[Love] was like a groupie or something, he liked to collect people or something. He was always pursuing me. We were both born on the same day, March 15, though I'm three years his senior. I was meditating years before the Beatles made it popular. I had learned TM: a guy in New York turned me onto it. I saw this guy whose life improved because of it. He was a waiter at the Village Gate and we used to go outside and do a little 'research' together, getting fresh air upstairs or somewhere. Then I saw him some months later, and this guy looked really clear and really wonderful. He said, 'I've been up in Boston and I started getting into TM.' That was around '66 I started doing that.

"I wasn't really doing music in a public way in the Seventies. This Mike Love thing happened. I came back from Big Sur and made a bunch of records. Mike was very shaky emotionally at that time, and the Beach Boys were very shaky. I was some sort of stability for him and them. I would go out like a spiritual counselor. I was helping Mike, who is hard to help, because he can be his own worst enemy. He has good intentions, it's just that he is so megalomania and paranoid. . . . He does have a sensitivity, but it's just misplaced.

"Also, when you make money before you learn how to play, that's a hard thing to live up to. They knew I was an artist.

"That was a time when the Germans had some kind of tax program where they gave you a four-for-one write-off, so he had some international attorney who raised like seven million dollars to record with. That's when I recorded *Big Sur Tapestry* [Pacific Arts, 1979] and *Autumn in New York* [Destiny, 1979], which I did with strings. I also did *Pathless Path* [Unity, 1979]."

CALL OF THE SPIRIT

After living at Mike Love's compound on Mesa Lane, a beautiful cliff-hugging property in Santa Barbara, when not in Big Sur, Lloyd scouted for his ideal piece of real estate in the area. His property on Ladera Lane, on the road out of Montecito and heading up into the rugged foothills, is very close to the idyllic Vedanta Temple as well as a property that once belonged to the Jesuits, fulfilling his desire to remain within nourishing proximity to both spiritual and natural resources.

As Lloyd says, "I moved up there because I would go to vespers [sunset prayers service] and hear those nuns chanting. I also had a metaphysical thing happening.

"They had a lot of good books in the bookstore. I said, 'Have you got anything with sweetness about the spiritual life? I don't want all this stuff about getting beaten over the head.' I had been with Catholics when I was a little boy, grades one through three. I couldn't learn anything. They were beating me on the hands with rulers all the time. . . . I wasn't stupid, I was just blocked because of the way people treated me. If you came to me and said, *Play some bad shit!*, well, I might not be able to do it. It has to happen tenderly. If the audiences are open and receptive to the music, then it comes. But if they're sitting there saying, 'What's he going to do?' Like playing in places where people are drunk and talking a lot, well, I'm not going to play. I haven't done that for years."

Lloyd's spiritual churnings and investigations, through TM and other modes of Eastern philosophy, led him eventually to Vedanta, an ancient Hindu religious practice emphasizing the idea that God is within the self, and that the paramount goal is self-realization. In the modern era, the outward migration of the Vedantic faith was facilitated through the nineteenth-century Vedantic saint Sri Ramakrishna, and his disciple Swami Vivekananda, who came to the United States in 1893 and subsequently lectured and sowed the seeds of Vedantic Societies in America, including a relatively strong order in California. One of their flagship temples is in Santa Barbara, nearly neighboring the property where Lloyd and Darr planted roots in the Eighties.

"I used to do TM years ago, back in the Sixties, before the Beatles. . . . Once you get off into something, if you're like I am, you want to go deeper and find the real cats."

Turiyasangitananda

Another jazz figure in Southern California who was entrenched in the Vedanta practice was John Coltrane's widow, harpist/keyboardist Alice Coltrane, who lived ninety miles south of Santa Barbara, in Woodland Hills. Her spiritual passions culminated in her establishing a Vedanta Center in a remote spot near Malibu, and changing her name to Turiyasangitananda. She also became the head, the swamini, *of the Sai Anantam Ashram, nestled in a secluded property between Agoura Hills and Malibu. Before she reemerged as Alice Coltrane later in her life, recording the fine album* Translinear Light *(2004) and doing some live playing with her son Ravi on tenor sax, and others, she would make appearances as a lecturer and musician on local cable TV. (Some Southern Californians recall happening upon her, as if in a half-dreaming vision, while flipping through TV channels, speaking in her entrancingly steady, calming voice, and playing modally meditative, rippling music on harp and synthesizer.)*

Lloyd describes his spiritual evolution, the real seeds of which were in his California "wilderness years":

"I had had ten or more years of deep solitude and I had cultured something," he told me in 1994. "I also met my present teacher, Swami Ritajananda, who became very close to me. This was a very interesting relationship we had. He was a holy man who was the real thing, the highest sense of the word. It was very powerful. . . . He didn't lay any trips out. We had a very warm and deep relationship. I built the guesthouse next door for him. He just died this year, at eighty-eight. I'm dedicating this recording [*All My Relations*] to him. When I say it's the real thing, you just have to trust that. He was someone who had mastered the problems of life.

"It wasn't so much what he said. He was a realized soul, so being in his presence you would get a quality of feeling that things would resolve. It was very beautiful. Maybe sometime I'll be able to talk about it, but right now I can't, because it's too new for me that he's gone. He spent more than a decade with me. He lived outside of Paris, and he would visit me in Big Sur and also here in Santa Barbara.

"I always knew that something was happening. I didn't know that I would play again in a public way. At one point I accepted that. When I accepted that, things became simpler for me somehow."

Inner values and concerns aside, Lloyd also wisely invested himself and his resources in California real estate. "I love property. I bought property—this place [his Ladera Lane place] and some property down on the beach. Then the whole California real estate rush cycle came. I was able to live in my lifetime because property values had escalated so much. So I sold some property and invested a bunch.

"Then the crash came, and that really wreaked havoc in my financial body. People stopped paying me. People walked away from things that they owed me for. I really saw how the system works, so to say. That's why I have some real notion that you really have to have your basis in peace rather than in prosperity, because that prosperity thing shifts. It passes from hand to hand.

"Oftentimes, a few people at the top pass the money amongst themselves. Everybody else struggles and gets whiplashed into things. So I got whiplashed in one of those political things with the Congress and the savings and loan and all that kind of stuff. The values plummeted in real estate. I had really quality properties, which plummeted fifty percent. . . .

"I had a goal in mind. You know the Jesuit novitiate down here [also on Ladera Lane], it's on one hundred thirty-eight acres, and it's for sale. I had a notion to amass an economic base where I could buy that and have it as an institute and retreat for artists and musicians. I also wanted to have a base where I could give grants. While I was working on that, the crash came and I got badly affected economically.

"It affected my dream. It deferred it, so to say. A wealthy man will go build hospitals or universities to make his peace with God. That's what traditionally happens in this culture. I wasn't trying to be a do-gooder or anything; I just felt like, this music is our indigenous art form here. You go all the way back to Louis Armstrong or King Oliver or Duke or whatever and go up through Bird, Lady Day, Coltrane, Jimi Hendrix, Booker, anything you want to deal with—European music. There's such profundity here. You take Ravel and Stravinsky and those guys. Everybody wanted to tune into jazz and get something from it. They did it in a herky-jerky way, but the real deep essence of it comes from here."

DARR

Lloyd's work, life, and path over the past four decades have been intricately intertwined with those of Dorothy Darr—his partner in life and matters of heart and spirituality, and a multidisciplinary artist whose paintings and photographs have graced many a Lloyd album cover. She has also designed various homes of theirs, from their humble Big Sur dwellings to their current lavish hilltop hacienda, and is Lloyd's manager and documentarian. She has made a series of documentaries on him over the years, including *Memphis Is in Egypt* (1995) and *Arrows into Infinity* (2012, co-directed with Jeffery Morse), and a film called *Home*, a chronicle of the Lloyd and Billy Higgins home recording process for the duet project, *Which Way Is East*, recorded in 2001, shortly before Higgins's death and released as a two-CD set by ECM in 2004.

Darr gave me a brief history of her life in the arts, and her path toward life with Lloyd:

"I grew up in a very artistic family. My mother was a sculptor and poet, and my father is a painter and art historian [an authority on Gaugin]. Very sensitive and creative people.

"I grew up in Amherst, Massachusetts. In terms of the educational process and my childhood experience, that was a high point. When I was in junior high, we moved to Richmond, Indiana, which was a low point. Coming from Amherst, where it's basically a white population, but we had black people living there, we didn't think in terms of black and white. It was very foreign to me. Indiana was so racist and conservative. There were the Minutemen, a militia group similar to the Ku Klux Klan, who were on call, any minute, if something bad were happening.

"My teacher would be talking about *niggers*. For me, it was probably the biggest culture shock in my life. I came home and cried at the dinner table. There was corporal punishment: They'd have these big paddles with holes in them and they'd beat children with them. The holes would make it hurt more. There were crosses burned on people's lawns. There were racist arrests, which I heard about again and again in this town.

"I wanted desperately to leave there, and I finally did as a senior in high school. I found schools in France that didn't cost anything—all I had to do was get there. My father took a group over there.

"I came back and went to Rhode Island School of Design, because I thought that was the best art school, as opposed to going to the Academy of Art in Paris, where my friends wanted me to go. I was very disappointed. It was in the transition stage from being a very fine fine-arts school to being a more commercially oriented school. I didn't like hearing the administration giving us pep talks about what big salaries we would make because we had a RISD diploma.

"I transferred out and went to the Maryland Institute in Baltimore, which was much more fine arts–oriented. But I discovered that school is school, and they all have their limitations. It's mostly just a good laboratory, a place to do your work and not have to worry about anything else."

Personal artistic involvement and creative urges aside, Darr's work with Lloyd stems from her passion for music. "I always loved music," she says. "When I was in fifth grade, I joined the Columbia Record Club. The first record I got was [Nigerian drummer]

Olatunji. I practically had the whole thing memorized. I found out later that Charles played with Olatunji.

Lloyd: A lot of what people think is Latin stuff in my music comes from playing with Olatunji, all the stuff in "Forest Flower" and tone poems and stuff.

Darr: I first heard his music in Montreal. When I was at RISD, a friend and I decided to go up to Fall River, Massachusetts, because we heard Charles was playing up there. It was a classic bill with Frank Zappa and the Mothers of Invention, then Charles, and then the Vanilla Fudge [sings "You Keep Me Holding On"]. The emcee came out and said, 'Now we have Charlie Lloyd.' Charles came out, didn't say a word. He played and I was mesmerized. They played an incredible set. Most of the audience seemed to be there for the Vanilla Fudge.

We felt very bad about the people who had been rude. I wanted to go backstage and express my appreciation to Charles.

We were offered a job in Philadelphia, for the Schmidt Beer festival, which was the summer of '67. It was one of the forerunners of other music festivals. It was designed to get kids off the street and they could get in for a dollar. They had Sly and the Family Stone, Sarah Vaughan, Country Joe, Judy Garland, Don Ellis, Louis Armstrong, Olatunji. It was a big interesting mix of events.

They had the opportunity to bring Aretha in and we said, 'You should do that because that would insure the success of your festival.' They didn't, because they thought she was charging too much money. My friend Vicki and I did the graphics and worked on the design end of the project. We had geodesic domes for the dressing rooms. We had big graphic designs on the fences at JFK Stadium.

I took the job because I knew Charles was going to be performing.

Lloyd: Ulterior motive.

Darr: It was. We just met then.

Lloyd: She was a good hostess. Actually, I met her at a concert at JFK Stadium. She was a hostess, and my little heart was aflutter. I didn't know it was a setup. She was there copping me. . . . See, you get perks when you're a musician.

Darr: But I wasn't a hostess. I was on the graphics crew.

Lloyd: But you didn't have to be back there with us. . . .

Darr: Then we met five or six months later and started a communicating relationship. Then I went away for quite a while. I went for a couple of years, and when I came back to the States, it was '75, and I moved to California. Charles was living in Big Sur.

Lloyd: She chose me. I don't know why she would do something like that. My childhood was so traumatic. The women I chose always turned out to be duds. I don't know what to say.

Darr: It was in his retreat. When I first talked to him, after I'd been in Italy, he told me he'd been living in a cave. It was pretty cavelike, a property on the cliff going down to the ocean. He had a series of goat houses. The one that Charles lived in first had a rock wall, with big timbers and glass and a dirt floor in one room.

Lloyd: Showers and john outside. Beautiful flowers everywhere. Ocean.

The reminiscing continues, as Lloyd and Darr revisit their early Big Sur days, when the pair were solidifying their multilayered partnership, and inventing a life for themselves in the mythic, sometimes semimystic beach town that was once home to Henry Miller (whose legacy is preserved at the Henry Miller Library), Langston Hughes, Robinson Jeffers, and, with an inherent transience, the Beats Jack Kerouac and Lawrence Ferlinghetti. To that list of notable American cultural seekers, escapists, and seers of varied sorts and intensities, Charles Lloyd must be added.

Darr takes out a box with notes and photos from their Big Sur period, providing a richer sense of the place, and their place within it. "I was going to give you a tour of our life in Big Sur," she says calmly, preparing for some intimate, insider's Memory Lane coasting. She pulls out a photo of a dramatic vista. "This is from the land, the Chief's Hill, looking down."

Lloyd: The Chief's Hill was the sacred place in Big Sur where the Esselen Indians [Native Americans indigenous to the Central

California coast] had their ceremonies. We're the stewards of that land, and we still have it.

Darr: Charles had been fasting and was in silence. Across from us was a house they were going to take Roosevelt to in case the Japanese bombed—Tassajara.

I designed our house in Big Sur, which was like a Japanese country house in the woods.

Lloyd: Beautiful, man. In the forest, looking out over the sea. I would go outside and play.

Darr: We had a property with an old cabin on it, owned by a plumber in Big Sur. As the mountains come down there's a V and the cabin was there. And the ocean was right there. So the idea was to create a simple, open house, almost like a barn, with *shoji* screens. That was what we built up there. I had a separate studio and there were a couple of old buildings on the property, which were outbuildings. But the living space was just one big open room with two panels of shoji screens to create sleeping areas. We had a wood-burning fireplace. It was really beautiful.

When Charles had his health crisis, when he nearly died in '86, we realized that we needed to be closer to doctors. We actually were here when that happened. Had he been up there, he would not be here now. So that was how we shifted permanently down here.

Lloyd: We used to go back and forth.

Darr: Well, we were there nonstop for a long time and then, when there was the big landslide, we got shut out. We were back and forth until then.

Lloyd: Isn't that great? The roads closed and we could go down to the road and have picnics. I'd be able to hike in and out. It was great. . . . The car would be on the other side of the slide. You'd hike up and down the side of this mountain and get in the car and go into town to get supplies and bring them up and down the hill, stuff like that. It humbled you.

When you live in this majestic land, you have a sense of the importance of how small we are and the fragility of the whole thing. We had mountain lions come around the property and deer and all

Lloyd and Dorothy Darr, 2015. (*Photo by Paul Wellman*)

kinds of wild boar, bobcats, all kinds of stuff. I walked or hiked all the time, and I got so that my night vision came back to me, from ancestors. I was able to just see in the dark, you know. It's another kind of seeing. . . .

Did you ever read *Indian Tales*? You ought to put that on your list. It's by Jaime de Angulo. It's about the indigenous people who lived in our area in Big Sur, the Esselen tribe. Down here it's the Chumash, but up there it's the Esselen. Marvelous stories about them. And on our property there grew this plant, this datura. It's like a trumpet flower and a vine. It had medicinal purposes. They could brew a tea with it. It was a hallucinogen; they would have ceremonies up on this part of our land. I got the hit from it.

It was a power spot, too. They never built anything on this particular site. I had to honor that. . . .

Darr: You have to explain that the elevation is one thousand feet. It's a promontory. They would bring their offerings up to this ring, where the datura plants were. . . .

Lloyd: And yerba buena, too, another plant. It's a wonderful tea. When you have it fresh, it's wonderful. We couldn't have the datura. We didn't know how to make it into a tea. It's like a ceremony or art form. If someone made it today, they would go catatonic and would die. They don't know how to properly make the tea now so that you could survive the journey. . . .

But we had a wonderful, expansive life in Big Sur. . . . I learned timelessness really well, the presence of the moment and being in that. That's the intersection that [Billy] Higgins and I had together, strongly. We would get into "the zone," which is what we called it.

Big Sur to Santa Barbara

Lloyd's eventual call to Santa Barbara came through the side door. "Mike Love was trying to contact me from India. He kept pursuing me to start up a company. I came down and checked that out, and found an interesting pathway between my solitude in Big Sur and a cosmopolitan kind of access that you can have here in Santa Barbara. There was a quality of quiet here.

"Mike had started the Love Foundation here. He has a vision of doing stuff. It's just that his implementation doesn't work. He is a cousin of the Wilsons [Beach Boys Brian, Carl, and Dennis], you know, so they've got some genes in there. I was still in Big Sur, and later I would come down here from time to time because he had this idea of Love Songs, a production company. He built a first-class recording studio over there, where we used to record. I made *Pathless Path* there, *Autumn in New York*, and *Universal Living Room*.

"I was still pretty much in Big Sur. I was involved in TM in those times. Little did I know that the Vedanta Temple was here, and that I was being drawn here. What solidified it was the nuns, and going to vespers down there. The Vedas, ancient scriptures from India that are five thousand years old, they know a lot about that down there. I was studying with one of the nuns down there.

"I'm real one-pointed: Whatever I'm into, I go all the way. So I followed that to where it dropped me off here in Santa Barbara, through various routes, to Ramakrishna. I suppose he's the soul of this Vedanta Society down here. I was in Big Sur and I had a dream one night. I was drawn down here. I went to the bookstore and said to these nuns, 'You got anything sweet to read?' I read some of his stuff. It was a living teacher for me, because this guy was a deity or a saint for the fallen. I definitely had fallen. I had experienced lights and excess and such. I realized that none of that was working. It means nothing to have lived a life and to have not known the Self—with a big S.

"I'll tell you the truth: I'm really not very together, I'm just blessed. I'm fortunate in that this property thing worked out. I love beauty. I started buying property up and down the coast. Little did I know the big boys would come along later and want it. I could keep some of it, and some of it I couldn't. But it endowed me to be able to live in my lifetime with my creativity.

"It's a strange thing. I could be out there toiling in the gold mines with my trumpet and trying to get over, or have some producers make some funny music. I sure have made some music that I'm not crazy about."

DISCOGRAPHICALLY SPEAKING

Viewed as a multichaptered tale unto itself, the Charles Lloyd discography tracks the twists of his life's story, post-USC, in interesting and revealing ways. The most productive periods, of course, were the second half of the Sixties and then the extended, and continuing, ECM era—from 1989's *Fish out of Water* forward. Primarily, despite occasional special projects, these phases found Lloyd working in the fairly traditional acoustic jazz context of his quartet—sax protagonist up front, with a piano-bass-drums rhythm section in tow.

No such linearity or traditionalism governs the strange, and also strangely fascinating and sometimes inscrutable pathless path (so to speak) of his Seventies recorded output. While there are passages of the jazz-fueled Lloyd blowing that the world had known from the Sixties, that voice was often kept subdued in favor of his Eastern-leaning flute playing, as on *Geeta*, and work with musicians not necessarily practiced in the jazz arts.

His "wilderness years" records ranged from Hollywood slickness in instrumental form (*Weavings*, with a Darr painting on the cover and long-haired Lloyd in Native American face paint on the back) to proto–New Age electroacoustic wafting (*Pathless Path*, with Mark Isham on synthesizer and Peter Maunu on guitar, recorded at Santa Barbara Sound in 1979). While Lloyd's Seventies musical alliances were largely left in the past once he got back on the trail of his life as a jazz bandleader in the late Eighties, there were exceptions, as when Isham hired him to play on the soundtrack to the Alan Rudolph–directed film *Afterglow*, in 1997.

In 1979, as something of a soft opening for his later full-on reentry into jazz proper, Lloyd recorded the album *Autumn in New York*, in connection with Mike Love Productions, for the Destiny Records label.

This is one of the odd, mostly overlooked jewels in his discography, and his only album devoted to traditional jazz standards, such as the title track, as well as "As Time Goes By," "Nancy (with the Laughing Face)," "Stella by Starlight," and "But Beautiful." Interestingly, this artist with such a fragile relationship to John Coltrane also nicely takes on the tender Coltrane classic "Naima." A photo on the back cover finds Mr. Lloyd now having swapped his post-hippie mystical recluse sartorial manners for a sleek, pseudo–*film noir* gumshoe outfit.

On the album, Lloyd, who had been something of an overqualified musician on other projects and guest shots during the decade, unleashes some of his old jazz fire and lyrical luster, albeit in a perhaps self-consciously straight-ahead milieu. And there are some intriguing moments with Lloyd's horn weaving and haltingly soaring over tasty string arrangements by the great, underrated composer/arranger/keyboardist Clare Fischer (misspelled as "Claire" in the album's credits). Closing the album, Fisher's lustrous arrangement of his composition "Pensativa" is, on its own, worth seeking out. Lloyd's back cover dedication, a harbinger of his music to come, reads "Special thanks to the tradition of the masters."

During his "wilderness years," Lloyd was also captured for posterity on a number of pop records, including albums by the Beach Boys, whom he sometimes toured with. He can be heard on important Beach Boys albums such as *Surf's Up* and *Holland*, and the later lesser LPs *15 Big Ones* and *M.I.U. Album*, after the band's artistic brain and visionary, Brian Wilson, temporarily departed from the fold (and from the conventional societal swim of things). Mike Love, the controversial figurehead of the operation, still had Lloyd's ear, and soul, at the time.

In the early period of his self-liberation from the jazz scene as such, while "hiding out" in Los Angeles, Lloyd also played on Canned Heat's 1971 album *Historical Figures and Ancient Heads* and the Doors' 1972 *Full Circle*, appearing on "Verdilac" and "The Piano Bird." He also appeared on the 1973 Columbia album *Roger McGuinn*, returning the favor of his friend McGuinn's cameo on Lloyd's 1972 lovable hippie-jazz odyssey/oddity, *Warm Waters*.

Looking back on his foggy musical doings during the Seventies, Lloyd is circumspect, viewing the period as a means to an end whose fruition was still to come. "As a musician, you hear an ideal world. You make these creations. . . . Listen, I bow down to anybody making music, because that's another kind of step. . . ."

"Buckminster Fuller proved, years ago, that there were enough resources to support the population. He had it figured out, with the food thing and all. We could be harmonious. I went to study with him years ago in Massachusetts. . . . This was back before the Information Age caught up. It was in the Seventies, after the Sixties.

"See, don't dime on the Sixties. I don't think they're over; the idealism continues. I saw that as really being an opening of America's sphincter—pardon my lyrics. I think it was a time of possibility. But then, we congealed back into the Fifties again, almost, with Reaganism and all that.

"For me, ideas and stuff, music making, being able to live in your lifetime . . . I'm fortunate in the sense that I still have this stuff coming through me, and I can bear witness to it. That's of interest. I tried to be brainwave synchronous, or at least keep the illusion of it. I've got a watch that tells me the time and date and everything, so that if anybody catches me in an *out* moment, I can look at my wrist and say, 'Well, it's such and such . . .'"

He gazes at his wrist, and I comment, "You've got three watches on."

"Yeah. One of them tells me phone numbers and stuff. It's the Information Age now. I've got a lot of stuff stored on here. I don't want to be remembering all of that. It frees up a lot of space in my head. That way, I can be in different time zones. I've been traveling a lot.

"Now, see, before, I was quiet. I was in Big Sur and not bothering anybody. If it's only about yourself, you're missing the point. It's really about the fact that the more you serve, the more it comes. It's like the equation that those boys [the Beatles] made, about 'the love you take is equal to the love you make' [a line from the Lennon-McCartney song "The End"]. All that stuff is true, I come to find out. So when you find that out, why would you want to do all this corporate deviance stuff?"

PETRUCCIANI

"I meditated for many years up in a cave in Big Sur. A weird thing happened. I began to not be *out* of touch, but more *in* touch than I've ever been when I was in the midst of a New York traffic jam.

That's not to say you have to go into a retreat to be peaceful. It was a time in my life when I had to go and do more internal purification, more work on the self and to really investigate. I had seen many of my friends and heroes die at a very early age. Witness Booker Little.

"I'd been quiet and silent all these years, until Michel [Petrucciani] came around. I couldn't believe it. That was like an apparition. I had been living in a tree in Big Sur. I had a compound at that time, until I had more friends and people. Dorothy painted and she needed a studio. I built a bunch of structures. Dorothy did—she's a renaissance woman. She can build, she can paint, she's an architect. The best cook on the planet. Just love personified.

"She built a beautiful Japanese teahouse for us and a main house. We had guesthouses all over the property. I used to call them Lady Day's House, House of Bird, Bird's Lair, Trane Foundation, and stuff like that. . . . Michel stayed in one of these houses. He came over and he had an entourage. Two people had to carry him over, and his brother came over, and then his mother came over later.

"That touched me, because I was not into making music in a public way. I played in the woods and I liked my quiet life. I had come to that thing of inner journey. I have always been about that. I love people, but there's something about me needing solitude. I need to come from deep quiet into activity. I've always had that in my nature. My father was like that. He was filled with solitude, and yet when he would coach his team, he was out there carrying on. So what happened was that during that thing with Michel, I was so touched by him.

"Michel said one time when someone asked if he was still playing with Charles, he said, 'No, it's hard to play with him because you always have to be on your toes. You can't relax. He's always listening to you. I don't like that pressure.' People have counseled me about pressure. I'm the hardest on myself. I think if you do anything you ought to do it full-out. Life is really serious business."

I spoke with Petrucciani in 1987, around the time he released his all-original piano trio album, *Michel Plays Petrucciani*, on the

Blue Note label. His stunted stature was the result of the genetic disease known as *osteogenesis imperfecta*, causing brittle bones and pulmonary problems that would cut his life short: He died in 1999, at age thirty-six.

The diminutive virtuoso lived a short, storied, intense, and circuitous life. As a prodigy in France, he played with his guitarist father, Tony Petrucciani, and with French drummer Aldo Romano. But he felt the restless urge to flee his European homeland—California called him.

As Petrucciani explained, in his sometimes sly way, "When I came to America, I ended up at Charles's house."

He had made his way to Big Sur to visit his friend the French drummer Tox Drohar, who was staying at Lloyd's house at the time. Lloyd asked the young pianist—then only nineteen—to play, and the then-reclusive saxophonist was duly astonished by his technical prowess and poetic style.

Subsequently, Petrucciani said of his connection with Lloyd, "We played together and he asked me if I wanted to join his band. He told me I was the one who inspired him to go back on the road. I said, 'Well, I'm honored and, okay, I'll do it.' I toured California and then Europe and also Japan. So he was the one who took me around the world. After four years, I got him a Swedish bass player, Palle Danielsson. So we helped each out. Little by little, I wanted to work with my own band, my trio. Then I took Palle and [drummer] Eliot Zigmund with me."

I asked about jazz musicians who made a strong impression on Petrucciani at a young age, who drew him deeper into the musical fold.

"The first person I heard was Wes Montgomery, but that was when I was six. In 1970 my brother bought me a record by Bill Evans, and I didn't understand it. It was very modern for me, and my ears weren't ready for it. It took me a minute. Way later I discovered people like McCoy Tyner. I discovered John Coltrane when I was sixteen. I was at my friend's house and he put an album on. I said, 'Who is that?' I had tears coming out of my eyes, it was so poignant and so strong. I said, 'Jesus, where did this angel come from?' He said, 'That's John Coltrane.' So I went out and bought everything he did."

Contrary to what many in the Jazz press assumed, Petrucciani insisted that "Bill Evans wasn't really my major influence. He's a great love of mine, he's very dear to me. But I think my major influence is Wes Montgomery."

No doubt, the strong presence of guitar imparted through the influence of his father, and guitarist brother Philippe, affected his ears. "My father was listening to jazz. He used to pick out solos, and I would sit next to him and tell him the notes. Sometimes he couldn't hear it, and I could. I'd go sit down next to him and sing a note to him until he got it. It was like a game for me. I got very close to my father that way. I was six or seven. It was easy for me, because I could hear everything, even the fast licks. It was like a photograph: I could listen to it and dissect it."

Family ties notwithstanding, Petrucciani the Younger pursued a not uncommon path of self-discovery. Aside from his wanting to explore the birthplace and stomping ground of jazz, he noted, "I came to America for personal reasons also. I wanted to get out of my house. I was a teenager, and, like all teenagers, you're more or less a pain in the butt. I was. I hated my family. I hated the world. I said, 'Screw it all,' and went to America because I thought that would change me a bit.

"After I came here and met Charles, it really changed my life. But I didn't expect it to be that way. I was planning to go back to France. All kinds of things happened. I got married and was married for four and a half years. I met friends and found a new lifestyle that I really liked.

"It was not a musical idea. I knew it would be very hard to make a living in the States and be recognized, especially coming from Europe. When I came to see this guy [Drohar], I didn't expect to see Charles. It was really a stroke of luck. Either that or it was meant to be. I didn't say, 'Okay, I'm going to go to America, meet Charles Lloyd, and play for him.' It's not that easy."

What was clear was that the fateful meeting of the young Frenchman and the middle-aged jazz celebrity–turned–hermit, both seeking a way into the global jazz forum—in entry and reentry form, respectively—enjoyed a certain symbiotic benefit from their musical connection. Lloyd's imprimatur gave the pianist the public exposure he needed to launch into music on his own terms as a leader, and sideman with other artists.

For Lloyd, the pianist seemed to pull him back onto his earlier path after a dozen years of drifting, soul-searching, and recharging. Here was a virtuosic and versatile pianist, in the vein of Jarrett and pianists to come in the impressive Lloyd piano chair—including Bobo Stenson, Geri Allen, and Jason Moran—who could more than handle the role of harmonic anchor and foil, in a genuine jazz quartet format. Lloyd's alternative musical sideshow of the Seventies, it seemed, was over.

And the jazz world was, if somewhat reluctantly, ready to listen to what the more jazz-inclined side of Lloyd had to offer. In its brief tenure, the Lloyd-Petrucciani quartet performed in Europe and produced two fine live albums, *Montreux 82* (Elektra, 1983) and, for the Blue Note label, *A Night in Copenhagen* (1984), with bassist Palle Danielsson and Lloyd's trusty drummer Woody "Sonship" Theus. On the *Copenhagen* album, Bobby McFerrin, then a young improvisatory wizard who was starting to make his presence known, sat in on two tunes. After this album, Lloyd and Petrucciani parted ways, but reunited for a Blue Note tribute night at Town Hall in 1985 with a couple of allies from Lloyd's past life—Jack DeJohnette and Cecil McBee.

Steve Cloud, the influential Santa Barbara–based promoter who has been Keith Jarrett's manager for many years, managed the renascent Lloyd for a brief period. Cloud was instrumental in getting Lloyd back into the jazz scene, starting with tours and live recordings with the quartet featuring Petrucciani early in the Eighties, and later in the same decade helping Lloyd secure his long-lasting record company home at Manfred Eicher's ECM label.

As Lloyd puts it, "Steve Cloud is a white boy who has ideals, living in a world of sharks. He was always trying to get me to do dates. So when Michel came though, I decided, 'Okay, this is right. The world needs to hear him. He has this beautiful gift. I call him an avatar. He's someone who has a beautiful gift. He should come and prepare a road and then go back to wherever he goes. He had a full-blown gift. It's not about age or anything like that.

"After presenting Michel, I went back into my silence again. But I found that I couldn't stay in the silence. As you know me, I have this conflict; I have to share something.

"In Europe, they kept inviting me over all the time. There were these musicians who sat at our feet, with Keith and Jack and Cecil, when we were youngsters in our early twenties. There were these kids named Bobo Stenson, Palle Danielsson, and Jon Christensen. They were sitting at our feet and they were imbibing the stuff. So when I get invited over there later, I get these guys over there who play on my record, because I hadn't been playing over here. Actually, Palle played in the quartet with Michel. And I met Bobo on one of the tours in Italy, and he and I had a vibe together. I knew we should play together someday. . . .

"I'm good at picking the right combination for the sounds that I hear. All my groups have always been orchestras. They dance on a lot of shores. People always say, 'Well, Charles Lloyd sounds like this and sounds like that.' I've lived all of that. I won't keep going on about that. Over there, they rolled out the red carpet for me. I played major concerts all over the place, in Europe and in Japan. Since I hadn't been on the scene, it was the Andy Warhol syndrome, your fifteen minutes."

DIVERTED BY A DIVERTICULUM

As it turned out, Lloyd's long-delayed reentry into jazz world would still take years to fully manifest. He may have been "bitten by the cobra" of jumping into jazz in a broad world forum through his eye-reopening, Petrucciani-featured work, but had to put that jump on hold when he was struck in 1986 by an intestinal disorder called Meckel's diverticulum and required emergency surgery to remove six feet of his small intestine.

For Lloyd, the experience was at once traumatic and rejuvenating, strengthening his resolve to resume his musical mission. As he remembers, "It was after playing for a friend's wedding. The next day, they were cutting on me. I had never been in the hospital before. I didn't even believe in that whole kind of thing. I've been involved in trying to purify in all kinds of ways, checking out diet and all that. I know about what's in the foods and all that are not set up to inspire much nutrition.

"I've gone through a lot of stages and a lot of study. Because I was born in Memphis, I still love barbecue sauce, as I call it, and that whole kind of thing. But I find that to put it on corn is much hipper than to put it on those animals, and it burns cleaner in the system. My grandfather had a huge orchard, so I got to play in that and taste a variety of plums."

Leading up to his malady, Lloyd says, "I was hiking in the mountains and I came back. I laid down on the slant board and had a glass of orange juice. I had excruciating pains in the abdominal region. Lo and behold, something from birth called Meckel's diverticulum had wrapped its way around my small intestines and had strangled them. We didn't know what was happening. Fortunately, I wasn't in Big Sur at the time. I was down here in Santa Barbara.

"My friends here got the best doctors for me. . . . See, that was a teaching for me. I was down on the medical society. I thought that was all about cutting people open and charging high fees and hurting people. . . . Arnold Ehret's *Mucusless Diet Healing System* pulled my coat some twenty years ago. That's when I started fasting and changing my diet, and seriously looking at the fuel I was burning. You can talk about ideas all you want, but it's also very important what you're putting into your temple. If you have lofty dreams and ideas and want to laugh on the higher mountains, you've got to burn cleaner fuel. It's that whole thing about the environment and such.

"See, I saw things coming. Like the surgeries I had on my body and my throat. My doctor said, 'You've had too much smoke, too much cigarettes.' I said, 'Man, I don't smoke cigarettes. I never smoked. I smoked the herb for a bit, but that was more than twenty years ago.' He said, 'Oh, my goodness. Well, you can't be around cigarette smoke.' I said, 'I knew that when I was a little kid, man. That's what the venues were full of, cigarette smoke. I hated coming home with my clothes reeking of cigarette toxins.

"When I had this weird surgery . . . that cost about twenty thousand dollars, just to spend a week in the hospital. I didn't have insurance, because I wasn't a believer in that. I now realize that I have to be more open-minded. . . .

"It was a humbling experience for me. I remember telling them, 'Now I don't want you guys cutting on me. I know what you AMA guys are all about.' [The doctor] said, 'Hey, your belly's getting more and more pregnant.' Peritonitis had set in, and the blood had been shut off by this little thing wrapping around my lower intestine."

Speaking of the experience of this life-threatening medical emergency in an interview in 1990, Lloyd said he "learned now to be more quiet. Although I'm speaking with you, I think the bottom line is that I don't really know much. I have a large capacity for respect for that infinite grace that blows through us. I'm about sharing that, and about sharing my music again."

MY LUNCH WITH CHARLES (AND DOROTHY AND STEVE)

In 1988, as Lloyd was getting himself back in gear, he was invited to play in the Soviet Union for the first time since his 1967 visit with his famed early quartet. Before heading over, he performed at the Lobero Theatre in Santa Barbara.

Working on a pre-concert story about the Lobero event for the *Santa Barbara Independent*, Charles and I met for a lunchtime interview at the Santa Barbara restaurant Downey's. We were joined by Lloyd's wife, Dorothy Darr, and his manager at the time, Steve Cloud.

Charles Lloyd: You want to go to Russia with us next Monday?

Dorothy Darr: As our faux manager/writer.

Joe Woodard: That would be great. Are you serious?

DD: It's an arts festival in Leningrad. They will take us through Russia. It's, like, the twentieth of May. Fly to Moscow, then they fly us to Leningrad for four performances.

JW: Who's in the band?

CL: We're trying to figure that one out. We were thinking about the European group I toured with last summer, with Bobo Stenson, Jon Christensen, and Palle [Danielsson].

DD: But Bobo can't go at that time.

CL: I got another bad cat for you—[pianist] Tad Weed. He's from Detroit; he's a bad cat.

I'm open, but I'm real stubborn when it comes to compassion. You know what Michel [Petrucciani] said when he had his own group—which he's had now from forever—and someone asked him, "How do you like playing with Charles?" He said, "It's great playing with Charles, but the problem is that you have to be great every night, because he's listening and that's too much responsibility. Now, I can relax."

What kind of statement is that to make—"Now I can relax"? Oftentimes, with his trio, it sounds like he's relaxed. He went with me and played last summer and he told me, "Man, I got to put my career on hold. Playing with you is where it's at, and that's what I gotta do." He said, "Man, I'm going with you this summer. I have to be where the music is." If you put your words on that, I expect you to live up to that.

Because the manager was into control, it didn't happen. So we divorced him.

DD: The manager was a problem. I don't know if you're hip to the French mentality, but they're very nationalistic. He didn't have room for Charles to be in the picture. He wanted it to be all about Michel.

JW: That's too bad.

CL: I gave you a tape of the stuff we did in Europe?

JW: Yeah, I played it on the radio, on KCSB.

CL: It was hot. I heard a little of it on the radio. We were rehearsing that day. Michel said, "Man, I play this all the time. It's the greatest stuff I ever heard. I try to play the blues like we were playing, but I can't play like that. How did we do it?" That saddens me. . . .

Music is way better than life. I'm embarrassed to tell you that. . . . But there's nothing like being inside of the inside of the music. All I'm saying is that it hurts that you come out of the music and the world's still a madhouse. You thought maybe something had changed.

DD: There was an old swami who came to Santa Barbara last week. He hadn't talked at all about music, and someone translated it, and he talked directly to Charles and said that even though life is suffering, when we express music, we have to express it with an open heart that transcends suffering. You were saying that the world is still the same when your heart is open, after you've made the music.

CL: And you're real vulnerable. After I play a concert, you know, people would come back and I'd be happy to see them sometimes. I don't know what to say. I'd say, "How ya doin'? How ya doin'? How ya doin'?"

Anyways, that's why I had this naive notion as a young man. I feel pretty much like an infant on one level, and then, on the other level, I feel like an ancient. It's an interesting dichotomy. . . .

I always tried to get this orchestra together that can swim upstream and play on all shores. You have to have a wide berth of stuff. Sometimes, I hate it when people play a ballad or they play funky or this way or that way. That's not what it's about. . . .

As a young man, you think you can change the world. Then later on, you want to change yourself. That's a hard number, too, because the deeper you get into yourself, the more you find that "Jeepers, I've got a lot of stuff to straighten out." I'll tell you, I'm on a roll now. It doesn't have to do with the music biz, it has to do with the life force. I can't sit down and come out and rip and play, and then these little brothers, like [bassist John] Patitucci, are just drooling. They're so excited. He's bad, man.

DD: I heard him a little more than a year ago on [KCRW radio host-producer] Tom Schnabel's show [*Morning Becomes Eclectic*] with his acoustic group. I heard something pretty special. Last year, I called him about doing the date here.

[Steve Cloud arrives.]

CL: The other day, I was walking across the [Lobero Theatre] parking lot and there was a brother way off in the distance, in coveralls. They make brothers wear coveralls because they have to go in boiler rooms. . . .

DD: Well, there's a designer in Paris who has made that his trademark.

CL: Well, that's a different situation there . . . that's like my watermelon T-shirt. Did you ever see my watermelon T-shirt?

The Japanese are very reverential. They'll clap and stand outside your hotel room and come to the airport and stuff. . . . [But] this person finally got up the nerve to say, "Excuse me, but isn't the watermelon on your T-shirt kind of derogatory?" I said, "No, we don't deal with that aspect of it. It tastes good."

[Lloyd momentarily turns his attention to the waitress.]

CL: Anyway, the brother was walking across the parking lot; he was way off in the distance. I was admiring the building. . . . So the brother said, "Hello." I said, "Well, hi, man."

DD: No, he said, "Nice day." I've heard him tell the story. This is the third or fourth generation of him telling it.

CL: Yeah, right, he said, "Nice day, huh?" I said, "Yeah." The brother thing is interesting. . . . Color's not a thing, it's a patina. It doesn't have a place where it lives or is generic. The whole thing started out in Africa . . . and then it moved up to Sweden and it got bleached out, man, the patina.

When we first landed in Sweden with Keith and Jack, they had to protect us, man. Them big blond Amazons was attacking us. You've gotta be careful over there—I swear they'd be fighting and jumping on cars and stuff.

What I'm trying to say is that, because I come from Memphis and have that underdog thing, I would feel that there's a camaraderie based on the idea that this cat is suffering. Somehow, that might be the wrong approach or the wrong reason. . . . When I was in Russia, I saw a brother once and I said, "Hey, brother, what's happening?" He said, "I beg your pardon?" Ever since then, I don't mess with no brother. I found out that the patina don't have no localization.

So anyway, I was coming across the parking lot and this brother said, "Man, I'm looking forward to your concert. I really enjoyed the last one. I was really surprised to see [bassist] Gary Peacock." That was kind of out there, in Santa Barbara, for anybody to say that. . . .

So I said to the brother, "You got the tickets?" . . . because these brothers never have tickets. [to Steve Cloud] Has it sold out yet? Of course not. I'm telling you, man. I've been thinking about canceling. I can't play to no empty chairs. . . . I love the Lobero. I used to bug Steve all the time, "I want to play the Lobero." So I finally played the Lobero. . . .

JW: Have you been listening to a lot of music lately?

CL: Yeah, I've been *liking* music.

JW: Seems like you've gone through periods where you don't really listen much.

CL: Yeah, I have to get away sometimes. Sometimes I don't have the stomach to take most of what they put on the vinyls. Radio and stuff inspires me. [to Joe Woodard] You're a blessing. And Schnabel down there, he has a lot of knowledge. For a young cat, he knows a lot about the music. I'm impressed with that.

JW: When was it that you were last in Russia?

CL: Sixty-eight. [to Darr] You was with me.

DD: Charles says we want to go on the Langston Hughes trail.

CL: Yeah, the Langston Hughes trail.

DD: In the Thirties, the Russians wanted to bring a group of blacks to Russia—like the blacks of America. Langston was going to do this screenplay, and then there were these dancers . . . none of them were really actors. The director of the film was German. When

Langston finally got hold of the story, it was so out to lunch he said, "This is going to have to be totally rewritten." So they're over there for about six months. The Russians took care of them. Wherever they wanted to go, they could go. Finally, it got down to that, no, it could never be done.

The group traveled around outside. Langston wanted to tour the Afghanistan area, so he left the group and wrote stories from there.

JW: So, Charles, yours was the first jazz group to perform in the USSR?

CL: We were the first music group ever invited by a Soviet music committee. It wasn't an official sanction. Benny Goodman or Louis Armstrong had gone before me, but the Russians had heard me from a radio broadcast in Finland. The Soviet Arts Committee invited me over. That's how it happened.

JW: Are you writing music mostly on piano these days?

CL: Yeah, I do it there, man. And then I come over to my saxellos [a variant of the straight soprano saxophone with a slightly curved neck and tipped bell] and stuff.

JW: Are you the kind of writer who gets besieged with ideas while driving in the car?

CL: No, I have a problem with that concept. When I'm driving in my car, I really want to be driving. . . .

I've got this architect-designer guy. One day, I saw his car on the freeway ramp, broke down. He turned his car around on the ramp and came over to talk to me. . . . I said, "What the fuck you doing? You could get killed out there." He said, "I stopped because I had an idea, and had to write it down. I had an idea about how to construct this tennis court." I said, "You want to talk to me *now*?" I was trying to help the cat, and he was trying to kill himself.

Remember *Ninotchka* [a 1939 film directed by Ernst Lubitsch], with Greta Garbo? A guy was trying to hit on her, and she says, "Suppress, Comrade, suppress." So I suppress. . . . It's hard on me, but I can re-till the soil and find my stuff. The mind is a marvelous servant but a terrible master. I try to get it to work for me. . . . I was writing something and I needed another part for it. All of a sudden, I sat down and started composing. It was different than having an idea.

I was bored in the past. I would never sit down and write. I would write on matchbooks and tell guys what to do. Now I'm writing things down. I realize now that this is what's happening. You know what I think it is? When you're fifteen, you have to go outside and play football. When you get to be thirty, like I am [grins], you have to be productive.

I went to see Steve Lacy down there [in LA]. I was sitting at home and a neighbor called me and said, "There are these guys who want to talk to you." I said, "What do you mean? Are they bill collectors?" It turned out that it was this guy [saxophonist] Steve Potts, who was a student of mine thirty years ago. I was shocked. I hadn't seen him for twenty years. He's been living in Paris. He joined Chico after I did.

When I was going to USC, I left there and taught briefly at Dorsey High down there [LA]. I taught music appreciation, and on the first day I said, "I want you to write down what you like in music." This one kid in the back—sweet most of the time—wrote, "Well, I dig jazz, like Mingus and Monk and Trane and all. You're probably not hip to that, but I am. I'm not into this Debussy stuff. So when you get around to that, tell somebody to wake me up back there." In the meantime, I'm playing with Ornette and everybody every day, or at least every night. It got to be a joke with us.

There he [Potts] was and I was so happy to see him, and he was burning, too, man. He followed me to New York and stayed at my place in New York for a week. He's a real sweetheart. I was backstage sitting around talking to him and the drummer, Oliver Johnson. We used to jam a lot in San Francisco in the Sixties, with Chico and Gábor and Albert Stinson. So Oliver said, "You know, somebody just asked me the other day who's the best-feeling bass player. I thought about it and I had to say Sparky." When he said "Sparky," a flood of warm feelings just triggered in me. Albert Stinson's nickname was Sparky. So I went home and wrote this piece for Sparky, like a requiem. That hurts me, because he died in his twenties. When he was playing with Chico, he was about seventeen. He played with Larry Coryell and other people. He ODed. He had a real strong style [sings a riff].

Have you ever heard the one we did on Reprise called *A Different Journey*? That's Frank Sinatra and [record producer] Mo Ostin's label. Mo was the accountant for the label [sings a melody]. Stuff's so strong, and Sparky was the bedrock of all that. I wrote this little piece for him. It's got a little Galveston, a little Houston around it, a little Mexico and California. You have to understand, if destiny didn't change the game, this would be Mexico, you know? It is, frankly. If you ask INS, or whatever you call immigration, I don't think they'd say so. That's cold, man.

SC: Baja is probably one of the most perfect wildernesses on the face of the Earth. It's wonderful. I went down there for two weeks.

CL: I almost got killed on those roads. I got married down there, in Ensenada.

JW: Mingus was fond of Mexico.

CL: Mingus was great, man. He could take any kind of musicians and get them to play his music. And if they weren't playing it, he'd stop the orchestra several times and make sure they did.

JW: Did you play with him?

CL: No. I got there a little bit too late. He died in '78, but he could have died in the Sixties.

DD: I saw him in '74 and he was still so strong.

JW: What will be the basis of your upcoming concert? Do you have an idea of what you'll do, and what kind of material you'll play?

CL: Remember last year? I came out and, how to say, I'm shy. It was very embarrassing to everybody, because I'm struggling so. . . . We've been practicing every day for a year. . . . These pieces are coming through, and they testify to the climate and the state of the . . . I don't have the words for it. But the interesting thing is that I've been observing that it seems to be getting deeper and with dark harmonies. Duke Ellington and Strayhorn and some of the old cats are coming through.

I was in the South of France, hanging out with Duke and Strayhorn just before Strayhorn died. It's like a cycle, like twenty- and thirty-year stuff is coming back and I'm reliving hanging out with Johnny Hodges and Harry Carney and going to Sidney Bechet's tomb with Johnny Hodges. . . . When I look back on my life, I've been real blessed. Somehow, all of this is coming through and I'm just dancing and singing. I don't know what say about it. Deep, beautiful ballads, soulful colors and stuff. I may play a couple of Strayhorn pieces, I'm not sure. Maybe "Upper Manhattan Medical Group" or "Something to Live For."

Towards the end, Strayhorn had this trachea thing with the tube. He was short and very elegant and refined. Just to see him was like seeing a deity. People talk about, in those bios, they talk about geniuses and stuff, and we had those cats on the planet. . . . I'm content to be in that lineage. That's all it is.

It's real scary, in a sense, because for me, being a private, quiet person, it's like scary a little bit to step onstage here in my own domiciles and play, in a sense. I was so shy last year. But once it gets rolling. . . . But see, Steve [Cloud] is intent on getting this thing rolling from the start this time, because he don't want to stay there until midnight this time. He wants us to say it and get it done.

SC: You went out burning in Saalfelden [an Austrian jazz festival].

JW: So will this concert feature new pieces mixed with older tunes?

CL: Well, it's unknown at the moment. Like I said, this new music erupted onto the scene and I feel like I'd like to hear it. I think I've got more material than I've got playing time. Also, I feel like stretching out. So if I've gotta start out burning. . . . Usually, if I start out a concert burning, it stays on fire.

SC: But that makes for a better balance.

CL: Really? I can tell when it's right.

See, Joe, I got a problem. There's a lady here in town who has a little music store. Before the concert last year, I wanted to tighten up on my piano studies, the Hannon piano studies and all that stuff [sings a scale]. . . . [I said,] "I'm gonna be giving a concert and I'm going to have [pianist] Henry Butler, and he'll sing 'Sometimes I

Feel like a Motherless Child' like Paul Robeson, and then play piano like Art Tatum or something. You should come to the concert. You'd like it." She said, "Okay."

So afterwards, I went by her store and she wasn't there. Her sister was there. I said, "Did she like the concert? We're doing another concert. You should come." She said, "I've been thinking about it and debating whether or not I should come. But the problem is that I loved it so much last year, I decided I can't come, because I can't stand to be disappointed."

That was like a dagger in me. It's hard for me to get up onstage and play, anyway. I'm not an exhibitionist or anything. I mean, I'm free once I get going. A few friends have been calling me up, giving me nice roses. But that one barb sticks in there—she can't come because she can't be disappointed. For somebody to say that to you, you know . . .

JW: You whetted peoples' appetites last year.

CL: What does that mean?

JW: They're ready for more.

CL: You think you're ready? How can we find out? I want to find out from the audience how many was there last year. I want the ones who were there from last year. I want to see, before I come out, who was there from last year, because I'm thinking that if you want me to start out burning, they would have to have enough openness in their being to allow me to come out and burn without getting acquainted.

Tell the people, when you write, I don't want no new ones to come. I don't want nothing but veterans.

DD: Charles, you want everyone who has the initiative to go.

CL: No. I only want people to come who were there last year, or who have had experience in their life.

SC: In Saalfelden they were one hundred percent new.

CL: Get outta here. That little eight-year-old kid up on the stage has been listening to me since he was three.

DD: There was an eight-year-old Austrian kid who first heard Charles when he was three. He begged his father to take him to the concert. He had this Charles Lloyd T-shirt on. He stayed the entire performance right in front of the stage.

CL: Let me tell you something: Dress to please others, eat to please yourself

If I dressed the way I dress at home, I'd get arrested. I couldn't come down and play. Dorothy gives me nice costumes. I don't mind wearing them. But I don't wear that kind of stuff at home. Some people don't understand me. When I play, I wear some different kind of clothes than I wear here.

[Lloyd chats for a moment with the waitress.]

CL: What was my theory? Oh, about the people in Saalfelden. So we played outside in this tent, in the mountains. It was beautiful. Huge meadows were all around, and they've got tons of Eddie Bauer tents all over the place and it's a Woodstock-revisited vibe. People are just milling around. They've just been living there for four days, in these tents. The audience is scattered. We start playing, and before I know it, the place is filled. Steve said people didn't know me, but they know the stuff, but they know the elixir is here. And they got in there. That was hip, man. I like that. My theory is that people can hear more than they're given credit for.

America, Ornette, Miles, and More

In a 1992 interview, Lloyd offered social and musical musings, as well as touching on Ornette Coleman, Miles Davis, and the tug and elusiveness of higher truths.

"I know that we all have to learn how to play changes. If you don't learn that, and keep faking through life, the Peter Principle comes around. That's not going to get you anywhere. All those people who bought the idea of the gold-plated watch when they retire—that dream is gone. It's better to go for what you believe. Ignorance is still a problem that plagues us, this huge institutional racism. It's really our big cancer, and something that we need to find a way to be bigger than.

"But I still have great faith in America. I had this weird experience in the Sixties when I was really disenchanted with the

situation here. I traveled around the world and saw that all cultures and societies had big problems too. In many ways, they're flawed and not dealing with things. That's what keeps leading me back to spiritual life. I can find, in that, that there's a way of knowing . . . what we are in terms of not being about desire manifest.

"I see two things. It's a real dark hour and something always comes through to manifest the light. I want to be about a force like that—that's all I can tell you. The musicians I have loved the most have done that. Trane was definitely a spiritual seeker and a great saint and sage. Look at Ornette. I can't say too much about his Prime Time thing, because I haven't really heard that. But I was very moved to go hear him speak with Charlie and Billy [referring to a special trio concert with Haden and Higgins, at the Broadway Theater in downtown Los Angeles, the same building where Coleman worked as an elevator operator in the Fifties]. That was quite beautiful. As for the other band, I don't know how I feel about that.

"I always had funny feelings about Miles and what he was doing. Without any commercial consideration, if Miles today continued to be Miles, well, you talked to him . . . don't get me wrong, he definitely was a great artist and he made a huge contribution. But in my observance of the process, I think he would have taken that statement of integrity after he got himself back again, back in the late Fifties. But you can't say that—he left such a wealth of music.

"I think Trane is untainted in his purity of music. We all do things that we wish we hadn't, but I think that there's a thread that runs through Trane. Someone said that at the end, he was thinking about putting the old quartet together again. He was doing some serious research. Miles did some serious research also, but his results were so mixed, with the lifestyle and his vanity. I'm suspect of wealth. We all have a desire and vanity and ego, but it's better to face and be confronted with where we really want to lay down the gauntlet, or where we're going to dance.

"If I painted my 'do or got some plugs put in or got some stuff happening with it, I'm sure it would enhance market value. If I put some synthesized beats to the music, I think that I could get out and play more. Well, I think that I've gone so far out on a limb

in terms of trying to know what's behind silence that whatever
mistakes or shortcomings that I have keep being uplifted by my
continued quest for the higher truth."

GETTING IT TOGETHER

By 1989, two decades after he jumped off the late-Sixties fame bus, and with his mid-Eighties health problem behind him, Lloyd moved into the next phase of his musical life—his ECM years. In retrospect, he comments on the wisdom he accrued during his long hiatus from the public spotlight.

"Those were great years for me, because I had a quiet retreat. All retreats are for a purpose, then you're propelled back into activity. I do the music now because I love it. I don't have a career mentality. We get reviews from all around the world and they really speak of me as one of the, pardon my language, I can't say 'masters,' but they speak like that because I'm becoming an elder. The thing is, for me, that I feel like I'm a late bloomer, that I'm still growing in the music.

"The whole thing about the search or the quest [is that] people are uncomfortable in their own skins. I lived in Big Sur and was always trying to get somewhere. There are sixty miles of coastline and five hundred families live there, yet I was still trying to get more intimate with nature. My nearest neighbors were a mile and a half [away] on either side, but still I wanted to get intimate with nature. I would round the bend on the property and, *whoom*, it would be like three-D kind of stuff.

"Then, in the music, whenever I record something, I listen to it and I try to get inside the music. It's like it's all forbidden. When you get out of the way, and there is no you, there is just the vision of the music. That's been happening.

"If you live in your world, it's expensive to live simply. In working on that dilemma more and more, I come to find that there is another simplicity. There's liberation amidst chaos. Right in the middle of a traffic jam in Manhattan, you've got to be centered, too.

You've got to be out of the way, but you've got to be present, too. It's like restful alertness to the max.

"That's why I mess around with all these cats, like Rumi [the thirteenth-century Persian poet and mystic] and all these swamis. They have this way of sidestepping doodoo. A different way of putting it is like someone went to the sea to measure the depths of the ocean. For me, I'm finding, more and more, less and less. It's like when the guy goes to the Zen master and says, 'I want to learn all about the truth.' The master says, 'We'll have a tea ceremony,' and pours the tea. The student tells the teacher that he has studied this and that. The master keeps pouring the tea, and the student says, 'It's too full, it's too full.' The master says, 'Precisely.'

"It's between the cracks of all that that I'm working on, the utter simplicity of just getting the fuck out of the way. It's beautiful."

6
THE MUNICH CONNECTION

SINCE 1989, LLOYD HAS been blessed by his involvement in the comfortable and warm embrace of a unique record label—German producer/career-maker Manfred Eicher's ECM, which beautifully suited Lloyd's vision. This serendipitous relationship of artist and label came as a surprise to some, including Lloyd himself. By any measure in the jazz world, the long haul of his rich ECM era has been very good to him and, symbiotically, to ECM.

Although Lloyd had dabbled with reentry into the jazz cosmos in the Eighties, through the Petrucciani prism and other half-steps in the right direction, it wasn't until his friend and then-manager Steve Cloud connected the business and artistic dots with ECM that Lloyd's full-blown return was made manifest. Almost immediately, with his introspective first ECM outing, *Fish out of Water* (1990), the long-awaited return of the wunderkind Charles Lloyd, now soaring again in midlife, became a reality.

At the time of his relaunch, Lloyd told me, almost with a self-cautioning, jinx-leery hesitation, "If I don't get exciterated, my stuff will happen, because it never happens when you want it to happen. In some ways, it's too little, too late for me. But on the other hand, there's still a child in me that wants to sing the song and I've just got to figure out how to keep doing it.

"I'm real slow. It takes me a long time to write, and a long time to recuperate. My writing is all about these hikes in the hills and mountains and being up in my place in Big Sur and stuff, and also going down in the jungles of the town. Don't misunderstand me: I don't subscribe to that notion about it only being in the sylvan setting that you're creative. I think that if you can't create in the middle of a traffic jam, you're in a world of trouble, too. But I go down into the towns and walk around. I go into the New York jungle from time to time. I don't do it a lot, but when I do it, I'm at ease with it."

During a conversation in Lloyd's house, deep into his ECM saga, he looked back on the matter of finding proper equilibrium between purely aesthetic interests and the realities of the marketplace. As Lloyd said, tongue only halfway in cheek, "Maybe I should be like Charles Ives and go start an insurance company, and then not let people have policies anymore."

In a way, you're pulling an Ives, in that you're able to do your work without compromising or bowing to the whims of the marketplace.
Lloyd: Ives would print his music up and give it to folks. I like notions like that. I've always been about that. I have this tremendous sense of dignity about some part of the being. I refuse to have the Mack truck debauch me.

Dorothy Darr: It has its pluses and minuses. It's true that Charles has always done what he's wanted to do, and in his way—which is great. Except that a lot of people resent that fact in the established business community; he has survived in spite of their stuff. In another way, he can't call his shots completely because there is a large amount of resistance.

CL: I wouldn't sign with Impulse! [Records]. I said, "Hey, guys, I'm viable. Let's get real about this." They've got a hidden bottom line and all that stuff. I found it and said, "Okay, here's the way it works. There you are and here I am. Let's make it an enlightened situation." They were willing to be more real with me than anyone else.

DD: It was so close to happening. The fact that it didn't happen is surprising. However, everything happens or doesn't happen for a reason.

CL: Joe, when I'm gone, let 'em know that, in the tradition of Paul Robeson, I had to stand up to the system. The folks at Impulse! thought I was too difficult to deal with. That's not really so. Basically, I wanted to be treated fairly, and they don't treat people fairly. Do you know what they said? They said, "You're the one now. . . . We're going to let you through now. . . ." They were all over this. But they said, "You're going to have to do it our way."

That's the same thing Atlantic said to me at a certain point. See, if I do it their way, there won't be any room left for me in there. They'll make me a product. I see all these little kids they launch now. They'll spend forty thousand dollars to make a record of them. Nothing happens with them, or if it does, *then* they'll focus on them. But they've got these other records for, years later, to put out there. . . .

You only do this music if you have to, and when they know you have to, they want you to pay. They came here and said, "He obviously doesn't need money. What does he want?" I got this back-channel stuff. They were saying stuff like, "Is he hungry enough?"

Basically, I was told what I should have done was to play the system game, do the happy-slave act and let them go ahead and make the bread and get me out there, and then next time, my time will come. Well, they wanted to tie me up for seven records. That's never good for the artist. That means that they can cut you loose at any time, but you can never cut them loose.

At least with Manfred [Eicher] and ECM, it's a real slow burn, because Manfred doesn't do the promotion and stuff. But I've been able to get four records done with some quality to them.

IN MANFRED'S HOUSE

The house that Manfred built maintains a disarming degree of integrity after four-plus decades of producing a musically diverse yet aesthetically focused catalog of music.

Lloyd recounts the process of his getting to ECM; "There were a couple of labels interested in my work at that period of mine. Manfred said he'd be interested. Stephen [Cloud] single-handedly convinced me to record for ECM, because all those other people were more 'chips on the table,' so to speak. . . . He felt that this was a place where I would be treated properly and that they would be honest and straightforward to me. That was an interesting concept because, in the American system, you can't find the bottom line in these contracts. Believe me. I tried to read one of them: Dorothy wouldn't let me. I was offered a contract with lots of bread on it, on the front. But she wouldn't let me read it. It was forty pages, and it was all about slavery. It had nothing to do with anything that I was interested in inside, so I declined the bread.

"I like honesty and integrity. I have a simple notion of 'Do not do unto others as you'd not have them do unto you.' I'm trying to practice that stuff.

"Speaking of Manfred, he's a very special guy. This conversation about the ECM sound and all that is kind of off-kilter. When I first came up, there was a phase where you could make your recordings and you could grow with your work. They don't do that anymore. They've got these guys from schools who come down and tell you which guys you keep and which guys you don't. You have to live in your lifetime with your work and evolve. I've been at this house [ECM] for twelve recordings now, and here's the beautiful thing: Manfred, man, he's a special guy, and they're all special folks.

"Steve steered me to the right place. If I picked up one of those offers in those other companies, I think it would have hurt me in places that I can't talk about. I'm a tender warrior. I don't want to be some other kind of thing."

Looking back on the 1990s, and his rejuvenation and maturation processes during that period, Lloyd clearly recognizes the central importance of his ECM pact. In the middle of his life, after his dizzyingly meteoric youthful flight into (by jazz standards) mega-fame, followed by his protracted escape from public scrutiny and renewed focus on artistic intentionality, Charles Lloyd finally found an enabling energy source in a record company and aesthetic ethos based in Munich.

"Out of all the music I've ever recorded or witnessed," Lloyd effused, "[Eicher is] one of the producers who I could say, 'He's an artist.' This cat brings something to the table. He's not just in there drinking his chocolate milk. He's got nuance value. He's one of the creative participants. He can suddenly just bring a little something at the right time. He and I are both strong-willed, so sometimes we go at it, but we always end up with a love fest. That's a special brother.

"I take my hat off to him, because he also is principled in the sense that he does what he loves, and for the right reason. He's not driven by being an accountant or a lawyer from the Wharton School or IBM or whatever that thing in the music industry is about now. It's like the film industry: When Jack Warner and Harry Cohn were there, you'd have King Vidor, you'd have Hitchcock, you'd have John Ford, you'd have Howard Hawks and Frank Capra. People loved movies.

"See, it's got to be a love thing. It's got to be a passion for what it is and when it is. From *Fish out of Water* straight on through, I think we've done some good work together. . . . That's a body of work that I'm proud of.

"It also happened at a time when, fortunately, I had come out of a 'Pick yourself up and start all over again' phase. How's it go? 'Think of all the things men have had, fall and rise again, pick yourself and start all over again.' Dorothy Fields wrote those lyrics [for the song "Pick Yourself Up," with music by Jerome Kern]."

Musically speaking, Lloyd's reentry program in the late Eighties also entailed some interesting, sideways rapport with forces from his past. His first European band featured bassist Palle Danielsson and drummer Jon Christensen, both members of Jarrett's "European quartet" in the late Seventies, and Swedish pianist Bobo Stenson, a classically trained dynamo and, when required, an ultralyrical player. Stenson's artistic voice is similar in many ways to Jarrett's, to the degree that some have said that Stenson's ECM career was slowed down partly because of his artistic proximity to the label's flagship pianist.

As it turned out, Stenson was possibly Lloyd's most ideal pianistic foil to date. He is a powerful, poetic, and versatile player, and also a sensitive team player who can keep his cool and resist the scene-stealing that Jarrett tended to do in the late-Sixties band. Listening back to Lloyd's fiery late-Sixties records, one gets the impression that the saxist could have been a sideman to the key-boardist; Lloyd's discography from the Nineties on, however, shows a more balanced ensemble equation, partly because of cooler musical heads and a prevailingly impressionistic repertoire.

Lloyd was to find an even stronger group rapport once the masterful Swedish bassist Anders Jormin cemented the core unit, along with the drum chair passing from the then-fragile Chistensen (through a brief and not entirely logical encounter with drummer Ralph Peterson on 1991's *Notes from Big Sur*) to Billy Hart, a drummer with whom the ensemble gained cruising altitude on the albums *The Call* (1993), *All My Relations* (1995), and *Canto* (1997). That American-Scandinavian band was among the strongest Lloyd has yet commanded.

FISH OUT OF WATER

On Lloyd's first ECM release, the album *Fish out of Water*, strong new vibrations are clearly already in place right from the very tender opening statement of the title song (and they will continue through the entire Lloyd-on-ECM saga). Lloyd opens with a few extended rubato measures of melody, in his willfully understated, breathy tone, his signature flourish of rapidly arpeggiated notes swooping to the arrival note. His intonation wavers in an expressive manner, in keeping with the saxophonic voice of his devising, and his Scandinavian comrades—especially the ever-masterful Stenson and the artfully elastic time poet Christensen—are naturally, instantly at ease with creating a loose yet engaged atmosphere in the music. That delicate balance would come to define the next decades of Lloyd's music. He had found home, labelwise.

As Lloyd told me, just before *Fish out of Water* was released publicly, the title song "was written just before our tour. It just came through. I walk, I swim underwater, and do whatever. I agonize over the condition of what it is, and yet my heart breaks out into song.

When it breaks out into song, that's devotional sharing. So that piece is just so organic to me, in its light and liveliness.

"I've played this music a lot and I haven't found it to OD me or tire me. It actually builds me more. That's encouraging to me, because I have to try to step back and be objective about my work. I'm touched that it still has this touching ability for me. I feel that, as the artist, if it touches me, I think it will touch others. I think we all share in that one breath. We just breathe it in different tempos. It's something that I'm still trying to get at. It's that thing I talked to you about, that thing in the tone and getting to where that essence is so *there* that it speaks a universal truth.

"I'm always trying to get to the universal. I know that's a weird thing to say, because one sound can't speak for all sounds. But . . . I always think about my tone and I always work at that. It's getting better. That's encouraging to me, that my tone is growing and it's getting deeper and it's getting lighter. You know, I still feel anger about things . . . but I try to transmute that into something of joy that I also feel, because I just refuse to be without hope, man, or without my dreams. . . . It's a call for love and a hope for sanity and the higher truth to stop being so hope-blind and hypnotized here, and asleep. I hope that, in the music, there is this awakening factor that will touch that part in peoples' beings that is vibrant with kindredness of that oneness—because there's only one life here.

"Everyone is progressing. We're just progressing at spiritually different rates. But I think there's something that can bypass intersections or lines of demarcation. That's what I'm about and try to get at in a song. That's why I go through intense suffering at not doing the music in pedestrian ways. It's like an intangible suffering. When I witness the scene that's available—as you do too in your field, and you talk about it—it's easy for mediocrity to get packaged or for someone to do biz on something. But we're not doing biz. It's our nature to write and to paint and to make communication. It's all the adoration of the divine.

"Some of that came through better and deeper and with a quiet blessing than I've had heretofore. Also, the whole orchestra shared in that and in the vision. Something was captured there."

At the time of Lloyd's long-awaited reemergence, blessed with and bolstered by a strong and empathetic band and the imprimatur of a supportive record label environment, he was particularly reflective—and also a bit wary—about the forces finally coming together to revive his public music life.

"I keep spinning it around," he told me in a long interview in September of 1989. "It keeps coming through that, in the absence of a perfect universe, with music, you can make a place that's different from the world you live in. We all want to make the world a better place. I'm sure everyone does in their way. . . .

"So what happens for me is that this music keeps coming through from a very deep place within me. Like that first piece, 'Fish out of Water,' it's what you are, too. We are spiritual essence and here we are in a polluted atmosphere.

"I don't know what this music is. I think it's whatever it is for you. Labels bother me. When I think of Duke Ellington, he is the music. Labels bothered him. Mingus, in an even more adamant way, complained about the label of 'jazz.' It gets back to that thing of Lenny Bernstein jumping up on the stage at the Five Spot and hugging Ornette. If Ornette had gone down to Philharmonic Hall and done that [to Bernstein], he'd have been arrested. There's something about the patina and the presentation of it and all. I guess I'm really about tearing down those barriers.

"I remember when I was a youngster playing this music, it used to feel like we could be busted for what we were playing, because it was such a wild, blatant truth. . . . I think that this so-called jazz expression is so beautiful in that it's such a music of freedom. I suppose I always identify with that situation because of the patina thing and my being born into that in this lifetime.

"As I looked back to my ancestry, I've traced it all the way back to Mongolia on one side of my family and then to the Native American

Cherokee thing and to the Irish thing in the grandparents, and obviously the African thing. . . . It's that whole thing of the melting pot. It's just mankind.

"I'm hoping that this record really reaches people on a sensitive level and that I'm able to go play in controlled environments, where . . . I can purify enough that I can deliver, and that it can be a sharing. Without that, it's pretty much a barbecue smorgasbord. It's a vulgar arena. . . . But I must tell you, there are two sides to this coin. On one side it's painful, but on the other side there are so many brothers and sisters out there who are open to the experience."

As is Lloyd's wont when lost in a twining convergence of ideas and observations, he eventually circles back to the topic at hand, in more real, ground-level terms. He gave a vivid picture of the dynamics at work during his first encounter with Eicher and the ECM ethos.

"So I go in the studio [Rainbow Studio in Oslo, where many an ECM album, classic and otherwise, has been recorded], and those guys had traveled with me and they said, 'Manfred Eicher's a detail man, and it will take us a while to get going, but once we get going, everything will be fine. The first day won't work and then he'll record for three days and it will hit on the third day.'

"I didn't sign up for any of that. I just went in and started playing this music. I had all these pieces. I played them and I'd finish one, and then I would start another. I'd finish that, and start another. Nobody bothered me, and I played about six pieces. I liked that, nobody bothering us when we played the music.

"The problem in my Atlantic years was that I remember I would go to record, and the producer would be on the phone talking to folks. The engineer would be drinking some chocolate milk or something. When I would hear the sound that came out, it wasn't what was in my mind's ear at the time. So I was never comfortable recording; I always liked the live experience.

"But this thing happened with *Fish*. After several pieces, finally Manfred comes on the talk box and he says, 'Would you like to hear something?' I said, 'Sure, okay.' I'd heard that he was a strong personality. And, quiet as it's kept, you might not recognize it, but this soul up here has a little strength, too—from my grandfather.

So I go into the control room and listened to the playback, and I started crying. What happened was that what I heard in my mind's ear, he had gotten. You could hear every instrument. It's in there, it's open. You can take the journey. I was so touched by the nuances and detail and such quality. Jan Erik [Kongshaug] was the engineer. . . . I just started crying. I took the dust off his shoes. I'm not 'Tomming,' I just took the dust out of respect, because the guy had pulled off something. Ever since then, he and I have been tight. He and I have had some adjustment things to take care of over the years. You know how marriages are. You're not goin' to get out of here scot-free.

"This recording happened in the middle of the tour we were doing in Europe. Going in, Dorothy and Steve were so beautiful. Bharati [Darr's spiritual name, and also the title of an airily balladic song on *Fish out of Water*] is the mother of the universe. They're so caring. Steve is so quiet in his way. We had these other opportunities, these other companies before they got me to do this with ECM, Windham Hill, and other companies. I don't understand why you're all of a sudden hot and then not.

"So it was the right thing to do to record for ECM, because this music couldn't have happened any other way. This Manfred Eicher—I had not met him before. At this stage in life, I'm a bit wary or weary of folks and what's coming at me, because of all these New York jungles that I've seen and all this rape and pillage. I wouldn't say anything to him. I just kind of went there and we met. We were just jamming. I'd seen photos, which Steve showed me. I could see that he was fastidious.

"He and Jan Erik work, really work together, and the studio and just the way they mic and the simplicity of it—we're just in this gymnasium room in this old building. As in life, they had to go downstairs to get them to stop the jackhammers in the restaurant, but, man, something really special happened. It was the right thing to do.

"As we began to record, I recognized what I was thinking in the music. This was what blew me away about Manfred—he *got* it, man.

In 'Fish,' there were these dynamics that I was hearing. We ran a tape down and he ran out into the room and said, 'What about those dynamics that were supposed to be there?' He just lightened up the atmosphere and took a load off my shoulders, because the musicians had it from what I was saying, but it just took it to a deeper level of listening. The record is really about listening, man.

"That's what we're talking about, what's missing in society, hearing your brother. He enabled us to go to a deep level of listening. And the amazing thing was, while this deep level of listening was happening, it was also being apprehended by the microphones and the machines, and it was done in a nonintrusive way. Most of my records have been live; I haven't spent a whole lot of time in the studio. Steve and Bharati kept insisting that I should do a studio recording to really capture this in its rightful essence. I tend to be impatient in the process, because the engineer is usually drinking his chocolate milk or his wine or whatever and reading his baseball scorecards, waiting for the next session or something.

"But this was truly a surrender of love. And everybody just was so wonderful. Manfred, I must say, he's got ears—the cat can hear around the corner. This is what amazes me, he can hear around the corner. I was very concerned about my tone. I have this way of hearing. I've never heard it captured so well on records.

"Did you read that book someone did on Marvin Gaye a while back? When he had his own studio down in LA, after Motown had come out, he worked very privately, late at night. He had his demons and stuff, but when he was working he found a way, with "What's Going On" and stuff. He would go in the studio and sit on the couch, behind the console, and sing his song very quietly into the microphone. He would do it in the control room with his engineer. They got to where they could communicate, and he could do his thing very direct.

"I told Manfred I had this thing about my tone. I didn't mention Marvin, but I said I had this singer in mind who, when he would record, he would be in the control booth and would just be singing quietly. I'm concerned about the miking, because sometimes I want to sing strong, and sometimes I want to sing in a quiet voice. . . .

"While I was out here [Los Angeles], I never liked the . . . wimp kind of sound. Down there in the Fifties there was that so-called West Coast stuff that was pretty vapid in a lot of ways. . . . Of course, we were all young wildcats—Eric Dolphy and Ornette and all. We were all angling to get to New York. But the thing is, as you grow, and grow deeper, you see the unity of everything. You can see beauty everywhere. What happened is that I was very concerned that the music could be very soft and yet very powerful and not [have] the wimp factor.

"Everything grows to shape us. Me, for example, being a lonesome child, that all comes through. It takes a long time to get comfortable with your loneliness and use it as a friend. Some people are very gregarious and can hang out and all that stuff nonstop. But I tell you something, man, you watch in the eyes of the cocktail drinkers around the party, with all the laughing and grinning. They're not but a few steps away from stark, raving terror in a lot of instances. I'd rather stay home and suffer my stuff and get to the bottom of it, because even a hundred years on the planet is just a flick of a second in terms of the ancient ones."

In Rainbow Studio, Lloyd explained, "I was concerned about my tone and I said, 'Hey, Manfred, when you're recording, I'd like to be able to play soft, but when I want to play at a different volume, do I have to back off the mic or push it or what?' And he said, 'No, you just play. We will get the music.' And so I played and I was very touched . . . because my sound is a different kind of sound. It's not like a tenor, in a way. I played alto for many years, and maybe it's light and yet dark.

"I was finally happy or pleased with my sound, and I never am; I'm always agonizing. A beautiful thing happened. Steve explained it to me. Those records that Manfred makes are technically perfect, and sometimes they're on the cooler side of cold. I really like the sounds that he gets, but sometimes it comes off a little cold, and I was concerned about my warmth being homogenized into something. Of course, I'm kind of paranoid from the Sixties. Manfred was flipping out. Steve said he'd never seen Manfred in the state that he was in. He said, 'What happened was that his technology and your warmth came together and this thing happened.'

"Actually, I didn't think he'd like my stuff, because of that. Steve actually didn't think that I'd be the one to record with Manfred, because he thought that Manfred wouldn't relate to my tone. But he's just flipped out over it. So it goes to show that there's hope after life anyway. But I was touched that he had this ability to hear around corners. He actually heard my intent, he heard my music, and he was extremely helpful in his very little production supervision.

"When I rehearse or when I do anything, I'm real intense and I'm driven. In the studio, I was very driven, and Manfred is very driven. He and I would have to console each other, because the musicians would disappear after every take. They'd have to go out and smoke and shit and drink beers and wine and stuff. That's just maintaining their level of toxicity.

"I said, 'Hey, Manfred, I'm here to work.' He said, 'I am too.' At one point, midway through the session, he came out in the studio. He wears all black clothes and shoes, all fashionable stuff. Tight black jeans, black denim jackets, and black T-shirt. Then he'll have a change of clothes—and that's all black. But he came out at one point and said, 'I hope you keep this band together. They're beautiful with you. I've used them before, but with you, they're very beautiful. I know they smoke and all that, but they don't talk during the music. They really are about the music.'"

Going back to when his first manager, George Avakian, deployed the shrewd strategy of "breaking" the Lloyd–Jarrett–et al. quartet across the Atlantic and then using the European buzz as leverage to bolster Lloyd's reputation in the States, Europe has always been a strategic reference and strong point of return for Lloyd, often more so than the US—and often to Lloyd's frustration over the years.

Of course, the Euro link is deeper than just a matter of marketing: As one who studied Eurocentric classical music and had ears open to musical ideas and attitudes from around the world, Lloyd's music has resonated well beyond American soil.

As he was easing into his ECM life and newfound critical favor with his Scandinavian-dominated band—Stenson, Danielsson, and Christensen—he came up against various elements of drama, or perceived drama, about his mix of American and European players.

"That's my band," he told me, just before *Fish out of Water* was released. "That's another thing I've experienced. In Europe, they want me to come with an American, Afrocentric band. That's what they want to see me bring. They don't understand that it's all about the music. I'm not playing with those guys because they happen to be in Europe. I bring those guys over *here*, too. . . .

"They don't understand what it was like for Billie Holiday to be with Artie Shaw and not be able to go into the restaurant. It was the same thing with many musicians, like Teddy Wilson with Benny Goodman. Those guys had to deal with racism. See, that's the other thing. I'm not holding Europe up to be cool or nothing. They've got their problems, as everyone does, with double standards in all kinds of cultures. I don't want to be redundant and get into all of that, but I sure wish we could see through our trips and that everyone could rise to whatever levels they aspire to without artificial whips and double standards and all that."

TALES OF CHRISTENSEN

For those of us who learned early lessons about the important Scandinavian jazz musicians through ECM records, Christensen is the stuff of legend, a drummer of uncommon subtlety and rhythmic impressionism.

Having not heard/seen him in his more wildcatting persona, imagine my surprise when, at the Montreal Jazz Festival not long after *Fish out of Water* came out, he not only waxed aptly lyrical in the tender passages but he channeled his inner Keith Moon elsewhere. Late in the set at the now-defunct venue the Spectrum (site of many a great jazz performance over many years at the festival), Christensen morphed into a madman at the kit, bashing wildly and grabbing the drum set's stem, picking it up and shaking the entire kit like a shaman.

Speaking generally—and about Christensen specifically—Lloyd discussed the timeless urge to achieve abandon and process energy as a musician. "Sometimes you have to rev up and get hot and get out there. It's a smorgasbord. It's the Glenn Gould [classical pianist famous for his sometimes eccentric interpretations of Bach] thing I was telling you about. In a controlled environment with Jon, it would be incredible. But in an environment where there's me following Freddie Hubbard and Diz and Oscar Peterson, it's not going to be that way.

"He's totally spontaneous. He may be real quiet while you're burning up there. You've got five thousand drunk whatever out there; all of the conditions aren't the best for the music. So, as a trouper, or some part of me that is a professional, recognizes that it wouldn't be good to play all ballads here—they'd *hang* you and shit. You have to go out and play some uptempo and stuff.

"I learned that with Cannonball. Cannonball never figured out what he was going to play ahead of time. The people would ask him for a program when we'd play colleges and concerts, and he'd say, 'Listen, lady, we don't know what we're going to play.' He'd go and play a couple of pieces and feel them out, and go from there.

"It's just that Jon is so spontaneous and he's a genius. But, you know, you might need to swing and get off the stage. And he might not feel like swinging that night. With the other fellas, it's different. That's the only thing: you can't get something to take out if you need something to go with him. You need to sit down and have a seven-course meal. That's beautiful, but sometimes you have to take it to go."

Slippery Peas

Lloyd: I played a great concert in Portugal with Jon Christensen and the king came. I don't know if he'll be doing that anymore. Jon spilled some food in the queen's lap.

Darr: He was invited to this royal dinner and he was sitting next to the queen. His knife slipped and his peas went into the queen's lap. He said, 'Oh, my goodness.' He started taking them out of her lap and the king said, 'I think that will be enough.'

BOBO STENSON

I spoke with Bobo Stenson in 1996, several years into his period of playing with Lloyd, and he was humbly appreciative of the opportunities afforded him through that connection, including coming to the US to play, a too-rare occasion for this great pianist.

"It's been a great experience with Charles. I'm very happy about that, with Charles bringing me over. That meant a lot to me, for my playing and everything, when you feel that somebody trusts you. It helps your self-confidence. . . . I've been playing with him every year since '88."

I asked if there is a special connection, a special relationship, that only happens when you play with someone for a while, instead of just doing a concert here or there. "Oh yeah. Sure. When you get to know each other, something happens, especially in the rhythm section. You get stuff going. You know each other and get the signals from everybody. You also work on the material a lot when you work a lot; it develops. That means a lot."

As Lloyd puts it, regarding his connection with Stenson, "It's beautiful. Fresh spring water from way up in the mountains. There is sensitivity, this boy is a poet. He can get very deep down, play some serious blues or whatever. I'm real happy with him. He's a gentleman, he's beautiful. And he's very, very soulful—even though he lives up in the north, he's very soulful.

"I still feel a great affinity with Bobo, and I think there's a special thing that has happened between us. He's a beautiful musician. The King of Sweden made him a national treasure a few years ago, and gave him a lifetime stipend of some serious bread that he can go into the sunset with. He called me, all excited, and I said, 'Great, now you can afford to play with me.'

"The thing about Bobo is that he's not only a national treasure of Sweden, but he's a national treasure of the universe. . . . I don't know why people haven't woken up to him, because he's seriously great on any kind of level. It's like Van Gogh and those cats would jump up and down to hear him playing. They may be jumping up and down anyway, wherever they are. . . .

"Bobo's my man. We've been together for years. He's a great artist. You know what, he's also a fine human being. He's a real brother, never no backstabbing or funny business. I've known him going on two decades now. He's just sweetness and light. I love sincerity and truth. . . Bobo is one of the rare souls on the planet. He stills carries the vision of deep beauty. I love his quality. As you well know, he doesn't get enough roses."

A Loner, and Phineas

"See, the piano thing is such a strong connection. I know now how to trace my stuff back, to look back. I've investigated my early themes of life. My mom wasn't really prepared to bring me into the world, so I got abandonment and fear-of-rejection themes happening as a child, because she was always giving me to some other women or some relative down the road. So I never felt comfortable. And then I'm a loner, so I had to be alone, because I had to do stuff myself, in a way, because I didn't have the nest. I didn't have the warmth at home.

"That's part of my loner or solitude thing. I just don't know when I'm going to be thrown out again, given to some other people, some relatives. That's something that I've just come to grips with, without going to these guys for years and sitting on sofas and stuff. I never told you this before; I just figured it out.

"I really love people, I love humanity. I think I'm a warm cat, but from the youngest days I can remember, I was always at somebody's house and it wasn't with my mom. So I became a loner.

"See, I played on this amateur show and Phineas [Newborn] came in and saved me from delusions of grandeur. I got all these slaps and left hooks really early. My mom didn't want me, and then there was this Phineas thing. I had just won first prize and *he came up to me and said I needed lessons bad. . . . It was a bitter-pill-that-turns-to-sweetness-later-on kind of thing.*

"When I was a little kid, he was like our Art Tatum, you know, or [Vladimir] Horowitz. He could play it all, all the classical repertoire. He could just tear it up, he didn't have to read no music. And then he could just tear up Tatum and Bud Powell stuff.

"It was like a home for me, it gave me a great love for the piano. That's why I've had all these great piano players with me. It's weird. People don't talk about it much, but if a child is around a certain kind of environment, it's like the tradition in Europe where you have bricklayers and sons of bricklayers for generations. Phineas was like my own father, he took me by the hand.

"I'm always attracted to the pianists. Getting back to the hit I got from Phineas . . . now I'm still spurred to study more. I want to be better at what I do. I always wanted to be a singer, although I'm on saxophone. So now, I'm interested in the content a lot. I used to say, 'It doesn't matter what I'm playing, just check out my tone.' I remember the old cats telling me that if you didn't have a great sound, forget the rest of it."

NYC, 1992

Although Lloyd's ECM albums *Fish out of Water* and *Notes from Big Sur* put him back on the map, especially in Europe, the size of his US listening public and its critical awareness of his new work was initially fairly small, particularly if one used his late-Sixties success as a measure. Some questioned the American-Scandinavian blend of his band and the ethereal lyricism of much of his music, compared with a more traditional American and Afrocentric band with a supposedly more rugged and aggressive approach.

Then, in the middle of 1992, fresh attention came to Lloyd in the United States when, within just a few days, he played in high-profile Coltrane tributes in Philadelphia and at New York's JVC Festival at Carnegie Hall. People took notice, and critics generally gave him glowing notices. In particular, a review in *The New York Times* by the paper's jazz critic Peter Watrous gave a revalidated Lloyd something to glow about and a renewed sense of "arrival."

Jazz festival concerts, given their general predictability, are set up for upsets. At a tribute to John Coltrane on Saturday night at Carnegie Hall, as part of the JVC Jazz Festival, the long-vanished tenor saxophonist Charles Lloyd came and gave a lesson in drama, playing miraculously graceful improvisations that had the audience pent up, waiting to explode into a standing ovation.

In the mid-1960s, Mr. Lloyd became a huge jazz star by popularizing the sound of John Coltrane, who died in 1967. It drew him scorn from critics: he quickly abandoned the jazz world for Big Sur, Calif., from which he emerged only occasionally. Mr. Lloyd, who came in as an outsider, clearly hasn't been loafing, because he performed three original compositions for Coltrane that had some of the more intense improvisations of the year. Backed by McCoy Tyner on piano, Chip Jackson on bass and Elvin Jones on drums, he repeated heated phrases, recalling the gospel church; stark lines alternated with windy flurries, and his tone moved easily from the guttural to the cottony.

Mr. Lloyd is a virtuoso, but unlike most virtuosos, he never let it show, keeping everything he played dignified. In his mixture of blues phrases, classical exercise quotations, howls and screams and gentle melodic sensibility, Mr. Lloyd has come up with a strange and beautiful distillation of the American experience, part abandoned and wild, part immensely controlled and sophisticated.

Bill Cosby had been the party responsible for enabling Lloyd's role in the Mellon PSFS Jazz Festival at the Academy of Music in Philadelphia, which happened the Thursday before Saturday's Carnegie Hall summit meeting. The Trane-based bill included the McCoy Tyner Trio, Elvin Jones's Jazz Machine (with guest Ravi Coltrane), and a final group set with Lloyd fronting Jones, Tyner, and Chip Jackson.

"Bill called," Lloyd explained, not long after returning home to Santa Barbara from his triumph. "He's been a fan for ages. When I was playing with Cannonball Adderley, he used to come out all the time. Cos was just starting out then. . . . I made a record called *Of Course, Of Course*. He loved it. He was always saying, 'Of course, of course.'

"Throughout the years, Cosby was always a fan, and supportive. Then we lost touch for many years, as I did with most people on a one-to-one level. But I figured I was doing some deep sea diving and had to continue because maybe I could bring back some pearls as opposed to getting fat and stupid.

"Recently, he called and said he wanted to do this tribute to Trane and he wanted me for the finale. It was kind of like a favor. [Promoter George] Wein's office called Steve [Cloud] and said, 'Okay, so everything's set up?' He didn't know what was going on.

"I was reluctant to do it, actually. I've had this association with people who said I was a Trane clone or a Trane this-or-that. That's not true. Obviously, as far as my major heroes go, he's certainly one of them, just like Ramakrishna is now. I just go for the highest. When I first heard him in '55 with Miles, he wasn't together, but I could hear something. He was coming out of Dexter. We all come out of somewhere; if you listen to the early [stuff], I was coming out of Trane and Sonny Rollins and Ornette, too, and of course Bird, and Lady Day. I was coming out of all that and Europe.

"So when he invited me to do it, the intention wasn't clear. George Wein puts all the cattle together, and they all go out and jam: the all-stars. I'm not about that. It's that he wanted me to come out and do whatever I wanted to do, whatever my offering to it is. And it was a funny thing. He told Steve that he felt that I would take it to another place. He heard *Fish out of Water*; he had heard I was back, and he was excited that I was back.

"All people know is what Freddie Hubbard said, that 'Charles Lloyd? He's up on a hill meditating somewhere. He's too far-out to think about.' I never lost my humor about all of this stuff.

"Sometimes, from a far place, from a place of quiet, you can . . . you ever heard of Warren Buffett? He's one of the most successful guys on Wall Street and he's not in New York. He's a billionaire, one of the big guys.

"Sometimes, far from the crowd, if you're connected to the source, you can do it. I was also told that if you have something, the world will beat a path to your door. This isn't necessarily true—we've seen great things that people don't know about.

"So I was reluctant to do this thing, but when he said that I would bring something special to it, it was just too muddled. It essentially wound up that I went and played and it was a very beautiful experience. Bill was very happy. . . .

"I like that he [Cosby] can be in the position that he's in and yet still have some sense of the music and still care about it. I think he's going to do a lot more if his focus could be on it, because he has definitely danced through America's living room. He has a respect for this tradition.

"In the meantime, he said if I do this, he would do a concert next year where he would open for me. Also, Steve called George Wein and he said, 'Charles can do what he wants to do.' For years, they thought I was difficult or odd or something. I just wanted to be treated like people do. If that's misunderstood, I don't know what to say about it, because I don't have any reason to go out and do anything stupid in my life. I did this in deference to Cos."

Darr adds, "Cosby told him to not cry the blues to the *Times*. He said, 'Tell him you're fine and you're doing this for me as a favor.'"

On this day, Lloyd reads the *NYT* piece aloud, and then the *Down Beat* review of the JVC Festival, in which the critic referred to the saxophonist's supposed deployment of the circular breathing technique during his performance. "I don't do circular breathing," insists Lloyd. "That's a circus trick. Booker taught me about that. He said he was doing a recording with Clark Terry and those guys and they kept holding these whole notes. He asked them, 'Hey, what are you doing?' They said, 'Oh they're just circus tricks, son. Don't get involved with that.'

REFLECTING ON TRANE, THE PROCESS, AND . . .

"There is the weird deceptive notion that someone who doesn't release albums on a regular basis is a recluse, or isn't playing the game by the rules. I may be more clear about it than most people who are out there all the time. There was a review that said that the quality of the music is better when it does come out than somebody who comes out with stuff all the time.

"I was saying to McCoy backstage in Philadelphia that there was still something so vibrant about the music. You see, I still experienced that greatness and that essence of what those masters were touching on.

"It's almost lost today. Young guys can play—and don't get me wrong, obviously everyone has to find their way. I'm really encouraged by these young guys coming up now, really sincere about the music and still in-process. And yet . . . it's a living experience, and when you get it from records, something is different. I don't know how to explain it. It's like McCoy said: 'We baked the cake and these kids today they get it in the box. It's wrapped.'

"There did seem to be a real synergy in the band. It was powerful. Before I came on, they were playing all Trane tunes and those saxophone players [were] playing all those licks. I just didn't want to go there and play the Trane tunes.

"So I went there and played my tribute to him. That piece 'Homage' is a tribute to him. That came from 'Africa Brass,' that piece that Booker Little was writing the arrangements for. I was living with Booker in New York at the time he was doing that. All those memories came flooding in, like Ornette's 'The Blessing' coming through. Playing with Elvin is such like breathing; it's effortless. I think he's really one of the great masters of our music. So is McCoy.

"I had jammed with Elvin at the Jazz Gallery in the Sixties, but I had never played with them before. We knew each other, and there was always mutual respect, but I knew it would be something vibrant. I also knew that what comes through me with them verifies the validity of my statement, as opposed to trying to step into the shoes of the master, which no one can fill.

"Coltrane is right up there with J. S. Bach, there's no question. In modern music, Trane smashed atoms. That living expression of what he left was so powerful. . . . They interviewed me for the radio there in Philadelphia. I said, 'The man was a saint.' His cousin was there and he said, 'I knew him. He was no saint. I knew his wives.' But they missed the wrong parts of it. It's not about that. It's about his essence and character.

"I think all experiences are great experiences, especially in this tradition of richness we have in this land here, this beautiful vibrancy of all these great masters. When you have Louis, Duke, Coleman Hawkins, Prez, Bird, Bud Powell, all that stuff coming on up through Trane and also that period when I was out here in California, with Ornette and Eric [Dolphy]. That was a real vibrant period. There was something we were doing that didn't hit the East Coast until later.

"There was more acceptance of the art form back there [in NYC], so we had to leave, but there was a cauldron here in the Fifties. There were other periods in LA, like the one [on Central Avenue] that Buddy Collette could talk about. You could trace that period . . . up to the modern times, when I came in the Fifties. I had a group with Scott LaFaro, Don Cherry played, and Billy Higgins. We made a beautiful recording. I remember my composition teacher from USC, Ernest Kanitz, came and said, 'Charles, I really loved your music, especially the slow movement.' That was the ballad, you know. There was this pianist, Don Friedman, out here. He's on my first record [*Discovery!*].

"I feel blessed. There was that period in Memphis under Phineas's tutelage and then my time out here with my peers—those guys, Eric and Ornette, were older than me, but they were still vibrant. We'd get together and play every day at someone's house or in clubs, unof-ficially. We would pay to play if we had to.

"This is a living music and I have nothing but bravos for Wynton and that whole scene. But, see, he's part of the process. His father was out here with me. . . . He was at the Marine base, El Toro, and would come to town and pick me up and say, 'Let's go play.' I can see how he brought the boys up like that. The little boy with the trumpet is brash and the older one's more eclectic.

"It's all music. I hold on to a sutra thread of something that I've lived. . . . My notion is to purify as much as possible and to continue to be a part of that process. Rather than having crutches, I'm blessed and fortunate that I can pick and choose what it is that I do. I always want to share it with people. Even in my deep exile in Big Sur, I really wanted to share the music, but I realized that there is something about culture in silence. I had to reflect on all of that.

"I was around all these great masters. I sat at the feet of Monk and Trane and Coleman Hawkins. I had to really reflect and digest that, real strong."

Just as his ECM connection in 1989 represented one major step in the revival of his jazz career, Lloyd's brief rapprochement with the Coltrane world a few years later seemed something of a vindication for this artist long linked to the Trane sound.

"I'm not a flake and a fluke and I'm not a Coltrane copier," said Lloyd, plain as day. "I have my own life and my music. Don't misunderstand me: Trane was a master. I got a bum rap. I never complained to you about this, but I thought about it a while back. Manfred told me there was some guy in Germany . . . that I was not liked in Germany and was called a 'Coltrane imitator' because there was some guy who controlled the scene over at George Wein. I don't know who this guy was.

"Years ago, there was a guy named Frank Kofsky, who was around in the late Fifties and early Sixties . . . kind of a house writer for . . . *Down Beat.* I wouldn't give this guy an interview, so he started being on a tirade about me. Trane was always real complimentary and a wonderful big brother to me."

ALL MY RELATIONS

In the summer of 1994, I visited Lloyd at his home in the period leading up to his third ECM album, *All My Relations.* I was summarily greeted by the sonic stamp of a bold quartet, with Bobo Stenson, Anders Jormin, and Billy Hart now in full flight on a generally more aggressive approach than heard on Lloyd's first two ECM albums. I heard more of the restless young man whose music burned back in the late Sixties, agreeably combined with the elegance of more lyrical and modal moments in the program, as on "Hymn to the Mother."

On the title track, which has been a staple of his for years, Lloyd displayed a stronger, fiercer saxophonic voice, in tone and line, as he did on the song "Piercing the Veil" and tunes paying tribute to his hero Monk ("Thelonious Theonlyus") and in the clearly Coltrane-ish fifteen-minute piece "Cape to Cairo Suite (Homage to Mandela)." On the closing solo piece, "Milarepa," he wields his Tibetan oboe in an invocation to the religious leader of his Vedanta faith.

Mockups of potential CD covers were scattered around the living room. Lloyd and Darr were, at that moment, torn over whether to go with a fashionably rough-hewn graphic design or an orange-tinted photo of Lloyd and his recently deceased guru, Swami Ritajananda. Despite his devout adherence to meditation and Vedantic practices, and many references to his spiritual life in song titles and interviews, Lloyd has sometimes been cautious about putting his spirituality up front and center. On this occasion, ultimately, *All My Relations* came out sporting a close-up of a stylishly suited Lloyd in mid-saxophonic flight.

In the afterglow of his new recording project—an album he was clearly happy with—being put in the can, Lloyd talked about the project and his group, which he liked to call the FSOL—"full service orchestra of love."

As he told me, before cranking up the freshly made sounds on his stereophile sound system, "I did another record last month in Oslo with the boys. This time, Manfred didn't bother me. I always get my stuff through. This time, I'd been playing in New York, and I was getting intense, and I didn't want to make another mellow record. Manfred likes the poetry and the darkness, with the black clothes. I just decided that I had to holler a little bit and howl at the moon. We went in and did some of that, and he didn't bother us at all.

"In defense of Manfred, people said he'd never let me do certain things. After a few years, you get to suss someone out. I was getting all this useless information, feedback, that 'Charles Lloyd is so mellow—it's not New Age, but it's real mellow.' And, man, you know, I wish I could be mellow. I've been working on that shit for years. I don't have that.

"Anyway, so I just went in and played my stuff. Manfred was very wonderful about it. I said to him, 'This is the record I need to make and you need to make too.' He's got a vibe of making a certain kind of record. It's on it, knee deep in the stuff."

Privacy, plus a View

Fast forward a few years, and Lloyd and I reconvened just after he released his 1997 album Canto—*his last recording with the great Stenson-featured quartet. That morning he was in a restless, wily mood. We met at his small beach-adjacent apartment, near the historic and swanky Coral Casino and the Biltmore in Montecito. As we talked, he was distracted by the sight of a gardener at work on the hedges around his unit's window.*

"Who is that guy climbing up there? I've got my machete. See, a brother should never get rid of his machete. Paranoia is healthy. They manicure too much."

We go outside and have a sit.

"When I first moved here, the bougainvillea came all the way up to here and it came around the corner. They had to replace the trellis because they said it was rotten, so they had to start over from the beginning with the stuff. I want it to come back. I like it big."

At one point, he yells at the gardener, working on the hedges outside his place.

"Don't cut it too short, Jose! I want to be private. Can you make it come back like it was? I'll remember you at the right time. Thank you, sir. But I want this one down so I can see the ocean. Thank you, sir."

There we had it. Privacy, plus a view—fragilely interactive values held dear by Charles Lloyd.

Abercrombie, Higgins, and . . .

In 1998, I met with Lloyd for a marathon interview session. After living for years in a smaller property down a winding road, he and Darr had moved up the road to a yawning hilltop spread with an exponentially more dramatic and bedazzling view of the land and sea beyond. There they built a Darr-designed lavish and beautiful yet also open-feeling and comfortable, hacienda-like abode, with various buildings and a multitiered central structure.

On this spring afternoon, Lloyd takes me on a tour of his new, nearly finished hilltop house, a rambling property with music piped into every room, a downstairs room that could be a recording or practice studio, views to die for, and a meditation/shrine room. As we work our way upward toward an upper berth room perched above the kitchen, Darr wanders in, and Lloyd tells her, with an impish grin, "I was just showing him your temple to Hyperion."

At the time, Lloyd seemed to have the word and notion of "Hyperion"—a Titan and the father of Helios (Sun), Selene (Moon), and Eos (Dawn) in Greek mythology and, to astronomers, a satellite of Saturn—on the brain: The next year, he recorded the tracks for the two albums *The Water Is Wide* (2000) and *Hyperion with Higgins*, the latter released in August 2001, a few months after Higgins's passing.

We settled into Lloyd's literal (and universal) living room. He scrambled around to find a particular DAT tape and cranked up his stereo, sending pristine sounds into the high-ceilinged livingroom, as well as various corners of the house. He turns to me, with a playful look, and says, "Check this boy out."

The sound of the band was unexpected coming from Lloyd, with a guitarist as his foil instead of a pianist, and a guitarist with a ringing, clean tone and a behind-the-beat, probing sense of phrasing and improvisational shaping. He reminded me of the signature player—and longtime ECM artist of note—John Abercrombie. After Lloyd played a couple of pieces, the latter being "Forest Flower," he waited for a response. I joked, "What was that tune?," coaxing a cocked head smirk from Lloyd. The guitarist turned out to be, in fact, Abercrombie, from a recording made at Birdland in New York the prior October, with a band that included bassist Marc Johnson and drummer Billy Hart.

"I dedicated the last album to Billy Higgins, so Manfred Eicher said, 'Why don't you do a special thing with Higgins?' I said, 'Cool.'

"Abercrombie and I had never played together and he'd been wanting to play with me, so I wanted to check it out. I hooked it up for us to play. After I finished my tour in Europe, I came back through New York. Bobo couldn't come over for it, he had something else he had to do. So I played with Marc Johnson, Abercrombie, and Billy Hart. It was bad. We did four days at Birdland.

"I'm recording with him and Dave Holland and Billy Higgins next month." The session would become the 1999 ECM release *Voice in the Night*.

Hearing Abercrombie and his exotic harmonic ideas, it must take you back to your days with Gábor Szabó.

That's the thing. In 1960, I turned Gábor on to Ravi Shankar and Indian classical music, and that's when he started bending those notes, plus he had his gypsy heritage from Hungary. I told Abercrombie I wanted to recapture some of that sound, from albums like *Of Course, Of Course* [1964]. He said that Gábor was a big influence on him, bending notes and holding one string while playing another one. He said he copped a lot of that from Gábor.

So Gábor left town [died] sooner, and this is kind of in homage and tribute to him. . . . I was just in Hungary a couple of weeks ago, in Budapest, and it was very soulful. People brought me all kinds of music and food and cloth and stuff. It was a very soulful experience.

I feel an affinity there, maybe partly because I had this fixation with Bartók. My fixation with him started naively, because I just liked that he used folk themes in his music. I've made a pilgrimage to his pad and to this Bartók museum they have now. It's ironic: After you die, you get all that stuff, even though he died in poverty over here.

Gábor died back over there. When I first went there eight years
ago, I was talking about Gábor and they didn't really know much
about him. But this year, BBC did a big program and they televised
that I was there. . . . I played to sold-out concerts. It was a big deal.
I have a place in my heart for that part of the world.

VOICE IN THE NIGHT

Voice in the Night, recorded in May of 1998 at Avatar Studio in NYC,
marked a new turning point in Lloyd's evolving second coming as a
jazz musician, appearing almost a decade after *Fish out of Water*. It
pulled him out of the piano-based quartet sound he had clung to for
most of the Nineties, and seemed a softer, more lyrical echo of his
late-Sixties music with Jarrett and company. This album also found
the leader moving away from his Scandinavian-European musical
connections, instead presenting American players in his band, as he
would continue to do for many years after.

On another, and not at all incidental, front, *Voice in the Night*
marked the first public expression of a brief-but-potent era of
enlightened artistic symbiosis with Higgins, his old friend from late
teenage days. Their suddenly renewed friendship and musical liai-
son would produce a body of work that was fascinating and often
unique (as with their belatedly released, free-ranging duet project, *Which Way Is East*), and all packed into the few years before
Higgins's death of liver failure on May 3, 2001.

From the earliest moments on, *Voice in the Night* proclaims a
fresh new ensemble voice (its title track being a tune that Lloyd
recorded in 1964 for his *Of Course, Of Course* album, as well as in
1968 for his *Soundtrack* LP with his Jarrett-era band). It is a lean
sound, particularly due to Abercrombie's half-earthy, half-ethereal
electric guitar work, and the delicate rumblings and ruminations of
the Higgins-Holland rhythm section. The calypso feel of "Dorotea's
Studio" (a nod to the new digs of the Lloyd-Darr compound) dances
lightly, rather than with the assertiveness Sonny Rollins might
have applied to a similar tune, and is part of a pleasing puzzle

of repertoire, including the fast (but easy) swinging minor blues "Homage" and the musing aura of "Requiem."

Lloyd also readdresses his trusty old greatest hit, "Forest Flower: Sunrise/Sunset," but with the ambling, resonating timbre of an electric guitar, which puts a new, more measured and matured set of clothes on the piece thirty-plus years after it created a sensation at Monterey. Lloyd's sax work befits the gentler glow and spirit of the musician at sixty, mellowed by life's experiences, inner spiritual refurbishing, and possibly also his tight, years-long alliance with ECM.

On *Voice in the Night*, from outside the domain of Lloyd originals, he also offered his rendition of a very contemporary pop song of the day, the inspiring, gospel-tinged "God Give Me Strength," penned by Burt Bacharach and Elvis Costello for their intriguing 1998 collaborative album, *Painted from Memory*. This Lloyd quartet did wonders with the piece, tapping into the inherent jazz-suitable qualities of it (something also demonstrated in Bill Frisell's version, released a few months later on the album *The Sweetest Punch*).

To close *Voice in the Night* on a more purely jazz-centric note, Lloyd called on the lush lyricism of Billy Strayhorn's "A Flower Is a Lovesome Thing," which would become a staple of the Lloyd concert canon after the album's release.

ABERCROMBIE

I spoke with John Abercrombie in 2000, just as his second album with Lloyd, *The Water Is Wide*, was released. This recording was from an epic set of sessions in December 1999 at Los Angeles's Cello Studios (formerly Ocean Way Recording) with pianist Brad Mehldau, bassist Larry Grenadier, and Billy Higgins. (This session also produced the tracks for the disc *Hyperion with Higgins*.)

The Water Is Wide's song list included the traditional folk classic title song, "The Water Is Wide," a trend toward including folk and pop song material that Lloyd would continue on the 2002 album *Lift Every Voice*. That later album, with pianist Geri Allen and bassist Marc Johnson in the mix, included the pop ballad "You Are So Beautiful" (made famous by Joe Cocker, also a Santa Barbara resident for several years), Marvin Gaye's "What's Going On," and the hymn-turned-anthem "Amazing Grace."

Abercrombie plays with probing lyricism and wit, and in interview mode he speaks with wry clarity, an incisively sharp observer of character with a well-calibrated bullshit detector.

Charles told me that when you started playing with him, you had a link—your knowledge of Gábor Szabó's work with him.

Yes, I did, in a sense. I don't think I play anything like Gábor. I first heard him play, not with his band, but it was with Chico Hamilton. When I was a student at Berklee, I went to the Jazz Workshop in Boston and I heard Charles with Gábor and, I think, Albert Stinson. It sounded so good to me, and I couldn't tell what they were doing. I told him I walked in and the guys were playing "Someday My Prince Will Come," that's about all I could tell. I couldn't find a downbeat and I didn't know where any of the chords were, but I knew what they were playing. I thought, "Either these guys are completely scamming me, or they're brilliant." I never really figured out which one, although I tend to think that they were playing really great.

I used to hear Gábor a lot in those days. I always liked Charles's playing. Of course, Keith [Jarrett] was a classmate of mine at Berklee. Then he went with Charles. I heard a lot of Charles in those days, in Boston, when I was still young.

So when I actually got to play with him, it felt very natural. I had to read his tunes, but as he said, "Well, you already know my music." I kind of do, not specifically, but I know the sound of it, because I heard it a lot. It was an easy hookup, musically. We've never had a problem that way. I think it was partly because of the Gábor thing. I'm really not like him, but there's a little tad in there, too.

I remember when I was playing around Boston, I used to play in a rhythm and blues band. I had one featured solo a night and it was on a Cannonball Adderley tune called "Jive Samba." I had a couple of little features, but I remember on this one night, I played this little Gábor solo, and it became my Gábor spotlight, with a drone on an open string going and then moving up and down another string. Everybody called that my "Gábor thing."

So there is some Gábor in me. There are all these kinds of weird people lurking around inside of me, these various influences. Sometimes they'll pop up and all of a sudden I'll find myself sounding like someone that I've heard in the past. All of a sudden I'll start sounding like Kenny Burrell or Wes [Montgomery], or Jim Hall, for sure. But sometimes it's an obscure thing and I don't know where it comes from. It's just because I've listened to a lot of music. I never tried to copy a lot, but I just listened, and it kind of gets in there in different parts of your brain.

I heard you with Charles at Jazz à Vienne [a wonderful festival in France, near Lyon, where the primary venue is a 2,000-year-old Roman amphitheater]. It was a pretty bizarre gig.

That was amazingly bizarre. It was hard to even hear on the stage because the rain was so loud when it hit the roof of the stage. I think I'd been playing two tunes when one of the rented amps blew up. And they hurried another one up, and it fucked up, and they brought out another one. Somehow I had a lot of fun playing, even though I could hardly hear what I played. I was also really afraid, in the rain with an electric guitar. If you got wet enough, you could get zapped.

The crowd followed us in the rain. They stayed there for both sets.

It was a sea of umbrellas. At the end of your set, it looked like lightning hit something and knocked the mains out. This happened almost literally on the last accent of your last tune. It was a strangely mystical moment or something.

Anything can happen with Lloyd. I don't know. I remember that gig very well. As messed up as it was, and although it was bizarre, it was sort of fun to play. I really had a nice time and it was great to hear Pat [Metheny, who was also on the festival]. They put us at this ridiculously expensive place, the restaurant-hotel La Pyramide, one of the most amazing restaurants in France.

That was a tour with about five gigs on it, stretched out over about ten days. We played Vienne and Montreux. They were all pretty big festivals. In Montreux we played a thirty-minute "Forest Flower" encore and got everybody angry. Claude Nobs [founder and manager of the Montreux festival] was furious. . . . Waiting to go on were Rickie Lee Jones and Elvis Costello, who are the biggest jazz people we know [he rolls his eyes].

Claude Nobs said, "Charles, you must play another tune. The people love it." And he said to me, "John, why do we not see you so much anymore?" "Because you never hire me." So we went back down and Charles started "Forest Flower" and we didn't finish until a half-hour later. He picked up the tenor, the flute, and the oboe, and went completely nuts.

Meanwhile, you could see people backstage really flipping, giving him the finger . . . but not giving him the ax. Apparently, it was written up in the papers as being quite a scene.

I didn't see Claude afterwards, but I hear that he was pretty upset. But he knew that it was Charles who played that long; we wouldn't have played that long. We were just following the leader. He took us out there and that's where he wanted to go. In a way, it was kind of a nice feeling. I know we screwed the schedule up but this festival is such bullshit anyway. There's very little jazz on it.

That doesn't mean that Elvis or these other musicians aren't interesting, maybe even great. But it was just a feeling of "Fuck them, fuck the festival" a little bit. That was my feeling and I think it was Charles's too, although I don't know for sure. Apparently, Rickie Lee Jones was very upset. We heard a little bit of her on the way out, and, God, she sounded dreadful. I know she can be okay. But what has this jazz festival become? Montreux is the worst offender; North Sea [Jazz Festival] has gotten close. They had heavy metal groups at Montreux, groups with tattoos and safety pins.

You can understand rhythm and blues and you can almost understand Rickie Lee Jones and Elvis Costello, but most of them had only dabbled in jazz. There were very few dyed-in-the-wool jazzers.

Herbie [Hancock] was there and Pat [Metheny] had his trio. There was just a handful of real jazzers. Everything else was just pop.

AFTERGLOW

One of the rare musical ventures outside of his work as composer-bandleader (apart from a thrown-together *Acoustics Masters 1* project for his old label, Atlantic, in 1993) was Lloyd's appearance on the soundtrack for the Alan Rudolph film *Afterglow* in 1998. The connection there was the film's composer, Mark Isham, who had worked on Lloyd's album *Pathless Path* (1979). At that time, before he found his professional groove as a film composer, Isham was a synthesist and trumpeter known for his work with intriguing pianist/bandleader Art Lande's group Rubisa Patrol, which recorded for the ECM label.

Lloyd recalled the experience of playing for the *Afterglow* soundtrack, which included a brief improvisational outing, with Higgins in the band. As he noted, "That free thing we did on the soundtrack you heard . . . they said, 'We've got a frenzy kind of scene. Can you go out there and do something for us?' I said, 'Sure.' We went back and listened to it and Higgins said, 'I don't know if Hollywood is ready for this.'

"Actually, Rudolph was cool. This was beautiful: He cuts his films to music. He was at the session. Isham is his musical guy. He said [to Isham], when he was editing *Afterglow*, he was listening to Charles Lloyd's *Notes from Big Sur*. Isham said, 'That's interesting. I know him. Maybe we can get him.' Rudolph says, 'Oh, we can't get him.' Of course, you can get anybody if you really want to get them. I made sure they really wanted to get me. They said they did.

"Rudolph was just beside himself with joy. So it was easy for me. Isham said, 'I'm going to try to write some stuff in your style.' I said, 'Why don't you let me write something?' But no, that's not the way it works in Hollywood. So he made some little sketches. He was very respectful. He said, 'I'd like to have some trumpet on there.' I said, 'Well, [pianist] Geri Allen is in town, so she could bring [trumpeter] Wallace Roney, too.' Isham said, in a hushed tone, 'Well, *I'd* like to play.' It was his tea party. He brought vibraphonist Gary Burton. Actually, I told him he should get Bobby Hutcherson, but he was not around. But he [Isham] was very open to whatever I wanted to do.

"Actually, bringing those musicians to his session, I think they added a lot of authenticity. There's some real stuff on there, some real source kind of stuff. Now, pardon my seeming lack of humility, I feel that I'm one of the young elders of our music. I was trying to tell him it was really important . . . to have the tone of the real stuff, regardless of how it was going to be treated in the end. I told him we should go in there and play complete pieces. I said, 'You can chop it up and do whatever you want to later.'"

When asked if he'd had much interaction with the world of film music over the years, Lloyd replied, "Not a lot. My music has been used in various films, in lots of documentaries—a lot of nature films use my music. And actually, years ago some porno used 'Forest Flower.' I thought 'Forest Flower' was about divine love, but they were moaning and groaning. The reason I know about it is because Eric Sherman—who did a film on me, *Journey Within*—found out about it, so we had to go do some research to get an injunction. They didn't license the music or anything like that."

7

DIALOGUING WITH MASTER HIGGINS

LLOYD'S HIGHLY FRUITFUL, ALTHOUGH sadly brief, artistic and personal relationship with Billy Higgins during the latter part of Higgins's life was profound for both musicians. The spirited, intuitively connected pairing proved something magical in the jazz world for that fleeting period. When Higgins played in Lloyd's ensembles, he lent them a grounding, centering force and a lightness of being.

In a way, the relative freedom of the Lloyd gigs offered Higgins a lifeline to a looser jazz way of being, with some ties to his seminal work in Ornette Coleman's groundbreaking "free jazz" performances of the late Fifties, after a lengthy period when Higgins had settled into more straight-ahead groupings, such as pianist Cedar Walton's mainstream jazz trio.

On recordings, the Lloyd-Higgins partnership is represented by only five titles: 1993's *Acoustic Masters I* (with Cedar Walton and Buster Williams); 1998's *Voice in the Night* (with John Abercrombie and Dave Holland); two albums drawn from 1999 sessions (with John Abercrombie, Brad Mehldau, and Larry Grenadier), 2000's *The Water Is Wide* and 2001's *Hyperion with Higgins*; and the fascinating double album of Lloyd-Higgins solos and duets, *Which Way Is East*, which was recorded in Lloyd's home in January of 2001 (only a few months before the drummer's death) and released in 2004.

LLOYD ON HIGGINS

Lloyd is particularly expansive about the deep bonds and special musical affinity and camaraderie he and Higgins enjoyed.

Lloyd with Billy Higgins at the Jazz Bakery, Los Angeles, 2000. (*Photo by John Ballon*)

"I met him when I was eighteen years old. . . . I was going to USC and went to a jam session at a place called the Stadium Club. He was there playing. . . . After all those years in between, we came together. I feel so blessed that we came together at the end. He had also worked on himself, like I had. You know, behind every saint is a sinner, and in front of every sinner is a saint.

"He made it all the way. Not only that, he just had such a beautiful spirit. We're all spirits on this human journey. Two years before he checked out, he said, 'There's nothing left. It's all spirit now.'

"He is music. For me, he is the nuance master. No one had more together with nuance. He's there, taking care of time, and then he steps out with some counterpoint on it. The religiosity of it—what this thing is all about, you've got to have the drum.

"When he left [when Higgins died], Max [Roach] called and said, 'You okay?' Then I lost it and started crying, got emotional. He called the next day and said, 'Charles, I'm coming out.' So Max and I went to the funeral. Max wanted me and Max to play at the service, but they wouldn't let us play; it was their [Muslim] tradition. Billy was all about music. In fact, at his mother's funeral, he played a piece of Max's. Dorothy was there and she made sure they let Max speak.

"Mr. Higgins—there's nothing to say about him. . . ."

"Higgins and I . . . have a connection. The thing about Higgins that people have to realize is that . . . he seems like he's minimal, like he's not doing much, but he's always rambling and always has these Latin beats that he plays. He's very creative, doing instant modulations all the time.

"I'm not big on labels, but I know there was this East Coast–West Coast thing [in the Fifties]. We were just a group of young outsiders, who were playing. We weren't playing in Hollywood, we were just playing in each others' houses. You know how musicians get together. There were a few venues. There was a place called the Hillcrest [a Los Angeles club on Washington Boulevard, near La Brea, made famous by Ornette Coleman's gigs there in the late Fifties], and some other places, like the Stadium Club.

"Ornette never had a gig in those early days, around the Hillcrest time. There were brothers who put on concerts that we'd play. That was a different time. There was this big interest and love in the music around us. There was a buzz. If Miles came to town, we'd all be there. But we were unknowns, so we didn't have big audiences, plus we weren't from there. I came out here in '56, and I think around '59, Ornette and his group took off for the Five Spot [a famed club in New York City's Bowery neighborhood]. So they left before I did, and then Eric left in '60, with Chico. I replaced Eric when he joined Mingus.

"So I would see Billy in New York, but then Billy had some serious substance problems for years that made it difficult. That's common knowledge, and he rose above all that, but during that time, he made all those Blue Note records, with Herbie [Hancock] and Dexter [Gordon]. He's on "Watermelon Man" [Higgins appeared on the Hancock jazz standard in its first appearance on Hancock's debut album as a leader, 1962's *Takin' Off*] and records with Lee Morgan and Jackie McLean and Bobby Hutcherson. Billy was all over the place.

"The thing about Billy Higgins is that he has always been great. From the start, he had his own stuff. Billy Hart was telling me recently, the last time Billy was playing in New York, Elvin Jones came and sat right down in front of the drums, and Elvin is the baddest cat out there. Higgins is another kind of master. He's got a lot of moves. He's always smiled, always beatific.

"The only reason I mention the substance thing is that, when you go exploring every night like we do, you've got to come back somehow not the same. It's fatiguing out here, going through so many tollbooths. . . . For perceptive, sensitive people, it's a bit too much. But Billy always had this Bodhisattva thing. . . . That's not right to say Bodhisattva, because his tradition is Islam. He had this Sufi thing, where he was always above the situation. He was Smiling Billy. He lights up everything when he plays.

"When you play with him, he can cause you to seriously hurt yourself, because you feel so good. You can be reaching for more than you thought you could reach for. And yet he's not loud. He has always been known for being tasteful. Drummers have a bad rap for that. Through the years, we had this strong connection, because when you're boys and you start out together, there's always something there. We had this connection and then we didn't see each other for a long time. Then we'd get together every now and then.

"Around the time of *Acoustic Masters I*, we came together and recorded. That was the first time we recorded in a public way. He had been playing with Cedar Walton, so it was Billy, Cedar, and [bassist] Buster Williams and myself. A lot of people liked that recording. Billy kept wanting us to play together, so I played some gigs with them, at Catalina's [in Los Angeles], Yoshi's [in Oakland], and a couple of different places. It was fun. He realized that a lot of things he feels and thinks coincide with what I'm doing. He tells me, 'You've got a lot of moves. You do a lot of stuff.' Then he started going with me and playing a few concerts. So it's like we've never been apart, and we just got back together again.

"Then there were all those years up there meditating and trying to find my own way and all that. The first time we played together, it was like 'Whatever you've got together, I'm right there with you.' It spurs you on. It was really a great lesson in enunciation and rededication, all of that, to hook up with him again. He's one of the masters of the drums in our music. This is our indigenous music.

"When he had his liver problem—he had a liver transplant . . . Before that, we were supposed to go do a big tour with he and Dave Holland and myself. He wouldn't tell us that he couldn't go because the doctors told him he was on call for this liver transplant. He just didn't want to face that he couldn't go. He was going to go anyway, but he just wasn't strong enough to do that. Finally, we had to go without him. We took [drummer] Idris Muhammad, went to Europe and Israel.

"But everywhere we went, we played 'The Blessing' [an Ornette Coleman tune] before each concert and I'd tell the people to keep a positive thought for Mr. Higgins. Everywhere we played, I tipped my hat to him. He had to have two transplants, but his spirit prevailed. That's more proof to me that we are spirits. We have bodies, but what I'm really about now is reflecting.

"You know the story about the young bull and the old bull? They're on top of the hill and the young bull says, 'Let's run down and have some fun with a couple of those cows.' The old bull says, 'No, let's *walk* down and have fun with *all* of them.'

"I'm learning that kind of stuff now. I can see the whole picture now, witness values and faith and the whole thing. I still love the music more than ever. By the grace of God, I'm still here. I could have been out of here in 1986, when I had surgery. We'd go to see

Higgins when he was at UCLA [Hospital]. I remember one day
Tootie Heath and Billy Hart were there, all these cats. We were all
trying to brighten Higgins's spirits, and he was entertaining *us*. He's
just that kind of cat.

"What I'm saying is that I'm still of the old school. To this day,
people ask me all the time, what young musicians have you heard
that knock you out? I still haven't heard anything special past Trane
and Bud Powell and Bird and Diz and Miles and Bill Evans and
Duke and Strayhorn. Nothing has come through better than that
yet, you know. I feel fortunate and blessed. That's not to negate
youth. I'm happy about youth in that it takes a long time to learn
how to use that stuff.

"Like the old guys told me, 'Junior, it will take thirty years to learn
to campus your tone and all that stuff.' But I have a little experience
now. The thing about Higgins is that he can be so lyrical, too. He
sings, and I'm trying to sing; it's a conflagration of a bunch of love-
birds. I'm like an anachronism or maybe a dinosaur by now . . . but,
you know, the Creator's been good to me, and I feel like I stood on
the shoulders of all these great masters, the people I just mentioned.

"We were playing at Yoshi's and Higgins and I were staying at
the same place. He called me up to his suite and said, 'I want to
talk to you.' He said, 'You and I are together. We've been soldiering
for a long time. We're veterans of many campaigns. You know, we're
doing this for the Creator.' I said, 'That's right, Mr. Higgins'—he's a
couple of years older than me, so he's my elder. He said, 'I got my
little drum with me. I think we ought to walk out into the audience
tonight and touch the people.'

"I said, 'I'm not going to walk the bar, Mr. Higgins. I love you,
but I'm not going to walk the bar.' He said, 'No. It means a lot to the
people. You'll see. We don't have to be about vanity no more. We
don't have to prove we can play. We know we can play. Everybody
knows it. We've got to do this. Let's just try it.'

"This was along about the second night of the gig. He gets his
drums and starts to march. I follow him out into the audience. Man,
by the third night, you couldn't get into the place. There was a line

around the corner, everybody wondering, 'Are they going to come out into the audience tonight?' It was touching.

"He has big humanity. He's got his World Stage place down in Los Angeles. [In 1989, Higgins and poet Kamau Daáood cofounded the World Stage, a community performance and educational center in the Leimert Park area of Los Angeles.] He and I now have a duo group, just he and I. We are also going to make a duo record. He plays guitar and sings, as well. I play all these funny oboes and flutes and stuff, and maracas. I was playing them once and this lady came up to me and said, 'Oh, Mr. Lloyd, where did you study? I've never heard anyone play maracas like you.' Higgins said, 'Study? [Lloyd laughs] You can't study for that.'

"He's just so lively and soulful and beautiful. I would visit him in the hospital or at home and he'd be so sweet. He reads his Koran and has his family, a beautiful wife and kid. He's special. So we have this duo group and we play with Bobo [Stenson]. He loves Bobo. I said, 'How come you love Bobo? He's not from here.' He said, 'Because you know Bobo is from here in the sense that we planted the seed over there in the Sixties.' That group of musicians—Jon Christensen and all those guys—say we really influenced them.

"Billy Hart said that, too. He said there were three rhythm sections that influenced modern jazz: It was Miles's rhythm section with Herbie, Coltrane's rhythm section with Elvin [Jones], McCoy [Tyner] and [Jimmy] Garrison, and then my rhythm section with Keith [Jarrett] and Jack [DeJohnette] and Cecil [McBee]. He said those laid the foundation of a lot of stuff that happened. Billy is a student of the stuff.

"Higgins helped me a lot with my last vestiges of vanity. I don't have much of that kind of stuff happening. I have big humility before the music. I'm always humbled before I play, because it's like a gift. When you go exploring like we do, on a high wire without a net, you can get into some serious difficulties out there. The way we play is like the analogy of a racecar, a Ferrari going around these curves, and right at the point where the tail breaks loose and could slide off the cliff, that's the edge where the stuff happens.

"Playing just consonant and simple melodies, and only on the chord in a particular chord progression, without sweet-and-sour sauce, isn't happening. Without dissonance, the consonance don't have the uplift to it. An artist either speaks for freedom or he speaks for slavery. That's basically where I'm coming from. If you speak for freedom, you have to step up in all ways.

"Again, our foreparents in this music—those elders—paid a lot of dues. Mr. Armstrong, Mr. Ellington, Mr. [Sidney] Bechet, Prez, Mr. [Coleman] Hawkins, Trane, and all of them. . . . One thing that I notice in common about them is that there is such sweetness, love, and saintliness about them. Even Mr. Hawkins would be there drinking his scotch, but he'd be looking at me with this radiance. It was the same thing with Trane—this big humility.

"I just think that the artists should be treated better. Also, great music should be looked after. I once said to a guy in the music business, 'I don't understand this guy. He calls me and tells me how much he loves my music and is going to do the right thing by me, but they're not doing the right thing.' And he said, 'You've got to understand—they don't really love art. They love to *sell* art.'

"Things like that pain me in a sense, because I would like to be better in all ways. I think we all have polarities and propensities. No one is perfected here, as to good and evil. That's what I'm trying to address here. It's a proven fact that the seeds you plant bear fruit. No one can get around that, you know."

THE WATER IS WIDE

Any subject in the air during a conversation or interview with Charles Lloyd is apt to take multiple detours and digressions, by the nature of the man: He is one of jazz's unapologetic and avowed digressionists. On this day, the ostensible subject was his then-new (2000) album *The Water Is Wide*, the first of two albums from an inspired set of sessions with a magical confab of a band that was destined to be fleeting, with Higgins, John Abercrombie, the masterful pianist Brad Mehldau (at the tail end of the period when he lived in Los Angeles), and Mehldau's regular bassist Larry Grenadier (with Polish bassist Darek Oles on the album's last track, "Prayer"). A photo of the crew in the CD booklet, shot by resident camera-wielder Dorothy Darr, shows the players in various stages of glowering sternness, flanking Higgins, with his blissful, archetypal wise grin, in the center.

The album incorporated material from outside the original and/ or jazz canon: *The Water Is Wide* takes its title from the essential traditional folk song, which here is steered toward a Lloydian, gospel-jazz ambience. The record opens with a version of the Hoagy Carmichael–penned jewel "Georgia," with extra lyricism sauce on the side. And Lloyd leans into the realm of Ellingtonia, with Billy Strayhorn's "Lotus Blossom" and Ellington's lovely meditation "Heaven."

Motherless Child

To get to the subject at hand on this afternoon, Lloyd drew circles in the sand, ambulating around the large issues in and around the music. In this case, that meant reflecting back on his childhood.

"Because my mother wasn't prepared to be a mother, she was always leaving me on other people's doorsteps. So I felt unappreciated and unwanted. . . . I couldn't understand why I couldn't be with my mother and stuff like that. But I made some connection with the Creator. That's the only thing that saved me, somehow it led me to the music. I heard a manifestation of the Creator . . .and the sincerity of the seekers in these cats who were seriously interested in elevating their instruments.

"Mr. Higgins and I talk about that to this day."

"It's still so refreshing each time we [Higgins and Lloyd] play, man. It's like a fresh dive into an infinite pool of creative intelligence and beauty. And he has elevated his instrument to such a level that he can play what it is, where it is, as it's supposed to be—play in the *now*. That's why all the cats love Master Higgins. He seems to be a minimalist, but he's got moves. Like Muhammad Ali said, before you know what hit you, 'Watch how fast I hit you' [slaps his hand].

"Higgins has got the dance. For me, to have hooked up with him again was something. We both went through a lot with 'the life' and all of that. I got to a place where my personal life was wreaking havoc, and I was suffering in there. I felt unappreciated in the business of it, being the low man on the totem pole. When you go exploring every night, you find beauty, and you want to live in your lifetime with your creativity. It's like a birthright. . . .

"Look what Higgins does. He has his World Stage. He's always giving. We did a benefit for Higgins up in San Francisco, after his transplant. He came out and he was in a walker. We drove right up to the door of the place. Two thousand people stood up and said, 'Mr. Higgins, we love you.' He gets up on the stage. He couldn't play at that time, four years ago. He gets up on the stage and he says, 'We've got to do something for the young people.' What a big soul. He's always reaching beyond. . . .

"We play with each other every chance we have now and talk on the phone about life."

Dr. Jackle

"When I was going to college, I had a gig in Glendale with Higgins, Terry Trotter on piano, Bobby Hutcherson on vibes, Scott LaFaro on bass. It's a wedding gig I got. We wanted to play [the Jackie McLean tune] 'Dr. Jackle' [sings its fast bop head]. . . . This young couple is getting married and we lighted into 'Dr. Jackle' because we wanted to send this couple off with all of the blessings of the Infinite.

"We thought if we did our job right and played this music right, this marriage would be blessed. All the angels would smile on this marriage, because we brought all our love, all our passion and intensity to the music. We were young cats ready to play it. We were playing for the Creator. We knew we had something special.

"You know, we got about four bars into 'Dr. Jackle,' and the father ran up to the stage and said, 'Please, please, stop. No more.

I'll pay you now. No more.' I hadn't seen Billy in years and we got together and laughed, remembering that story.

"When you play this music, you should be telling the truth. That's why that father in Glendale was like that. I bet you anything that couple is not together now."

Coming back to *The Water Is Wide*, Lloyd says, "I want to tell you about this recording, why it's special. See, when Higgins was in the hospital sick, I was praying strong to the Creator. A lot of people were, because Billy is so loved. . . . I went around the world and asked people to pray for Master Higgins.

"Then I dedicated *Canto* [a Lloyd album released in 1997] to him. After that, I was having dinner with Manfred [Eicher] one night and he said, 'You dedicated this last record to Higgins. Why don't you all do a special project together?' I said, 'Man, right up my alley.'

"Higgins and I have this little duo thing we have together. He plays guitar and sings—African stuff and blues—all kinds of stuff. At the San Francisco Jazz Festival he played all different instruments, I played percussion and flutes and stuff. We have a whole orchestra, just the two of us.

"I got Abercrombie. Holland and I had already played together. We were supposed to do a tour with Holland and Higgins and I. So we did *Voice in the Night*. We did it in New York. It was beautiful.

"One time, I looked over at Higgins. He had a funny look on his face and I said, 'Whatcha doin', Higgins?' He said, 'I'm trying to think of something to play.' I said, 'You never had to do that.' He laid out this little march kind of thing, [and] another kind of beat on this Latin thing. Higgins knows what to play. He keeps it sailing, no matter what it is.

"Mr. Higgins and I were riding in a car in Brazil. He said, 'I can't do this stuff anymore from a physical standpoint. It's all spiritual now.' His vehicle now is not what it was, but at the same time, when the Creator gives it to you . . .

At the San Francisco Festival, three thousand people gave a standing ovation. The next morning, I was in Higgins's room having breakfast. I was saying, 'Man, I want to keep this feeling all the time.' He said, 'What's the matter? You ain't the Man. You can only have it when He gives it to you.'

"That's the thing about him—his deep spirituality."

Unseasonably Irritated

Lloyd recalls a moment when he grew irritated with pianist Geri Allen, whose baby was crying during a rehearsal. "I kind of blew it and I was in a state. That night when we played, it was amazing. Higgins said, 'I told you . . . you need to get upset before you play.' Higgins was always beautiful.

"What we went through together and where we arrived in the music, that's been a touch of benediction for me. I feel in service, and that's one thing we had in common. Another thing was his practice. I was coming out of India, in the sense of [the Hindu philosophy] Vedanta, and I studied [Tibetan Buddhist yogi] Milarepa and all those guys. He [Higgins] comes out of Islam, but we never had any arguments or disagreements. We'd be recording and take a break. I'd go meditate and he'd go in there and do his prayers on that prayer rug in there [points to an ornate rug in the adjoining room]."

"The other thing was, he had never played music in the forest. He was so thrilled to be here. For five years or more, we offered to have him up here. He'd say, 'Okay, I'm coming up, I'm coming up . . .' but he'd get deeper and deeper in the mud. I'd go down there and do things with him, and go to the World Stage. He was a beacon.

"The other thing that Higgins gave me," Lloyd comments, pausing, was that "it was my last finishing school. I played with Tony [Williams]. Tony had all this stuff and was coming out of Roy, that natural effulgence that came out of him. I played with Roy Haynes. I played with Elvin. I tell you something, Higgins was the finishing school—he'd be playing something and then play counterpoint on top of that and turn it around and dance on that, and keep dancing on you. There's nothing you can do. He was modulating all the time. That's why Ornette's stuff sounded so great, because there was Higgins dancing. Got to have the dance going."

"He was the mayor of Leimert Park [the LA area where the World Stage was situated]. I'd go there and play with him. We'd play at Catalina's [a Hollywood jazz club] or somewhere and then go to the World Stage. People would be going crazy. . . .

"Man, we went through so much together as kids in New York and tragic magic. He became an incredible spirit. Many times he said, 'We must do something for the children.' He was always thinking of others, and not himself. The last time we played for him was in San Francisco back in March. He spoke on the microphone and said he wanted to come back and play soon, but he didn't know what the Boss had in mind. He left town [died] in May, on May 3 [2001]. . . .

"He's done so much for this music, maybe made more records than anyone. [Higgins played on more than 700 recordings.] I can't tell you how miraculous it was. The beauty of it is that he still resides here, in our hearts. He will be manifested in the spirit of the music. So, to Master Higgins, we dedicate our efforts. God bless . . ."

In reflecting back on the all-too-brief yet richly symbiotic period spent with Higgins, Lloyd often seems wistful, as if forces brought them together in a fateful way. The upside of this twist of fate was their dense rush of musical interactions, and a fair and fairly varied amount of recorded evidence of their work together, but the saxophonist also recognizes the missed opportunities in the many years between their youthful playing together and their latter-day bonding.

Speaking about Higgins one day after the drummer's passing, Lloyd mused that "We rarely saw each other in New York [in the Sixties]. He kept me away from him, because he was deep into it [heroin]. He didn't want me to go that far, because Cherry also had.

So he kept me away from it and I hardly ever saw him during that period. Much later, he told me, 'Man, the reason I stayed away from you is that I just didn't want you around me at that time. I'm glad of that, because you were able to pull out and take care of yourself.'"

Referring to Higgins in the final, frailer stage of his life, Lloyd noted that "he said, 'See, this thing is all gone now. This is all spirit now. I can't play anymore from the physical plane. It's all pure spirit.' That was two years before he left. We were playing concerts in Brazil, and all over the globe. I remember we played in Marciac [the Jazz in Marciac festival in Southern France] for five thousand people. The people just went berserk. He was like a little kid when he played. Afterwards, he was slumping down.

"We were doing this thing down there at Bones and Blues in Watts [a monthly concert series presented by the Watts Labor Action Committee], one of the benefits for him. He had swollen up. We put

Billy Higgins, Catalina Bar & Grill, Los Angeles, 1998. (*Photo by John Ballon*)

him in Cottage [Hospital, in Santa Barbara]. . . . We were going to have one of his little protégés to play with me and Kamau [Daáood], the poet [who had also worked with LA's famed Pan-Afrikan Peoples Arkestra (founded and run by the legendary Horace Tapscott) and many other jazz groups]. Somehow, the protégé couldn't be found. Higgins, being the magnanimous spirit that he is, he could hardly walk—he was bloated—wanted to play. I was worried for him. We started playing for about twenty minutes. I went over to him by the drums and I said, 'Master Higgins, are you all right?' He said, 'Yeah, I'm fine when I'm playing. It's just this other stuff.'"

Higgins on Lloyd

Twice, I interviewed Billy Higgins, who was generally as press-shy and man-of-few-words as Lloyd is expansive in conversation. Once was for a *Los Angeles Times* piece on his World Stage phenomenon, an inspiring story. I spoke to him again within the last year of his life, for a Lloyd article, just before the August 21, 2000, release of *The Water Is Wide*.

When did you reunite with Charles? Did you play together between those early years and now?

Not really. It wasn't until about five years ago. I made a record with him [*Acoustic Masters 1,* for Lloyd's old label, Atlantic Records], with Cedar and Buster. That's when I started playing with him and getting together again. But he wasn't on the scene for a while.

Did you have a particularly good time in the studio working on this new project?

I tried to. Charles is doing good now. People are getting to hear him, which is great. If you're not on the bandstand, you can't be heard. The way things are going now, he's on the bandstand much more, and he feels better about the music.

He really has a strong feeling about you and your playing.

Yeah, well, we've always enjoyed each other's playing, but we hook up as people, too. We've got a lot of inside stuff going, and that really helps.

Is there any point of comparison between Charles and Ornette in terms of an openness of approach to the music?

They're two totally different kinds of people, but they're looking for the same thing in that way. They're still looking for that bull's-eye. That makes them the same in a lot of ways.

You don't play duets with many horn players, do you?

Well, I did that with Harold Land, and also with somebody who just died, Walter Benton. But at that time, duets were not really popular. They're not really popular now, but that doesn't mean you can't do them.

It's tricky, isn't it?

It's tricky, but it's different. One-on-one is always different; you can come up with a lot of things like that.

You have to find somebody you can converse with, right?

Definitely. It's funny when you're speaking a language and nobody understands what you're saying. You have to have some kind of camaraderie or empathy going on. It doesn't make any difference where we are, we can do that.

Does your long relationship with Charles make it easier to get into the duet mode with him?

Could be. When you're with somebody, it's not always a band. If we were on an island somewhere and nobody was there but us, that's what it might be like. It's good for a drummer to play with just one melodic instrument like that. The drums are also melodic, but that means that you have to think that way. That's a very good practice.

I would recommend that for a lot of people, even saxophone players. They're feeding off the drums anyhow, but when it's just mind-to-mind, it's very different. Nothing gets in the way of anything. You have to play different, that's for sure. You don't have the bass player there, so you have to play those kinds of parts. You have to cover it up with something, or else it will sound very empty. That means you have to think musically.

It sounds like you have a good ally in Charles.

We have understanding. That's the best thing about playing music. I've played with a lot of different saxophone players, and piano players—I've played with Cedar for so long. These people have such a great empathy for music. I feel like I'm still learning. I want to get it right this time. It's great to just play the music and be inside, locked in with people.

When you're playing music *with* someone, it's deeper than just getting on the bandstand. It means so many different things, especially with the spirit. It's always good to look forward to. It's better than laying bricks. Unless you're an expert bricklayer—some people can do it good.

WHICH WAY IS EAST

Several months after we talked, Higgins took some time to take creative refuge and set up shop at *chez* Lloyd, resulting in the multicultural, free-minded, and impressionistic mosaic of recorded duets gathered together for the two-CD album *Which Way Is East.*

"For years," Lloyd explained, "he'd been saying he'd come up [to Lloyd's place in Santa Barbara]. So in January [2001], he brought up every instrument he owned, filled up the living room. He came in. There was a rainstorm. The house was full of drums and guitars and *guimbris* [three-stringed Moroccan lutes] and stuff like that. He always called me 'Aki.' He said, 'Aki, you and I have an inside thing.'"

Higgins sang, played supple, Brazilianesque classical guitar parts, took to a wide range of drums and hand drums, while Lloyd stretched his own instrumental palette to include surprisingly deft and lyrical piano parts and vocal moments, along with the expected coterie of reed instruments including Tibetan oboe, and the maracas he has been known to go to town on since the Sixties. (Dorothy Darr was both de facto recording engineer and chronicler for the project.) When the album came out on ECM three years later, Lloyd was excited to talk officially about the adventure of making the album, which was documented in a sweet film by Darr called *Home.*

This new album is quite amazing. It documents a magical musical relationship and covers so much territory—known and otherwise.

Before you embarked on the project, did you establish any general guidelines for the two of you, in terms of how to approach the sessions?

First of all, we didn't embark on it as a project or a session. Billy and I had been talking about getting together ever since he recovered from his liver transplant. One of our first concerts, post-transplant, had been at the Masonic Auditorium in San Francisco. We started to cover a lot of territory. Billy played guitar and sang, I played piano, and we both played our other regular instruments. But we knew there was a lot more to delve into. Billy always said that he and I had "an inside thing," which lent itself to open explorations.

At any rate, he had an open invitation to come up [to Lloyd's home] and hang. We started talking more seriously about it in the fall of 2000, and also about the idea of documenting it. I borrowed some old analog [recording] gear from an audiophile friend, Tom Mitchell, and he gave Dorothy a crash course in recording with it. By January when Billy finally came up, he was in too delicate a state to have anyone else around, and the hours were unpredictable.

But, we didn't discuss an approach or concept, we just started playing. Billy arrived in a rainstorm with every instrument he owned crammed into his nephew's vehicle. And I had taken out all of my instruments, including my alto saxophone, because that is what I was playing when Billy and I met in LA when I was eighteen and he was nineteen. We set everything up in the living room and just started.

I love the title, **Which Way Is East,** *right down to its absence of a question mark. It becomes declarative, or something akin to a Zen koan.*

Picking a title is the most difficult thing for me. I have hundreds of them. Some stick and some don't. If you saw the DVD [*Home,* a documentary about the album's recording process], you can tell how it got started.

When we were in Munich last fall, Manfred wanted to call it *Journey Within* because he had always liked that earlier recording from 1968 with Keith and Jack. But as he watched the video and heard [Billy utter] that phrase ["Which way is east"], he said, "That's it—a perfect title."

For me, it has many meanings, but it is best left to the poetry and imagination of the listener to think about it rather than to explain. East has many implications.

Did your and Higgins's various leanings, musical and spiritual, form a particular bond, in and apart from the music?

There was never a disagreement between us about it. Billy was a devout Muslim and I follow the path of Vedanta, which teaches the harmony of all religions. But our bond was so deep on all levels, there was no difference between being on the bandstand or riding in a taxi.

Once, we were on our way to Avatar Studio in NYC, and a couple of blocks from the studio we got stuck in traffic. Billy could see that I was getting more and more agitated about the delay. He said, "Okay. Take three deep breaths, cross your toes, and say, 'Yes Charles, yes Charles, yes Charles.' I did that and then jumped out of the cab and walked the rest of the way.

This album seems like an ideal final tribute to the obviously strong musical link you had with Billy in the last few years of his life. Was the recording made with such an intention, or just out of a sense of wanting to seize the day, and the chemistry you two had together?

At the time, we didn't think Billy was dying. We knew he needed a new liver, but his doctor had said he had plenty of time. . . . The last day of his stay, as his nephew arrived to take him back to LA, I think Billy had a strong premonition when he said to me, "This could be the last time we do this together. It is important to have a rendezvous and a vehicle, the right space and the right time to be able to do this."

Lloyd had more to say about this album on another occasion:

One unique aspect of **Which Way Is East** *is its showcase on your fine and unfettered piano playing, which has previously gone more or less undocumented. At one point it's lyrical and almost Jarrett-like, pardon the parallel. Then, on "Devotion," it gets quite abstract and tonally unhinged, in an expressionistic way. Do you use piano as both a writing tool and an expressive outlet?*

I'm glad you like the piano. Geri Allen loved it too, and I felt highly complimented to hear that from her. The European critics call it "genius" and some of the US critics call it "sketchy." Keith played in my band for about three years. One night after the gig, we were sitting around and I played the piano. When I finished, Keith stood up and gave me a big applause. Did you know that he used to play saxophone and percussion during our performances? Those were some *out* days. You would have liked them.

Piano is my laboratory. I have always used it to compose with. My first foray into incorporating it into a concert was in 1983, when Michel Petrucciani and I were supposed to play a duo concert in Seattle at the Opera House. Michel broke his arm and couldn't go, so I had to go up and perform solo. There was a wonderful concert grand onstage, I started playing piano and saxophone alternately.

Have you been a bit intimidated to play it publicly because you've played with such greats, i.e., Jarrett, Bobo Stenson, Brad Mehldau, and Geri Allen?

Sure, wouldn't you be? I have to be in a very different kind of mood to play it publicly. If the piano itself, the sound of it, inspires me, I might be more inclined to play it in public.

Which Way Is East is definitely, and thankfully, off to the left of any jazz mainstream sensibility. In that sense it is less accessible, for instance, than your last two albums, which dipped into familiar cover songs such as "You Are So Beautiful," "What's Going On," and "Georgia." Do you have a sense of your relative position in the present jazz scene?

I can't help it if people have been hypnotized into sleepwalking. We have to wake up—that's why we're here. I'm a musician by nature. Showbiz heaven is never what called me. The music has always moved me and I feel blessed to have a song to sing. . . .

Higgins and I were deeply in service. It's the last night of the play whether they boo or applaud, the song must be sung. I thought this music we made together would be very accessible, especially hearing Billy sing like that? When he sings "If I done *anybody* wrong, Lord have mercy on poor me"—that alone is worth the price of admission.

It may also be viewed as a kind of special project, off to the side of your regular work. Do you view it otherwise, maybe as an important juncture that could steer you in the future?

Well, when Billy came, I was working at deconstruction. After he left, and with 9/11, I found some comfort in the material I chose, kind of like assuring myself that everything would be all right, again . . . sometime. I just made a new recording [*Jumping the Creek*, recorded in 2004 and released in 2005] with my current quartet with Geri Allen and Eric Harland, and I think it continues on this path of openness and directness.

A general and personal question: How is the future looking to you? Are we able to dip into optimism?

It is human nature to be optimistic. . . . I can only try to go forward and do what I love and do best, and that is to make music and share it with others in hopes of making a change for the better. Truth and love seem to be on trial these days. I always remember my grandmother and my great-grandmother, Sally Sunflower Whitecloud, saying, "Do not do unto others what you'd not have them do unto you."

So we must go forward in truth and love. All men are my brothers.

8

NEW MILLENNIAL
DANCE STEPS

9/11

AS TO THE OFTEN-ASKED question *Where were you on 9/11?*, Charles Lloyd has a poignant answer. On that day in 2001, in New York City—close, in fact, to the World Trade Center complex— Lloyd was preparing to open a weeklong stint at the Blue Note in Greenwich Village, a gig slated to begin its run that very night. But life in NYC, and the world at large, would not go on as planned.

That week would also turn out to be a transitional moment in Lloyd's musical life. When he and his band—with John Abercrombie, Geri Allen, Larry Grenadier, and Billy Hart—did open at the Blue Note on Friday, September 14, three days after its originally slated 9/11 start, he would bump fortuitously into a young drummer who would become his comrade and kindred spirit for many years to come, Eric Harland. Lloyd heard Harland in an after-hours jam at the Blue Note, a meeting that he would later view as some kind of kismet ordained by the spirit of Higgins, who had passed away four months earlier.

Looking back on that night several years later, Lloyd commented that "in the deep relationship I had with Master Higgins, it's like he said to me, 'I'll always be with you.' He left in May of 2001, and then on 9/11 I'm in New York and we finally started playing the Blue Note on Friday of that week. Well, the whole Village was shut down. They opened it up on Friday and they let the music flow. To uplift spirits, they had a jam band to keep playing into the night after we finished our two sets. . . . So there was Eric Harland playing in the jam band at the Blue Note.

"Check this out. We arrive in New York on the ninth of September, a Sunday. We usually stay down in the shadow of the World Trade Center, down there at the Marriott or another nearby place. The Marriott's gone. That was my neighborhood. We had loft spaces because of the cheap rent. . . . Those were the days, in the Sixties. . . .

"Dorothy's uncle and aunt, John and Sally Darr, live . . . in the Village. They're beautiful people. They had a friend who lived on Eleventh Street, just off Seventh Avenue, around the corner from the Vanguard. This friend offered us part of a townhouse. . . . We had a couple of floors. . . .

"The next morning, about six or seven o'clock, the jackhammers were going in the street, tearing up the street. Dorothy turned to me and said, 'We've got to move somewhere else. We can't stay here.' I said, 'When I lived in New York, it was jackhammers all the time. To me, I take it as a humility sutra. . . .'"

"When this thing [the attack on the World Trade Center] happened, I was in the room and was watching the news on television. An airplane hit the building. We couldn't believe what was going on. Then the second one hit. We walked out on the streets. It was just too much. My heart goes out. . . . There were all these fire engines going down. I used to live down there, with a fire station right next to me, on Tenth Street. I think they lost all of their people."

PRESS PRESSURES

Roughly three months after 9/11 I met with Lloyd for an interview at his house back on the other coast. He was in an unusually agitated mood, giving guff to a photographer who had come by to shoot him for a *Los Angeles Times* piece. Maintaining his best sour expression and barking at him, "How would you like it if I pointed a camera at you?," he was obviously not thinking kind thoughts toward the Fourth Estate on this day.

By way of possible explanation, Lloyd was still notably rankled by a feature article that had appeared in *The New York Times*, timed

around his Blue Note run. The article, by Ben Waltzer, a pianist as
well as a writer, ran on October 7, 2001, and was a less-than-glow-
ing appraisal of the saxophonist. Rather than portraying Lloyd as
a seasoned artist who had found his voice and his place in the jazz
pantheon, the article sometimes satirized Lloyd's mystical lingo and
status as a West Coast eccentric who seemed restless and defensive
in the Big Apple—despite having lived in the city and played there,
often to high critical praise, many times over the decades.

Waltzer asserted that "Charles Lloyd talking sounds like Dennis
Hopper imitating B. B. King reading Carlos Castaneda." Of their
interview, the journalist reported that "rather than engage in a dialogue, he regurgitated rehearsed anecdotes placing himself in the
firmament of jazz stars; the greats wanted to hire him, the comers
wanted to join him. . . . For a musician whose previous record, *The
Water Is Wide*, released last year, was widely praised for its pristine
tranquility, Charles Lloyd seems ill-at-ease, eager to prove his jazz
bona fides." Later, Waltzer states that Lloyd "has cultivated a sha-
manic persona, becoming the hippie's jazzman."

As Lloyd remembers, "This guy from *The New York Times* comes
to interview me, on Monday, the tenth. I asked him if he knew about
my music and he said, 'Yeah, I spent two weeks studying.' I was a bit
concerned because he had done a piece on Hank Jones, I felt that
he didn't give him his props. Hank Jones is one of the deities, and I
thought he made him into a journeyman, a man for all occasions. I
told him I didn't think he did Hank Jones proper.

"As we were talking, we took him to the bamboo garden to talk. I
told him about the jackhammers and he asked me, 'Well, what's all
this stuff about tenderness?' I said, 'I think the world needs some
tenderness and needs some tender songs. That's what I wanted
to express.' He said, 'Well, I like *Hyperion with Higgins*.' I said,
'I like it, too. It [i.e., both *The Water Is Wide* and *Hyperion with
Higgins*] was all done at the same time.' When I first did it, I told
Manfred I wanted to do these tender songs. I guess you get in the
studio and you don't want to be one-dimensional. You want to pick

up the tempo. It would be too static if I had the musicians record all ballads.

"My way of working is a full service, a full thing. We spent a lot of time preparing pieces, thinking about what we were going to record. There was lots of music. I was just pregnant with so much music. First of all, I wanted to record in Los Angeles, because Higgins was there. I knew his medical thing was there. I knew his support was there. He also told me he would like to record with his own drums. He traveled all around the world and used what drums he could. So he had his drums there.

"Also, I wanted to get the best sound possible. I wanted to capture all of his nuances, because he's a nuance master. Higgins never thought about competition. That smile came from such a deep reservoir of love. We all dip in the same well and the same sun shines everywhere, although its manifestation is different. Ever since we were kids, he had that.

"See, we were on this trail of finding the deities in the music. That's where we came from, a hunger for the Hyperions and to go up in there. The world never made sense. It still doesn't make sense. I can't sit around and pontificate on who's on top or why some man's on first. It grieves me to no end. . . .

"I was thinking about this kid asking me about tenderness. 'What's this tenderness talk?' When he finally came to see me play, on a Saturday night, I said, 'Man, you see what I was saying about tenderness?' He was saying, 'Oh, the music's so great. You should record this band.' That's disingenuous, man. That's not correct. I was so into a Mingus frame of minding this guy, but I don't live there. I don't live there. Also, I had to work with the humility sutra, with all these teachings I've learned about the ego and all this. I backed off.

"He wasn't around. He wasn't even born when I was playing in the Sixties. I talked about Higgins, just like I'm talking to you about him, and he didn't say nothing about that. . . .

"That's odious, man. I don't come off like that. You know, I was very loving and gentle with him. I was not agitated. Get this: I told him the story about Coleman Hawkins, who said, 'When a guy first plays in New York, he never sounds the same as he sounds in his hometown.'

"He made it like I was nervous because I was getting ready to play in New York. I've played a million times in New York; I *am* New York. I lived in New York when giants were roaming the earth. Let me tell you something: [For] any artist who is working on his stuff, it's a lifelong endeavor. You're always talking about the same stuff. You've got to be. Of course, it's always moving around, but it's always in the *now*. You know me, I'm not someone who sits around sleepwalking or talking about pet phrases.

"I don't feel no tension going to New York to play, no amateur hour. That didn't get through. What can I do if I can't communicate?"

Lloyd addresses a question my way: "Tell me straight up: Is it best for me not to speak to people anymore?"

"I don't know the answer," I told him. "I hope you don't judge the whole scene by one journalist who may have been operating with an agenda."

"What bothered me was that it was *The New York Times*. There's not a Sunday that goes by that I don't find *The New York Times*, no matter where I am.

"Of course, we were trying to raise bread for Master Higgins one time, and I thought it was because of what I said from the stage [complaining about a lack of coverage of the Higgins benefit concert]. I'm not really paranoid—I'm just sensitive."

During our conversation Lloyd was unusually sensitized and feeling ostracized—and even halfheartedly entertaining the idea of going on another hermitage from public life—yet he was also nuzzling up against personal truths and revelations.

"Charles Jr. [referring to himself] can step off onto banana peels and things. I have to keep him on track. That's why a sheep or a cow has to be fenced in when they're young. I kinda have to protect myself. . . . At a certain point, I still feel childlike. I have that zest, I'm blessed like that. Basically this thing is like school, and I'm trying to find some sense in it.

"I know what's been laid out. There's this whole notion of simple living and higher thinking, at least working with the mind so it can be a nice friend and not lead you astray into all kinds of things.

"Discipline for me has been a key to another kind of freedom. It gives me this kind of energy that I don't think I would have otherwise. I'm still, as I told that little boy in New York [the *Times* writer], I'm still ecstaterated," he laughs. "He thought I was trying to be Dennis Hopper or something. It's just that it was *The New York Times*.

"I'm trying to find a way through here where I can have full wakefulness and know that this is not my home. I still have a dream. I've been fed by this deep, indigenous art form. Since I was a little kid, this music has always electrified and uplifted me. . . .

"If you work on yourself and you're vigilant about it, then something happens. I made a connection earlier with the Creator when I was a little kid. That connection stays. I can talk to the Creator, I get guidance. Therefore, I can stay in a modality of simplicity and wakefulness. I like wakefulness. I'm on that track. Hey, people can be any way they want to be, but there must be some grace, there must be something in it. . . ."

LIFT EVERY VOICE

In the fall of 2002, Lloyd gave me an email interview on the brink of releasing his album *Lift Every Voice*, on which he is joined by John Abercrombie, Geri Allen, Marc Johnson, Larry Grenadier, and Billy Hart. Recorded in February 2002 and released in October of that same year, it is a double-disc album that radiates a sense of renewed spirit, and it found Lloyd stretching out into a new terrain of song choices. Alongside his originals, lyrically mystical tunes and vehicles for collective expansiveness, he appealed to the common public ear with select favorites like Marvin Gaye's "What's Going On," the American folk tune "Wayfaring Stranger," and the spirituals

"Go Down Moses" and "Amazing Grace," along with the first record-ing of Cuban singer Silvio Rodríguez' "Rabo de Nube" (which would become the title track of a significant Lloyd album a few years later, the first foray of his band featuring pianist Jason Moran).

It's a year after that fateful day in New York when you were to open at the Blue Note. Do you have reflections on that event and its aftermath?

Time has a different velocity now. It is as if the bulk of the year went by at the speed of light, while 9/11 and the week that followed remains frozen or in ultra-slow motion. I have thought about it nearly every day since. . . . It was devastating and painful to watch the whole thing from a few blocks away and be totally useless to the people who were still inside the buildings.

A year later? I reflect on how short our time is here. Don't put off to tomorrow what you can do today. And I realize how important it is to do our work. I am in service, and all I have to offer is the music. It is not *my* music, I am just a vehicle for it to come through. I reflect over and over that we are spirits on a human journey, and how important it is to understand the universality of things, and of how lethal ignorance and arrogance is. Let's focus on developing spiritual wealth over material wealth.

I go back to the philosophers, poets, and spiritual teachers who have told us for century upon century, "Truth is one, sages call it by various names." That's from the *Rig Veda*. So whether it is Buddha, Christ, Mohammed, or however you want to name or not name your deity/creator, it's all the same.

That was a beautiful thing about my relationship with my friend and drummer Master Billy Higgins. He was a devout Muslim, and I a steadfast follower of Vedanta, but there was never a quarrel or dis-agreement between us about our paths. Fear is not the answer. Fear only sets up barriers. And ignorance creates fear. So we must each of us reach deep into our inner resources for tolerance, understanding, and acceptance. It starts in our hearts and minds, it's about Love with a capital L. It needs to be practiced at home and in school, at work, and on the streets, in your car. You name it, we just need to be mindful.

That was one of the incredible and beautiful things about the streets of New York on 9/11 and the following week. In the midst of the haze and stench from the buildings burning, the dust of the fallout, there was a powerful feeling of love and community. Such a peaceful feeling of calm. Nothing was threatening. I had never experienced the streets of New York in that way. I have to believe that love is a more powerful force than man's inhumanity to man.

Does your new CD, Lift Every Voice, address or channel, directly or otherwise, your feelings about the experience?

Absolutely. There was such a need to try to help ease the pain of those directly involved, and also to ease my own pain and anguish. My offering is the music.

I was in shock and disjointed for quite a time. On the first night we played, which was September fourteenth, I opened with "Rabo de Nube," written by the Cuban songwriter Silvio Rodríguez. This became something of a theme song for the rest of the tour and fall. I was shocked to find out later that I had been so disturbed by the events of 9/11 that my fingering on my saxophone was off, and it was most evident on my live performances of "Rabo de Nube." I am happy that we captured a beautiful version on the new recording.

Your music always seems to balance strength and suppleness. Are those the two forces at work in making art that counts?

I think that every artist hopes that he will make an artistic statement in his art that "counts," whatever that means—is relevant.

You do a few arrangements of spirituals, including what has become an anthem of sorts—"Amazing Grace." You also do "Go Down Moses," "Lift Every Voice and Sing," and "Deep River." Do these tunes resonate with your own religious path?

Well, they are songs about finding your way, righting your wrongs, and making peace before leaving town.

Is it an album about healing? Are music's healing powers being put to the test in the current atmosphere?

I hope it is healing. There was something healing about it for us, the musicians, as we were all there together in New York. It weighed heavily on each of us. We put a lot of love into it. And I think that each individual served the whole so selflessly. Also, don't ignore the title "Lift Every Voice"—everyone needs to be heard.

Now, more than ever, people need to speak up and be heard, stand up and be counted, before the planet completely self-destructs. It's not only the threat of war, but the melting of the polar caps, tan oaks dying in Big Sur, polluting of air and sea, frogs deforming because the ozone is disappearing, and on and on.

Hussain Enters

In 2004, shortly after his jewel of an album *Which Way Is East*—duets with Billy Higgins—was released, Lloyd took another inventive step away from his conventional quartet context and performed a Higgins tribute concert, in trio form—with himself on horns and occasionally piano and two drummers, Harland and Indian tabla master Zakir Hussain. That May 2004 concert in Lloyd's favored local haunt, Santa Barbara's Lobero Theatre, was recorded by Dominic Camardella, engineer/musician and owner of the Santa Barbara Sound Design recording studio.

The resulting material, another blast of fresh ideas from the "junior elder," became the much-praised live 2006 album *Sangam*. ("Sangam" is an Indian word for the merging of rivers. Lloyd's album should not be confused with Norwegian saxophonist Trygve Seim's album of the same name, also recorded in 2004 and released by the same label, ECM.)

I interviewed Lloyd via email shortly before this Lobero Theater concert (which I unfortunately missed, although I later caught up with and savored this unique trio live at festivals in Berlin; Montreal; Guelph, Ontario; and elsewhere).

Zakir Hussain came from India and brought that improvisational mindset westward, in Shakti [an Indian music–jazz fusion group of the mid-Seventies that featured guitarist John McLaughlin] and his own assorted projects, and some of your instincts go the opposite direction, eastward. Do you two meet somewhere in the middle?

Playing with Zakir is an incredible experience. He comes from a tradition of tabla playing that goes back centuries. His father, Ustad Alla Rakha [a famed tabla player who often accompanied Ravi Shankar], was one of the baddest cats on the planet, and so is Zakir. Playing tabla and dancing with rhythm is in Zakir's DNA. But on top of that he can swing in the most musical and effortless way. As for the directions we go, we weave in, out, and around each other. I encourage him to sing now, which adds another dimension to the orchestra.

You had such an incredible kinship with Billy Higgins. Do you sense a new musical kinship forming with Zakir through these concerts, something to build on?

Yes, indeedy. I met both Zakir and Eric Harland in the fall of 2001, just a few months after Higgins left town. It's the H factor, and I think Higgins sent them to me. Whether it is Zakir and I in duo or the trio with Eric, as we did at the Palace of Fine Arts in San Francisco and as we will do at the Berlin Festival, Rome, Paris, Carnegie Hall, and UCLA next November, this is not a one-stop shop. Each time we play, something new opens up.

Eric is an amazing young drummer. At the age of twenty-five he is becoming a master. He reminds me of Master Higgins, in that he plays in the *now* and has all those moves. And no matter how intense things get in the music, he stays loose and alert. He and Zakir had an instant rapport.

CONVERSING WITH ZAKIR HUSSAIN

Ever one to rise to a challenge, especially the bringing together of diverse musical languages and viewpoints, Zakir Hussain spoke about being part of Lloyd's unique trio (along with Eric Harland) back in the group's early days, when it was just going public. (By now, ten years after the initial spark and concert, the Sangam group has proven it has legs and legacy, while retaining its credo of spontaneity.)

Hussain spoke to me about the project, which began casually but quickly became a *thing*, an entity unto itself, and one worth pursuing for the parties and listeners involved.

Sangam seems like a special, unique, group. Does it feel that way to you?

We really enjoy each other. It's great to work with the Master, because he allows us room to be kids and have fun. There's none of this "Watch me and do what I ask" kind of thing. It's more like "Okay, here it is. Fill in the blanks." It's a lot of fun to be allowed to have such confidence coming from such a great man. Charles is so supportive, backing us up to do what we like doing onstage.

In that sense, it's a learning process for me and Eric to be able to work together and see what we can come up with to support what Charles is doing. At the same time, the great master guides us without really saying, "Me boss, you subordinate." That's fun. The learning curve has really gone up immensely.

You've heard the record, but that was the first time we played together. Since then, we've done shows and a tour, and the group has really evolved. The music has actually become even more interactive and multidimensional. It's amazing to see. In fact, on the last tour we were saying, "Oh, this concert should have been the one to release on the record." But what that means is that we have some more stuff to do.

It seems that this was initially a special side project, which has now grown legs, right?

It started with a duo—Charles and myself playing at Grace Cathedral as part of the San Francisco Jazz Festival. They have this series called the Sacred Space Concert. I've done this before with Joe Henderson and once with an Indian musician, where we play as a duo, acoustic. It's more like a sacred kind of music.

The idea came from [San Francisco Jazz Festival director] Randall Kline, saying, "Why don't you do this with Charles." That happened, and it kind of took off from there. There was a special connection with Charles. I've been working with some very fabulous senior great legends of India, like Ali Akbar Khan. It was something like that, working with Charles. He was like this great Indian *Ustad* or master. That connection somehow became very deep. His interest in India and philosophy and his interest in meditation and yoga took root in our relationship. It just kind of blossomed.

It was his idea to bring Eric into this thing, because Eric had played with him in the quartet. I think it was a masterstroke.

I'm so impressed with Eric. He's one of the really great drummers of the future in jazz. But at the same time, he's already a master, at such a young age, in the way he interacts and plays and his sensitive touch and the space he allows other people to work in. I feel that. I'm playing the acoustic tabla and you'd think you'd be overpowered by drums, but that's not the way it is. It's like he's playing hand drums. Somehow, it just connected. Our eyes met and we knew what the next pattern would be and how we could interact.

You heard the record. It's totally unrehearsed. It was just "Let's get on stage and let's do something." I called Charles beforehand and said, "Master, what pitches of tabla should I be bringing, so it works with the keys you're working in?" And he said, "Just tune to the key of the universe." It's so typical [laughs]. So that's basically what the show was. I came in with some tuned pitches, and he adapted to those. We set up some pieces. It all just happened.

That singing that I do was spontaneous, it was not planned. These words that I had just came about. And there you are, and the album is done.

When I've seen the group live, there's such a great dynamic between all three, and especially when you and Eric get into these sort of conversations.

Yes, and that's because he's so sensitive to my sound. I guess the key word is that we *listen* to each other and find things to react to while we are listening. It's a conversation, as you say. It transcends just being able to play a rhythmic pattern or a flourish. It's beyond that in that we literally consider it to be a language spoken between three people. The boundaries don't matter. The way the phrasing is, it's almost like a language. It doesn't have to be metered.

That's so much fun, to be able to work with someone like Eric, who does that. And yet, that is a way to give back. There is eye contact that allows us to revert back to where we started from.

We have yet to rehearse, by the way. We have never rehearsed. We go onstage and we play.

And this is the pattern for the future?

Well, what happens is that we come up with ideas in a concert, and at the next concert, we refine them further. It develops as it's going. By now, we have four or five ideas that have sort of become pieces. They all evolved from various performances and good points were strung together. So that's what has happened now.

There are some of Charles's pieces that he has already done before, which we have adopted. We also have four or five vocal things which have come together as we have played. I think there is an idea of our musical statement that has come together after so many concerts that we've played together. So, hopefully, the next time we record, we will actually have pieces of music that have been put together in a song form.

In a way, I feel that that's not the way to go, because the way we are playing now is so much more fun. But who knows? Even these ideas that we have together are different every time we play. Something new gets added. I'm hoping that that freshness can keep going.

That sounds like a very organic process.

It is an organic process. It's interesting to watch musicians sitting onstage and then listen to them and see this tapestry being woven, and to see this creative process and hear how the process is cooking this little dish. It just happens right there for you. What's special about it is that it will not happen that way again, so it's a special, unique experience for the artist and the audience, just like Indian music is. It's a spontaneous, improvised creative process that involves the artist and the audience. Once it's done, it's done. It will never repeat that way. In that sense, it's a personal experience—it's designer [laughs].

MORAN ENTERS, AND A NEW QUARTET FORMS

Pianistically speaking, the Lloyd Quartet's Geri Allen period begat its Jason Moran period. And the group with Moran in the piano chair has indisputably been Lloyd's third great quartet (after the Jarrett and Stenson eras in decades prior).

Moran, recommended to Lloyd by the pianist's friend and fellow Houston-bred ally Eric Harland, was, by the mid-2000s, one of the more artistically alive pianists on the scene. Moran had caught ears that matter in a band led by cerebral saxophonist, post–M-Base (a musical/philosophical term coined by Steve Coleman in the 1980s to describe the work of the loose collective of African-American musicians he worked with) pioneer Greg Osby, as well as with Moran's own retro-futurist trio Bandwagon, featuring idiosyncratic bassist Taureen Mateen and potent drummer Nasheet Waits. Moran was and is clearly and defiantly a virtuosic and broad-minded artist who has found secret byways connecting early stride piano with free-minded contemporary notions. He was destined for the MacArthur "genius grant" he received in 2010.

Lloyd was lucky to cross paths, or musical thought patterns, with the fascinating piano man, and he did so in an empathetic ensemble completed by the fiery fine bassist Reuben Rogers, as well as drummer Harland. Lloyd quickly came to realize that Moran was a forceful and subtle addition to the "full service orchestra of love," and a European tour (a night in Theater Basel in Switzerland—April 24, 2007, to be exact) yielded this new quartet's first recorded statement, *Rabo de Nube*, released by ECM in 2008. That was also the first live album Lloyd had made in twenty-odd years, after having recorded most of his first great quartet's records in concert, and his first live album during the ECM era. Clearly, something was clicking, onstage and off.

On the brink of that album's release, we gathered at Lloyd's new "big house" with the killer view, and he talked about the roundabout process by which he intersected with Moran's musical saga.

"When I go into the music," he noted, "I've always been blessed to have guys and gals—in Geri Allen's case—with me who can take the journey. I'm like an explorer. I'm blessed that these guys keep coming and wanting to play. We were playing at Carnegie Hall with Sangam.

"Eric is from Houston. Jason is from Houston, too. I didn't know Jason. We were in different dressing rooms. Eric's mother had come up from Houston to visit. I went in his dressing room to say hello to her. Jason was there and I saw him, and I didn't know him, but there are certain people who you know just have the thing. I went over and talked to his mother. She's smart and charming. She said, 'You and Benny Carter, for me, are the ones.' I don't know how she put those two together. Maybe she said that because Eric had been playing with me. It's like that B. B. King song 'Nobody Loves Me but My Mother.'

"I was in there. Jason turns to me and said, 'Man, that music touched me all the way to my backbone.' Well, that's the Southern thing. I knew what that meant. I thought *This is good.*

"Then later, Eric said, 'Geri Allen had a scheduling problem.' Speaking of Geri Allen, she gave beautiful service all the time. She was just devoted to what we were doing. She was always just lovingly there for the music. That was a beautiful thing that she did. She had her own stuff going, and her own ambition, but she would come to me and say, 'I really want to play with you again'. . . . But she had a scheduling conflict. Usually, when people have a scheduling conflict, it hurts my heart. Billy Hart had a scheduling conflict, and I had heard Eric. . . . I knew Higgins had sent him, he had to. So I told him, 'We'll play together one day'. . . .

"So Eric joined. Billy Hart said, 'I'm ready to come back now,' but I said, 'Yeah, but I'm still finding out what this is with Eric.' I've been finding out what this is now since 2002. We've been doing this research with Eric. . . .

"I love Billy Hart. We had a really warm connection together. He started with me here in Santa Barbara, at the show at [the nightclub] SOhO. That was the first time we played. Man, we rehearsed about thirty pieces. It was a lot of music. He said, 'Man, I don't know what's going on, but I know that I'm very high from this experience.' I said, 'Well then, I want you to join the group.'

"I kept telling him that it was something really beautiful. I said, My music's really simple.' There was a lot of tricky stuff in the music, with the bar lines and different things. Bobo was still with us and we were dealing. But Billy was able to matriculate with us. We would hang out in airports and stuff. We had a beautiful life together.

"Billy Hart would say, 'Now, what do you want me to do on this?' I said, 'Just play your stuff.' He'd say, 'Man, you always say that. You don't know how hard it is to play your stuff.' I just play my stuff and I expect the other guys to do that, too.

"See, Eric was like that. We were on this wavelength. He was a young guy, seemingly. But he had studied to be a minister, and there was the ecclesiastic stuff and the Bob Marley and the herb gardens and stuff. He had studied a lot of stuff that prepared him, he had an openness of spirit. So he came aboard. So Jason said to me, 'The music touched me all the way to my backbone,' and later Eric called and said, 'Jason wants to play with you.' I said, 'Why didn't you tell me that earlier?' He said, 'Well, I thought he was on his own career and didn't want to play with nobody.'

"One day, I was listening to WKCR, the radio station in New York, and Jason was up there being interviewed. He'd play the piano, too. I thought, 'Okay, that guy understands.' So when Eric said, 'Jason wants to play with you. He understands '. . . so right there was that word, that universe: 'He understands.'

"This show [which became the album *Rabo de Nube*] was only into the fourth concert on a tour of maybe twenty concerts. What can I do if the stars align and the heavens open up and we're given the goods? We take the journey every night. It's not the same concert every night.

"[Lloyd's former bassist] Bob Hurst left, because he had the opportunity to go to these gold mines with Diana Krall. So he went to the gold mine. Well, that hurt me, because that band with Bob Hurst and Billy Hart and Geri had a tight thing, it was really

Lloyd in concert, Santa Barbara, 2006. (*Photo by Paul Wellman*)

something special. I had to deal with that. And then Eric came to me again and said, 'Man, there are things you like about Bob and then there are things you miss in Bob.' See, Bob didn't like Scotty [LaFaro]. When Hurst left, Eric said, 'I got a guy who has that thing that you like in Bob, but he's got this other thing that you miss, like

Scotty.' And so when this guy Reuben Rogers came, there was more elasticity in between the beat and between the moments. So when Rogers came aboard, it opened up the beat. It became juicy and it gained in elasticity.

"And then when Jason came after Geri, I didn't want to try to mimic what came before. You don't sit down in my orchestra and be other than what you're prepared for."

YOUTH, AGE, YOGAS, ORNETTE, WAYNE . . .

Now Lloyd was at the helm of a strong new band—his second all African-American group—in which the septuagenarian musician was at least double the age of his bandmates. He had peaked by age thrity, by some accounts, began rebounding and finding his regenerative artistic voice after the age of fifty, and was now onto something fresh and revitalized again at seventy. In this latest of his musical phases, Lloyd couldn't help but think about matters of mentors and protégés, historical continuities in jazz, and lessons accrued as one proceeds on life's path.

"The whole of our life is for this moment, and it's also to know the moment we leave this stage. This is again just passing through. I was a kid when I wrote all those pieces: 'Passing Through,' 'Man from Two Worlds,' 'A Different Journey.' It was prescient. I had some kind of vision, but I had to do some living and some *mistaking* and [slipping on] some banana peels and stuff like that. Finally . . . [I had to learn about] which foods work and which don't and don't imbibe too much, don't stay at the trough or watering hole too long, or chase the wrong lullabies, because some of them could take you out.

"New York was a wonderful teacher. I've told you that in the past. But, see, these young guys say something interesting to me: They say, 'When we play with you, it's not like playing with the other guys, because you was there. You come from the days.' So they need that. They say, 'We don't play with nobody who has this.'

"I'm like an old guy. I hadn't thought about that. We were playing on the gigs and stuff and they'd say, 'Man, he's done his homework.' I'm not thinking about it. I'm thinking about 'How can I go onstage, because I'm not prepared. There is the chasm. How can I get to the other shore?' See, I'm the other-shore kind of guy, but I don't know the mechanics.

"There are four yogas . . . *Raja* [meditation], *Karma* [action/service], *Bhakti* [devotion/love], and *Jnana* [knowledge]. So there are these different yogas, and the best one is Bhakti, which is love; I go with the love sutra. As a young man, I tried to have knowledge, I tried that path. Now, I'm kind of liking the path of service, which is Karma yoga, undoing karmas. Did you know about [eleventh-century Tibetan yogi] Milarepa? He had a rough life. He made a lot of mistakes and he had to undo them. That's the karma sutra. One of my musicians called me today and said, 'Man, I got some karmas I gotta undo, so I'll learn something.'

"There are two guys who I don't rub up against enough, but when I do, something amazing always happens: That's Ornette and Wayne [Shorter]. They're a little older than me. I remember when we were recording *The Water Is Wide*, with Brad and Abercrombie and Larry Grenadier and Higgins. We were in the same studio complex recording as Wayne. They said, 'In history, this has never happened before.' It was in Cello Studio, on Sunset. Wayne was in one room and we were in another room. . . .

"I remember [Shorter] so fondly, man. . . . We'd be on the road and Blakey would be in Toronto when Cannon [Adderley] would be there. The two bands would be there and we'd get together after hours and play all night. The thing with Wayne is that we could go all kinds of place in travel and in thought process. With Ornette it was different. You wrote something once that Higgins said [that] me and Ornette were after the same bull's-eye, but we just go about it differently. He would say to me, 'A chord can never resolve. People talk about resolution . . .' He would go on for two days about a chord not being able to resolve, just to be contrary [laughs].

"The openness of those moments of sharing, though, are pregnant with delights and elixirs and things you find, because we're not looking for glass beads, we're trying to go deeper. Sandalwood and beyond, diamonds and beyond, gold. It's the 'other shore' thing.

"We were always blessed with that. We didn't know anything about bread or a career or anything or jumping slick suits or . . ."

Dorothy Darr was in the room while we were talking, and she slyly interjected, "Well, I think you jumped on slick suits."

CL: No, I could dress because that was part of Memphis. Cats was sharp. Period.

DD: That's what I mean. You knew how to dress.

CL: I had that. . . . Then there was this guy Yohji [Yamamoto], in Japan. I go there and they give me clothes. They give me all this stuff. So what is it? He said, 'We listened to jazz since we were little boys. See that room in there? Go in and take whatever you want.' It's beautiful stuff.

MIRROR

For his powerful new quartet's first official studio album, *Mirror* (recorded in 2009 and released by ECM in 2010), Lloyd made the rare move of recording in a studio in his own hometown, which he hadn't done since the Seventies. Interestingly, it was the same facility he'd worked at so many ears earlier, but with different ownership and a different vibe: What had been Santa Barbara Sound, where the hiatus-era Lloyd recorded *Autumn in New York* in 1979, was now Sound Design, a state-of-the-art facility in an unassuming building.

Owner and engineer Dom Camardella, who had engineered Lloyd's live (at Lobero Theatre) album *Sangam* (and whose son Adam has been Lloyd's live sound engineer), was at the studio's controls, coaxing a warm and embracingly intimate sonic environment from the session.

Mirror is a luminous and lyrical set of pieces that range from gospel tunes ("Go Down Moses," "Lift Every Voice") to Monk songbook treats ("Monk's Mood, "Ruby, My Dear"), framed by a spare opening rendition of the standard "I Fall in Love Too Easily" and a meditative closer, "Tagi," a Lloyd original on which the saxophonist recites from the *Bhagavad Gita*.

In another earlier-era hometown connection, once or thrice removed, Lloyd offered his version of a Brian Wilson classic from the Beach Boys' *Pet Sounds* album, "Caroline, No." (On his 2013 duet album with Moran, *Hagar's Song*, he would pull another tune from the *Pet Sounds* album, "God Only Knows.").

In talking about *Mirror*, Lloyd asserted that "this quartet [with Moran, Rogers, and Harland] is my best formation yet. We share such a deep camaraderie and intuition about the music. Everyone has such a strong individual voice and mind, yet we come together as a unit. On top of that, we really dig to be on- and offstage together.

"We use organic fertilizer, and no GMO products. The music is nourished in the sun kitchen and has huge doses of love and trust."

I asked him if there was any particular statement made through this album.

"A statement in this project? I think I make the same statement over and over: Life is about finding freedom. Throughout civilization there have been inequities. As humans, we need to wake up and realize we are custodians of a very small planet in a much larger solar system and galaxy. The false moves of several centuries are now being compounded, and in this twenty-first century, tiny misdeeds are felt in a nanosecond around the world. So, it is past time to stop all that. We have to face the mirror of our own inadequacies. It's about growing whole, not growing old. . . .

"When I recorded *The Water Is Wide*, I thought the world needed tenderness. Then I got angry with the course of events, now sad. There is so much harshness all around us—we must be kind to each other. So I felt it is time for the tender sutras again."

A particular point of personal tenderness and nostalgia on *Mirror* comes in the form of Lloyd fleetingly breaking out his alto sax, the instrument of his youth. "I don't know about nostalgia," he commented. "It started with Master Higgins, when he came up and we recorded *Which Way Is East*. Higgins and Dorothy really liked it, and he called it my 'secret weapon.' I started playing alto when I was nine, so it is an extension of me."

I mentioned the seemingly disarming choice of closing *Mirror* with "Tagi," a meditative spoken-word piece he had been including in some live performances around that time (including at a jazz-and-poetry evening at Disney Hall in Los Angeles). I asked him if there was a point recently where he felt, *vis-à-vis* his spirituality, that he wanted to make explicit, in verbal terms, what had been only implicit before.

"I was hesitant to include the spoken word, which is a verse from the *Bhagavad Gita*. It is something that has been with me, interiorly, for many years. It is also a favorite of the band. Eric was trained as an ordained minister and gives it a special resonance with his low voice. I can soar on top of the rhythm section and it finishes with a joyful dance. I thought it was an appropriate way to end the recording."

FARANTOURI

In June 2010, Lloyd once again cast quartet orthodoxy aside to engage in a collaborative meeting with legendary Greek vocalist Maria Farantouri for some concerts in the ancient ruins of the Odeon of Herodes Atticus in Athens. This was hardly a typical jazz vocal occasion. And this unusual musical meeting was preserved as a beautifully expressive double CD, *Athens Concert*, released by ECM the next year.

Lloyd's initial encounter with Farantouri took place in Santa Barbara in 2002, when she was town in connection with an event at UC Santa Barbara. He met her through their mutual friend Jimmy Argyropoulos, and hearing her sing planted in him a seed of wonder and the long-gestating notion of a future collaboration. In Lloyd's liner note for *Athens Concert*, he waxes poetic and mythic, recalling that when he heard her sing in Santa Barbara, years earlier, "I felt such a power and depth of humanity; she is a modern wonder rising up from the ruins of civilization. She is Alethea, Athena, Aphrodite, Demeter, Gaia, Phemonoe—Mother of the Universe. The resonance of her voice stirred the memory of my love for Lady Day."

Their musical summit meeting in Athens, with Lloyd's quartet expanded by Greek *lyra* player Socratis Sinopoulos and Greek pianist Takis Farazis on a couple of tracks, was auspicious. Farantouri told me, "I'll never forget our first concert in the cool summer breeze and the moonlight above the Acropolis, which created the unique sensation of a beautiful journey.

"In my opinion, an artist must be ready to take up challenges, to keep an open mind to new ideas, to interact with different artists and to fuse different sounds. So my cooperation with Charles gave me the opportunity to experiment with and produce something new and unconventional."

I asked her about the unconventional merger of jazz and Greek music, and the process by which they came to conversational terms.

"At first," she said, "I felt that the jazz-meeting-Greek-music process would be complicated. But during the rehearsals, I realized that the idea we were going over in our minds would come out easily as a creative act, both for me and the audience. I would also like to add that Charles and I felt that kind of rapport from the first moment we met. Charles's music is a source of inspiration for all of us who work with him. Certainly our collaboration has enriched me in many different ways.

"I have always enjoyed listening to jazz music. It was a lucky moment when, visiting a friend of mine, I first heard Charles's record *Forest Flower*. You can imagine my huge surprise when I first met him in Santa Barbara. In my view, his playing has all those particular elements, such as the aesthetic spirit and eclectic style, that you have already mentioned."

Charles has drawn a comparison between your vocal style and presence and Billie Holiday, and other references have been made to parallels with Nina Simone. Were you inspired by these and other

*American singers, as part of the broad swath of music that informed
your own musical voice?*

It's true that Charles compares my voice to those of Nina Simone
and Billie Holiday, but for me it's very difficult to make this comparison because I don't think that our voices are similar. I admire
both artists very much: They are sublime, unequaled goddesses.
But I am not a jazz singer. I have been mostly influenced by
Mediterranean voices.

Although in the past I had the opportunity to record songs by
George Gershwin, Charles never expected me to be a jazz singer. On
the contrary, he wanted me to express myself in my own way. This
is why I was particularly flattered that he chose me to sing three of
his beautiful ballads.

*Would you say there is a special extramusical message implicit in
this project, maybe something having to do with transcending perceived barriers and promoting peaceful universality?*

Naturally, the message is present in the project. The fruit of our
cooperation is sufficient proof that music knows no boundaries,
that different genres can fuse and produce sounds with universal appeal in stark contrast with the destructive leveling process
of globalization.

THE WORLD AND . . .

In the midst of a 2008 tour of his house and archives, Lloyd
slipped into a thicket of sketchily connected notions, an exercise
in lateral thinking, touching on global politics, unity in life, and
other concerns.

"I've got all these tribes in me. . . . I never understand why, when
this is a small planet, we can't get together and do this dance on
this planet in a way filled with humility and gratitude to the Creator
that we're all here and to respect everyone. I believe in the harmony
of all traditions and approaches. If one is sincere, you will be met—
that's what I believe.

"I'm an idealist about this notion of the universe as a place where all God's children can sing their song and infuse something into the journey through here. Of course, you've got generations coming after us, so you want to leave the planet a better place. You get sensitive to the environment and how it's treated. Witness how things have gotten out of hand with this fossil fuel stuff and how we treat the land. There's this thing of the spirit and how people are closed off.

"Now, we're at a place where, with all these lines of demarcation, we need to manifest more sages than politicians. That whole arena is a depleted model. This, again, comes back to that beautiful word that Master Higgins used to use all the time, 'service.' We're here— what can we do to make a better planet?. . .

"This is what's so amazing: We still live in a place that has the greatest possibility for this experiment of the so-called melting pot or 'democracy'. . . . But it's very hard. I think about someone I studied with years ago, Buckminster Fuller. He had a model where we could all live on the planet and make it all work. But enlightened beings need humility and to rise above only self-serving interests, because it's gotten to a tight place now where if we all can't dance, there won't be a dance. That's basically where the song has gone to. . . .

"Chasing an old model of the universe, of only materialism, won't get us there. Somehow, we've got to realize that we're all spirits on a human journey and go forward with that, and be kind to each other. . . . I'm oversimplifying it, possibly, but I'm a dreamer. I'm a Pisces, I'm March 15, I don't know any other way. . . .

"There's something about balance, that's all I'm trying to say. I'm not trying to be a hypocrite. You have to look at yourself all the time. I'm like Jimi Hendrix, with 'Crosstown Traffic,' you know: 'Ninety miles an hour is the speed I drive.' You've driven with me.

"But at a certain point you have to give up things. I rarely drive now, I go with Dorothy. My mind is still a compound. It's a wonderful servant, but it can be a terrible master if you've got all kinds of dreams and visions and music dancing in your head. I go out hiking in the mountains or swimming in the sea, underwater. I'm thinking about intervals and sound and how things relate, how things move through space. I like something about that place where time ceases and the *now* is what it's about. . . .

"Higgins called once and said, 'I dreamed we were flying on our backs last night, playing "Forest Flower."' He was always like that. We would go down sometimes and play at his World Stage. Children and all kinds of people from the community would be there. He was always about that.

Musicians who played with me all love him so much. I'm so happy to have served with a great master like him. He was like a finishing school, because he had such high standards.

"In earlier times, he and I had gone through all kinds of tragic magic and all kinds of stuff that was not for your health. But we came through that. . . ."

"I don't like to travel so much now. It's gotten very difficult to move around like that, but I love to make the music. There are these prices we pay. But on the other hand, you can say you don't like to travel, but that's not true. It's all just a journey. Young people should be about loving the music, not the fast lane and the avenue and the business. There was no money in the music when I grew up—it was just the Holy Grail."

THE WINDS OF GRACE

In 2010, I asked Lloyd about his state of being and relationship with the musical muse. "I'm still drunk with the love of music," he asserted. "I approach the bandstand with beginner's mind each night, and hope that I will be met along the way. I hoist my sails to make ready to the winds of grace."

9
Postlude: Horizons on the Run

Montreal's Invitation

It seems a formidable challenge, if not a fool's errand, to try and arrive at some kind of summary "story so far" picture of the Charles Lloyd saga—a life that is simultaneously complicated and circuitous and surprisingly contiguous and logical. And yet a rare glimpse of him in such a perspective occurred in Montreal, in the summer of 2013.

That year, Lloyd was, in timely and logical fashion, featured on the Montreal International Jazz Festival's "Invitation" series, a set of concerts in which a selected artist appears on multiple nights, each night in a different instrumental setting. (The series was launched 1989 with another Southern Californian—Charlie Haden—presiding over several groupings, including his Liberation Music Orchestra, his Quartet West, and a memorable duo with the Cuban piano master Gonzalo Rubalcaba.)

At a festival he had played many times, the saxophonist was ripe for the Invitation series (splitting that year's roster with pianist Vijay Iyer): In the previous several years, he had branched out into contexts other than just his longstanding quartet format, and he had just released a duet album with Jason Moran, *Hagar's Song*. Lloyd, who had turned 75 on March 15, 2013, brought to Montreal his quartet, the Sangam trio (which had also performed during Zakir Hussain's Invitation series run in 2005), and a set of duos and trios with Moran and a brand-new ally for Lloyd, guitarist Bill Frisell.

Adding to the festive fizz and historical gravitas of the affair, Lloyd was also granted that year's Miles Davis Award by festival director André Ménard. The award, established in 1994, "recognizes the entire works of an internationally renowned jazz musician and his or her contribution to continuing the tradition of jazz." Previous recipients have included Wayne Shorter, Joe Zawinul, Herbie Hancock, Ron Carter, John McLaughlin, John Scofield, Dave Holland, Chick Corea, and other jazz notables.

Never mind that Lloyd and Miles had an alternately warm and sparring relationship back in the day; Lloyd's deeply entrenched voice and body of work going back over a half-century has certainly made a strong "contribution to the tradition of jazz."

On opening night of the Montreal festival series, Lloyd's quartet—with Moran, Rogers, and Harland—took the stage at the Théâtre Jean-Duceppe and did what it does best: played a set that was both contemplative and fiery, and attuned to the delicate balance of individual and collective energies onstage. At the end of the performance, Lloyd spoke to the crowd in his usual charismatic way: "This is a very touching evening for us, and especially for the kid [meaning himself]. It's always young in the springtime, but don't tell anyone that; I don't want the gendarmes to come and move us offshore. Thank you for your beautiful vibes. It means a lot to us."

Two nights later, he brought a more intimate ambience to the same venue, as he engaged in sensitive duets with Moran (on material mostly from *Hagar's Song*), as well as stepping into a promising new collaboration. As the saxophonist told this all-ears crowd, "Brother Frisell will come out and sing with me. I always wanted to be a singer. People think I'm a saxophonist. Be kind to us. This is our first time playing together. "

No special kindness was necessary: Frisell beautifully channeled his own early fascination with Gábor Szabó into a disarmingly natural musical connection with Lloyd, a partnership that has continued post-Montreal.

On this virgin voyage onstage together, they got along famously, in part because each musician has created a signature voice by working around the prevailing, sometimes hubristic clichés of their respective instruments. Just as Frisell stirs elements of dissonance

and run-on sentences or fragments, along with his tonal and tim-
bral explorations, Lloyd has honed his tone and voice to include
atmospheric detours, parsed overtones, left-of-normal intonation
feints, and a manner of blowing that can be both airily ambiguous
and cathartically charged.

The two found much common ground upon which to connect on
this night, on themes as varied as Lloyd's "Voice in the Night"—which
Lloyd had first recorded with his comrade Szabó on the 1964 album
Of Course, Of Course—as well as a sinuous take on Miles's "Solar" and
a tune from the Americana-flavored niche of Frisell's musical patois,
"Red River Valley." As Lloyd said that night, "We're dreamers, but our
dreams are bigger than the rivers and valleys. But we love the *now*."

HAGAR'S SONG

Released in sync with Lloyd's seventy-fifth birthday, *Hagar's Song* is
a burnished, intimate, and atmospherically rich musical conversation between him and pianist Moran. The two musicians developed
a finely honed rapport during four years of playing together, and
on this album, Lloyd falls easily into an inspired pairing with this
pianist of uncommon grasp, freedom-minded impulsivity, and
organically cross-historical vision.

There are touchstones of Lloyd's own history filtering through
the album's song set, from the saxophonist's continuing personal
explorations of Ellingtonia—Billy Strayhorn's "Pretty Girl" (aka
"Star-Crossed Lovers") and a relaxed sashay through Ellington's
"Mood Indigo"—to a visit to the Brian Wilson musical well for "God
Only Knows" and a lean and soulful take on Bob Dylan's protest
song with Biblical overtones, "I Shall Be Released," inspired by the
death of Lloyd's friend Levon Helm while the album was being
recorded (at Sound Design in Santa Barbara).

Most closely tied to Lloyd's own story on this album, though, is
the five-part "Hagar's Suite," dedicated to his great-great-grand-
mother, Hagar, a slave taken from her parents at age ten and sold
and traded. Lloyd's composition, an emotional canvas inflected with

quiet rage and sad rumination, pays homage to his ancestor's tragic life, but also serves as a lament for the still-present scourge of slavery. At the same time, the suite seems to touch on his own legacy of loneliness, and the alienation of his own motherless childhood.

Yes, there are non-Ellington standards in the mix as well, in the form of personalized dealings with Gershwin's "Bess, You Is My Woman Now," Carl Fischer's "You've Changed" (an often-recorded ballad associated with Billie Holiday, one of Lloyd's towering influences), and Earl "Fatha" Hines's "Rosetta," which nicely showcases the special modernist-historicist touch of Moran (a famed Fats Waller aficionado and reconstructionist).

The duo shines, in a mostly low-key, introspectively glowing way, but unleashes some free-play elasticity and intensity on Lloyd's wily original "Pictogram" and during moments in the "Hagar Suite."

"God Only Knows," with the spare, breathy spaciousness of Lloyd's melodic treatment and Moran's summoning of rhythmic juice and a handsome chordal flourish, is one of the most striking tracks in the Lloyd discography. Here we have 3:31 of wisdom invested with the fascinations and underpinnings of musical lives richly and curiously lived.

Brass Note

On April 12, 2012, Lloyd played his first concert in Memphis in forty-odd years. The city fathers took that occasion to honor this native son with a brass note on their Beale Street Brass Note Walk of Fame. This occasion also marked the saxophonist's surmounting of his resistance to returning home, where his deeply rooted memories of racism mixed with untold other ghosts from his early life, to accept Memphis's honors.

Lloyd's Beale Street Brass Note, Memphis. (*Photo by Justin Price*)

SEVENTY-FIVE AT THE MET

It can safely be said that, in his seventy-fifth year, Lloyd's career and personal musical bearings were solidly rooted, but with experimental options always tempting him from the wings. He was an artist who, having risen to meteoric heights as a heady and sometimes ego-dizzied young man, returned to the scene two decades later, older and wiser yet still resistant to smug complacency or laurel-resting, and blessed with a subtle voice anchored with confidence and his deserved status as an *éminence grise* in the world of jazz.

To celebrate his actual birthday in high and rarefied style, Lloyd brought an entourage of special guests to the Metropolitan Museum of Art in New York City, a pristine setting on the other side of town from typical houses of jazz. At the Met he performed with his trusty current quartet (Moran, Rogers, and Harland) and friends, including mezzo-soprano Alicia Hall Moran (the pianist's wife) and, nodding to his recent Athenian connection, singer Maria Farantouri and lyra player Socratis Sinopoulos.

In the house that night was *New York Times* critic Ben Ratliff—who has opined on Lloyd from various angles and attitudes over the years (and who, not incidentally, wrote an acclaimed biography of John Coltrane). His review, appearing in the *Times* on March 17, 2013, begins thusly:

> On a small stage facing the Temple of Dendur at the Metropolitan Museum of Art the WNYC radio host Terrance McKnight put on his most serious voice and requested a divine secret of the saxophonist Charles Lloyd. "Who does one talk to," he asked, "to have one's 75th birthday fall on a Friday night?"
>
> Mr. Lloyd replied, "The deities." But of course he did. This was the opposite of a setup for a joke. A joke would have been Charles Lloyd saying anything else.
>
> All Mr. Lloyd's music and affect suggests that he seeks guidance from the spirit world. He is a Northern California mystic [*note: Santa Barbara is very much in Southern California*]; since near the beginning of his career as a bandleader he's been an it's-all-one-music, process-not-product kind of thinker,

going beyond his training and rooting in jazz to collaborations with musicians from other cultures and languages. About 60 percent of his sound, individually and in his excellent new quartet (which on Friday he referred to as his "orchestra"), derives from John Coltrane in the early- to mid-60s, when that great saxophonist and de facto philosopher was still exploding the blues but also reframing his jazz as a kind of universal folk music with inherent religious feeling.

The idea of divine inspiration takes many different metaphorical forms, so let's say what we mean. A lot of people, Coltrane included, have talked about musicians being vessels or containers for the wisdom they're mysteriously receiving. That doesn't seem like the right image for what Mr. Lloyd does in general, and what he did, excellently, on Friday — which was, as Mr. McKnight indicated, his actual birthday.

A GLANCE BACK AT RIVERS AND "BECOMING" AND . . .

Rummaging through mountains of paper and archival whatnot pertaining to my interactions with Lloyd over twenty-five-plus years, I ran across a wayward snippet that still seemed to resonate, many years down the line. This was one of two liner note projects I had been pulled into, only to have the assignments retrained on alternate courses and to different ends. The subject of my would-be liner note was Lloyd's 1998 album *Voice in the Night*, recorded when he had just turned sixty—a transitional moment when he moved from his Scandinavian quartet to his group with Billy Higgins, Dave Holland, and John Abercrombie. At the time, things were changing, while heeding the logic of artistic continuity, resonating with the past and the tradition he had built for himself.

Here is an excerpt of my essay "Considering the River":

> Rivers run, maybe not in the open, but they course though us, ever propelling and allowing us to observe the trajectory even as we become part of its inexorable rush. We can acknowledge the residue of the past and the promise of what's to come, and gauge the effect on the moment, or sleep through the

journey. Charles Lloyd, even through periods of detachment from the public forum, has always chosen the former. He's a hopeless seeker, after a state of restless alertness, wielding the saxophone as a machete and a clarion instrument of truth, or at least the pursuit thereof.

Lloyd knows about rivers, as metaphors and actualities. He speaks of the deep resonance of his origins coming up Memphis, where rivers meet and the legacy of musical crossroads is undeniable. The influence, and confluence, of blues, jazz, R&B, and seminal rock 'n' roll is embedded in the city's nature, just as it is imprinted on the voice of her saxophonic son.

But he left Memphis to broaden his worldview, as an adolescent with big ears and a curious mind. He will also gladly point out that, apart from the American landscape, "Memphis Is in Egypt" (to borrow the title of Dorothy Darr's documentary). Truth be told, when the verbal spirit moves him, Lloyd will talk in a stream that may appear circular, and at times dizzying, but which, on closer examination, carves out its own fierce and clean, linear logic. It forms a strong, restless current, like his playing . . .

Art that Matters teeters, sometimes dangerously, on the precipice between invention and affirmation. It's an operative paradox. To say, then, that this recording both contributes to and departs from the current of Lloyd's musical path is to say that it speaks of a powerful and elusive truth. He's onto something.

That still-valid sense of a *something* has been a fixed focus on quality combined with a flexibility to move aside from conventional wisdoms or established patterns. Years ago, Lloyd spoke to me about the importance of being evolutionary as an artist—and human—based on what he termed his "notion of becoming."

"I still have this notion of becoming, the whole thing I got from Hindu ideas. . . . I never bought the rigidity of systems or just the mentality of how we're treated as artists. I was just trying to find a way to endow my creativity. My truth had to do with an inner kind of struggle. Gee, I'm far from being my ideal of developed in many areas, and yet I still keep my eye on that notion of becoming.

"So whether you have negatives thrust at you or not, you find the inner strength to go on. It's beautiful to have that from mom and from home, and from family. When I was younger, my peers and I had their parents' support and love. They said, 'Be the best that you can be.'

"That is not about competition. That's actually about sharing. We used to play nonstop. Booker Little's mother and father were so beautiful and such soulful people. . . .

"But your dream should be allowed to be nourished. I'm for inspiring and consoling, because I experienced so much heartfelt help and guidance from those who went before me. I sat up on their shoulders to look over the wall. What I really saw was that, in this gymnasium of the world, you have to find a way to evolve.

"It's simpler for me, because I've broken form now and I'm left alone. My heroes are gone. They still live in my heart, and yet you have to do that for yourself at a certain point. So my thing has always been an inner dialogue."

NOT ON THE ELEVATOR WITH WELK

Fast-forward to our long interview in 2006, when Lloyd was having an inner debate about whether or not to play "Forest Flower" at the impending Monterey Jazz Festival, on a show celebrating the fortieth anniversary of the sensation-fueling Monterey set that would beget the live album that effectively launched Lloyd into the stratosphere (marketwise), and helped put jazz into the titillated open ears of many in the Baby Boomer generation.

He was waxing nostalgic, in a slightly circuitous manner, as only he can.

"I remember one time Bob Dylan and I were talking. . . . He was saying he grew up in a time when you could find your community in each city you went to. It was the same thing, you know; it was a search and a quest. Wherever we'd go, the community of music lovers would find us. Then the party was on, because the setup of the world was always alien to sensitives and the poets.

"I would like to say that, for young people, [they should] imbibe the music and the culture and the richness of it, because it's something that will set you up for life. I'm still ecstatic from all of that. I'll never get over it, nor do I wish to. I love music. I heard that yodeling cowboy: I listened to the radio in Mississippi at my grandfather's place, you'd hear all that serious blues stuff, and then I'm dialing and find Jimmy Rogers yodeling, and that's music. To grow up in a beautiful place and hear that music . . .

"You know my history with Howlin' Wolf and Junior Parker and all these guys, and Johnny Ace. But the main thrust was these modernists, with Phineas and George and those guys, and Willie Mitchell, who had a big band that I heard in the fourth grade. They played like Dizzy's band, like with Gil Fuller, and those kind of charts, 'Things to Come' and all of that. There were all these sound mystics playing in Willie Mitchell's band. I heard that stuff really early on.

"That's the thing. If young people get to hear this stuff . . . it's not like being on the elevator with Larry Welk. It's like another kind of thing. It sets your spinal cord, the kundalini thing, moving in a direction. I think it plants seeds that grow up to be wonderful offerings, they grow up to be altar flowers. Now, as far as the world goes, I think it's a travesty that music is not even in the schools and such. When I came up, music was everywhere. Now they take the instruments away from the students. You've got people rapping and stuff nonstop. People have got to break out in song. . . .

"I'm here to sing the praises of that, that this son here was greatly aided in the journey, because it equips you to deal with all kinds of vicissitudes and waterfalls and Mack trucks. You can hear around the corner, you can see around the corner, and you're not impeded by any kind of false impediments, because you hear so well and there are teachings in the sound that open you up to your inner life.

"I had correlations like J. S. Bach and Bird. In this lifetime, I wasn't around J. S. Bach, but I was around in the lifetime of the music of Charlie Parker, the elevation and the swing and the brilliance of that, and the nuance. His name was Bird, and I knew he flew off of his penthouse terrace and flew all over Manhattan and sprinkled manna and upheld the dharma, like Superman. So as a young man, I knew that Bird was bringing it. That inspired me. Then you hear Art Tatum, and it's like five or six guys playing the piano. It sets you up.

"I heard so much great music in my youth that I'm still moved to try to go forward and make some offering in my lifetime, to give some gratitude or thanks for what that was and is.

"I think that's one reason why, when I had my near-death thing in '86, I realized that I had to rededicate myself to this tradition, which had been so uplifted and made me so drunk. And then Master Higgins, on his deathbed, told me, 'Man, we've got to keep working on this music.' I will do that, as long as I'm able, as long as I have a breath."

KEEP SINGING THE SONG

It's a rainy spring day, and the afternoon is waning and the light is dimming over the Santa Barbara Channel and harbor, laid out panoramically below Lloyd's hilltop outpost and enclave. At seventy-five he seems more committed to music than ever, his sabbatical mentality long since abated, even as he tries to maintain meditative equilibrium and detachment from music industry machinery and worldly hustle and hubbub. The ongoing creative spirit of Higgins is palpable in his work ethic and renewably affirmed spiritual attitude, and he seems to have both arrived at and resigned himself to the unceasing continuance of *arriving*.

We are at the end of another epic interview, and Lloyd seems a bit drained. Tapping into a mantra-like refrain, he declares, "I'm going to keep trying to elevate. That's what I do best. The thing that sparks me up so much is that I have all of these people wanting to serve with me. It's a very beautiful offering to be able to do this on such a level of commitment and dedication.

"I've been bringing it all these years and I'm still here. It's a calling and it's a blessing. As long as I'm able, I'm going to keep singing the song."

ACKNOWLEDGMENTS

THANKS TO Peggy and Harper for enduring fits and starts of high and low spirits, grousing, elating, and second-guessing in the midst of a long, tangled, and somewhat emotionally complicated but ultimately fulfilling project. Thanks to Jane Faulkner, for the use of the ocean-view-blessed hall. And thanks to my editor, Jim Fox, for both encouraging the creation of this book and helping give it clarity and a form befitting both the art of understanding and the art of getting lost. Those, not incidentally, are twin elements in Charles Lloyd's musical being.

Thanks also go out to the numerous publications whose assignments made possible the wealth of interview material from which this book was drawn. The list includes jazz magazines—a 2006 cover story and other features for *Down Beat,* and stories for *Jazz Times* and *Jazz Hot*—as well as Santa Barbara–based publications the *Santa Barbara Independent*, *Santa Barbara Magazine*, and *Santa Barbara News-Press*. These and other periodicals offered me the logistical, deadline-fueled excuse to convene repeatedly with Charles and allow him to tell his story—a story still very much in progress at this moment.